Paul J. Hopper was educated in England, Germany, and the United States, and received his doctorate in linguistics from the University of Texas. He has written books and articles on numerous aspects of language and linguistics, held academic positions at several American universities, and lectured widely both in the United States and abroad. He has been a Fulbright Fellow and a Guggenheim Fellow and is currently Thomas S. Baker Professor of English and Linguistics at Carnegie Mellon University in Pittsburgh, where he teaches courses on English grammar and linguistics.

A Short Course (IN) Grammar

A Course in the Grammar of Standard Written English

Paul J. Hopper
Carnegie Mellon University

W. W. Norton & Company

New York / London

For Justin

The text of the book is composed in Sabon
with the display set in Trade Gothic.
Composition by Gina Webster.
Manufacturing by Maple-Vail Book Group
Book and cover design by Mary McDonnell.

Library of Congress Cataloging–in–Publication Data
Hopper, Paul J.
A short course in grammar / Paul J. Hopper
p.   cm.
Includes index.

ISBN 0-393-97381-6

1. English language—Grammar. I. Title.
PE1112.H638   1999
428.2—dc21   98-35706
                        CIP

W. W. Norton & Company, Inc., 500 Fifth Avenue, New York, N.Y. 10110
http://www.wwnorton.com
W. W. Norton & Company Ltd., 10 Coptic Street, London WC1A 1PU

1 2 3 4 5 6 7 8 9 0

CONTENTS

Preface   xi

Chapter 1

The English Language: Preliminary Concepts   3
1.0   A World Language   3
1.1   The Historical Background   3
1.2   A Complex Language   6
1.3   Written Language   10
1.4   "Grammar"   15
1.5   Conclusion: Convention and Change   17
EXERCISES   19

Chapter 2

Words   24
2.0   Parts of Speech   24
2.1   The Meanings of Categories   24
2.2   The Categories   25
2.3   Nouns and Pronouns   26
2.4   Verbs and Auxiliaries   27
2.5   Adjectives   29
2.6   Adverbs   30
2.7   Prepositions   31
2.8   Determiners   33
2.9   Conjunctions (Subordinators and Coordinators)   34
2.10 Summary   35
EXERCISES   36

Chapter 3

Phrases   38
3.0   Phrases   38
3.1   The Notion of "Phrase" in Grammar   38
3.2   The Analysis of Declarative Statements   39

3.3   Diagramming: Some Introductory Concepts   40
3.4   Summary   42
3.5   Form-Function Diagrams   43
3.6   The Triangle Convention for Abbreviating a Tree   47
3.7   The Notion of "Head of a Phrase"   48
3.8   Some Important Terms   50
EXERCISES   51
APPENDIX: Some Tips on Drawing Form-Function Diagrams   53

Chapter 4

Sentences and Their Parts   55
4.0   Sentence Types   55
4.1   Sentences   55
4.2   The Classification of Sentence Types   55
4.3   Ellipsis   62
4.4   Diagramming Sentences   62
EXERCISES   63

Chapter 5

Objects and Adjuncts   66
5.0   Elements of the Predicate   66
5.1   Elements That Precede the Core Sentence   66
5.2   Phrases That Follow the Core Sentence   70
5.3   Objects   73
5.4   A Formal Definition of the Term "Phrase"   82
5.5   Subject Complements   83
5.6   Sentence Patterns   85
EXERCISES   86

Chapter 6

The Verb Phrase   92
6.0   The Verb Phrase   92
6.1   Forms of the Verb   92
6.2   Tense and Aspect   96
6.3   Modality   101
6.4   The Operator   104

6.5   Verb-Auxiliary Homophony   106
6.6   Problematical Verb Forms   106
6.7   Other Aspects and Modalities   107
EXERCISES   110
APPENDIX: Diagramming the Verb Phrase   112

Chapter 7

Prepositional Phrases and Adverbials   114

7.0   Prepositions and Adverbs   114
7.1   Prepositional Phrases   115
7.2   Forms and Functions of Prepositional Phrases   115
7.3   Prepositions in Phrasal Verbs   121
7.4   Prepositional Verbs   126
7.5   Adverbials inside the Core Sentence   128
7.6   A Survey of Basic Sentence Patterns   131
EXERCISES   131

Chapter 8

The Noun Phrase I: Pronouns, Nouns, and Determiners   135

8.0   Noun Phrases   135
8.1   Pronouns   135
8.2   Special Pronouns   141
8.3   Demonstrative Pronouns   143
8.4   The Impersonal Pronoun *one*   143
8.5   Nouns   144
8.6   Determiners   150
EXERCISES   154

Chapter 9

The Noun Phrase II: Modifiers of the Head Noun   158

9.0   Elaborations of the Noun Phrase   158
9.1   Compound Nouns   158
9.2   Possessive Nouns   161
9.3   Adjectival Phrases   162
9.4   Prepositional Phrases as Modifiers   170
9.5   Nominalizations (Infinitives and Gerunds)   171
EXERCISES   173

Chapter 10

Negation   176

10.0 Negative Sentences   176
10.1 Negation in the Verb Phrase   176
10.2 Negation Elsewhere in the Sentence   179
EXERCISES   183

Chapter 11

The Passive   185

11.0 A Review of the Auxiliaries   185
11.1 The Forms of the Passive   186
11.2 The Agentless Passive   190
11.3 The Passive of the Prepositional Verb   191
11.4 Functions of the Passive in Discourse   192
EXERCISES   194

Chapter 12

Coordination   197

12.0 Introduction   197
12.1 The Coordination of Full Sentences   198
12.2 The Coordination of Other Phrases   199
12.3 Disjunction   206
EXERCISES   209

Chapter 13

Subordination: Relative Clauses   212

13.0 An Introduction to Complex Sentences   212
13.1 Relative Clauses as Modifiers   213
13.2 The *wh*-Word Relative Pronouns   215
13.3 Case in the Relative Clause   215
13.4 Relative Clauses Based on Prepositional Complements   217
13.5 Some General Pointers on Diagramming Relative Clauses   221
13.6 Restrictive and Nonrestrictive Relative Clauses   221
13.7 Zero Relative Pronoun   223
13.8 Elliptical Relative Clauses   224
13.9 Other Relative Pronouns   224
EXERCISES   225

Chapter 14

Subordination: Noun Clauses I   228
14.0 An Introduction to Noun Clauses   228
14.1 Noun Clauses and Subordinators   229
14.2 Grammatical Functions of the Noun Clause   233
14.3 Noun Clauses as Complements of Prepositions   235
EXERCISES   240

Chapter 15

Subordination: Noun Clauses II   242
15.0 Noun Clauses, Part II   242
15.1 Indirect Statements and Indirect Questions   242
15.2 Noun Clauses as Adjectival Complements   246
15.3 Noun Clauses as Subject Complements   247
15.4 Noun Clauses as Appositions   247
15.5 Nonfinite Noun Clauses   249
EXERCISES   253

Chapter 16

Subordination: Adverbial Clauses   256
16.0 Pre- and Postcore Clauses   256
16.1 Subordinators in Adverbial Clauses   257
16.2 Adverbial Clauses as Noncore Adverbials   258
16.3 Finite Adverbial Clauses   260
16.4 Nonfinite Adverbial Clauses   265
EXERCISES   267

Chapter 17

Grammar and Discourse   270
17.0 Grammar and Discourse   270
17.1 Balancing Information   271
17.2 New and Old Information in the English Sentence   273
17.3 Pre- and Postcore Adverbial Phrases   279
17.4 Conclusion: Grammar as Control and Opportunity   280
EXERCISES   280

Terms and Abbreviations Used in Form-Function Diagrams   283
Index   285

PREFACE

A Short Course in Grammar came into being the way most textbooks do. Over several years of teaching English grammar to undergraduate and graduate students, I discovered that out of a wide range of available books none precisely fitted my needs and that I would have to rely on my own materials. At first these materials were supplementary. They reinforced the written exercises of excellent textbooks like Sidney Greenbaum's *College Grammar of English* with diagrams and explanatory handouts. But eventually the extra articles started to live a life of their own, and there came a time when I relied on them exclusively, without a textbook. Discussions with colleagues at other institutions convinced me that the special needs I experienced were not unique and that others would find my written modules useful. W. W. Norton & Company showed an interest in seeing them developed as a book.

The needs the book was to meet were quite specific. First, it must address the college or postcollege writer. This meant that the material had to be presented with sensitivity to an audience of educated adults whose previous exposure to grammar had been in high school or even earlier. This audience did not lack knowledge or sophistication, and would certainly have resisted being treated as beginners, but they needed a course that started with few or no assumptions about their previous understanding of grammar and that brought them to a level of knowledge at which they could confidently analyze most types of sentence they would use or encounter.

A second need was a judicious blend of theory and grammatical knowledge. The textbook must handle a range of frequently used grammatical constructions and study them with some precision. This meant presenting some system of diagramming sentences that would reveal their structure and their relationships to other constructions.

The third need reflected a practical problem that was familiar to many teachers of grammar: only a single term could be spared for this subject. However, the sort of formal refinement that was required called for theoretical concepts that would alone consume the entire semester. The dilemma seemed to be either to teach grammar anecdotally, without the two-dimensional diagrams that permitted constructions to be visualized, remembered, and extended to new examples, or to be resigned to teaching linguistic theory with only a minimal concern for the special needs of writers.

The present textbook seeks a compromise: a framework that will permit a set of useful grammatical concepts to be taught through a system of diagramming simple enough to be mastered in a single academic term. The grammatical concepts used, and the associated terminology, derive largely from the British school of grammatical pedagogy enshrined in Quirk, Greenbaum, Leech, and Svartvik's *Comprehensive Grammar of the English Language* (Longman) and Greenbaum's *College Grammar of English* (Longman). The general approach is monostratal—that is, it avoids as far as possible multiple levels of analysis and phantom elements.

The system of diagramming is a form-function one—that is to say, diagrams include simultaneous reference to forms like *Noun Phrase* and functions like *Subject*. Several textbooks (and theories) that present diagramming have recognized the need to combine grammatical categories with grammatical functions in a single diagram, but the display has not generally progressed beyond the Reed and Kellogg stage of double labeling, usually some variant of *NP:Subject*. The idea of combining a syntactic form diagram above the sentence line with a corresponding hierarchical underlining of functions below the sentence line is a useful innovation in grammar pedagogy. It was developed by Mickey Noonan, of the University of Wisconsin at Milwaukee, for grammar courses taught there by him, but has not to my knowledge been published. Professor Noonan is not responsible for any of the uses I have made of this idea in the present book.

The analyses themselves are basically quite standard, but some departures from orthodoxy have been made in the light of my own teaching experience. Linguists may note, for example, the insistence on equating the function of the head of a phrase with the entire phrase, so that in *An alert bystander grabbed him* the word *bystander* is a Subject by virtue of being the head of the Subject noun phrase *an alert bystander*. The alternative of assigning *bystander* the function of Head (reserving the function of Subject for the entire noun phrase) makes for problems of presentation when phrases consist of a single word (for example, one does not know whether to call *onlookers* in the sentence *Onlookers were shouting* a Head or a Subject). I am also aware of what I hope are minor inconsistencies that result from my conscious avoidance of X-bar, a convention that allows elegant solutions in places where phrase and category appear to conflict, such as in compound nouns. The theoretical complexity introduced by X-bar is, in my experience, more costly in terms of classroom time and student confusion than is warranted at the elementary level by the relatively small gain in analytic delicacy. Teachers who are granted the luxury of a second term of grammar can take up some of the issues raised by these decisions later.

The sociolinguistic posture of the book is somewhat conservative. It can be said broadly to be normative—that is, it is assumed throughout that a relatively fixed form of English exists, the formal written language, and that serious writers will wish to learn more about its conventions. This written standard is, however, carefully distinguished from colloquial spoken usage, as well as from casual writing, and students are reminded frequently that to aim for correctness in writing does not mean discarding their own accustomed habits of speech; students should not be made to feel they speak incorrectly and need a course in grammar in order to improve their speech. The opening chapter lays out some basic sociolinguistic notions such as genre, register, and regional dialect. The treatment of areas of written English where change is under way, or that have been the object of more or less random prescriptivism, is fairly liberal. The Passive, for example, is afforded its rightful place as a useful, important, and stylistically appropriate construction. The relative pronoun *which* is allowed in restrictive relative clauses (as in *The language which was used in the conference was English*). The objective form of the pronoun is recommended after *than*, as in *He is taller than me*. What might seem like an inordinate amount of attention paid to prepositional phrases is spurred by my conviction that prepositions constitute a central aspect of English style and that clarity and unimpeded written communication are significantly advanced by the ability of the writer to distinguish among fundamental types of prepositional phrase.

Numerous students and colleagues have participated in the production of this book. The primary guinea pigs for the successive drafts have been the graduate students in the Master of Arts in Professional Writing (MAPW) program at Carnegie Mellon. Their enthusiasm and good humor as they suffered through the obligatory "grammar course" in their first term are beyond compare; not only have they made grammar fun to teach, but they have over the years also given many valuable suggestions on how I might improve the text, and their input has crucially shaped it. My valued colleague and teaching partner in the grammar-style course sequence, Erwin Steinberg, has supported the project generously and given me the benefit of his long experience in the study and teaching of written English. Ceci Ford, Don Hardy, Barbara Muse, Dave Kaufer, Ritva Laury, Richard Cureton, Dianne Gigler, Julie Woodson, and Tom Straw are among those from whose input and support I have benefited inestimably. Haj Ross has been only a phone call away when I needed the advice of a veteran syntactician. My editors at W. W. Norton, Carol Hollar-Zwick and Jennifer Bartlett, were always available with the requisite combination of reassurance and expertise, not to mention patience with an author facing for the first time the complexities of commercial publication. The copy editor, Deborah Gerish, has worked hard on the manuscript, and her alertness and experience have saved us from many errors. Helen Hopper has shared lovingly and uncomplainingly in the intellectual and emotional toil.

A special word of thanks is reserved for Johanna Rubba, of California Polytechnic University, San Luis Obispo. She has commented meticulously on practically every page of an earlier draft, and her astute insights into questions of grammar, usage, and pedagogy have resulted, quite simply, in a better book. While holding her blameless for any errors I permitted to remain, I am most grateful to her.

Paul J. Hopper
Pittsburgh, 1999

A Short Course in Grammar

THE ENGLISH LANGUAGE: PRELIMINARY CONCEPTS

1.0 A World Language

English is spoken natively by about 400 million people and learned as a second language by perhaps twice that number. While these two figures added together still amount to less than the number of speakers of Chinese, the preeminent position of English in world affairs is owed to its global geographical spread and its prominence as a language of wider communication.

Besides being the national language of several important countries, for most of the twentieth century English has enjoyed a privileged status as the recognized world language of science, business, and diplomacy and is widely used in any sphere where a default language must be chosen, such as multinational conferences, air traffic control, and the administration of international organizations like the United Nations. English is the unquestioned *lingua franca* of the worldwide computer culture. It is the standard written language of international scholarship. Scholars all over the world recognize the reality that it is only through English that an international audience can be reached, and that a grasp of at least written English is essential to gain a truly international reputation. And English is on the way to becoming the official language of the European Union.

1.1 The Historical Background

The origins of English are in medieval England and, going back a bit earlier, the northern parts of Europe. English was brought to the British Isles by invaders from the coastal areas of present-day Germany, Denmark, and the Low Countries. Among these invading tribes were Angles and Saxons, two closely related peoples, and the oldest period of the English language is for this reason often known as Anglo-Saxon.

> **By the Way:**
>
> The exact origin of these two names is not known. Some scholars think it likely that the Angles inhabited a narrow land, *ang* being a word that meant "narrow," and that the Saxons were "axe-people" (*sax* = "ax").

A group of languages that are linked historically can be represented as a family tree, with languages standing in such relations as "parent," "sister," "daughter," and "cousin." Historically, English is a member of the Germanic group of languages. Some of the languages of the Germanic family whose names are probably familiar to you are German, Swedish, Dutch, and Norwegian. These languages are sisters or cousins of English. The parent language from which they are all descended is referred to as **Proto-Germanic**. No physical evidence, such as documents or inscriptions, of this language has survived. However, some of its features have been reconstructed through painstaking grammatical and historical comparisons of the Germanic languages that have been undertaken by scholars over the past two centuries. This research has also shown that there are subgroupings within the family. One commonly used grouping would show the relationships roughly as follows:

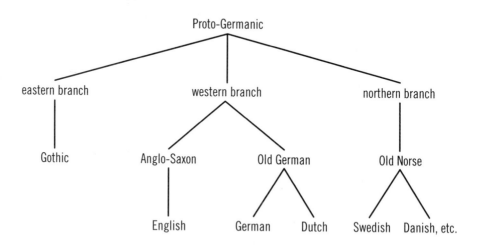

Diagram 1A.   Germanic languages.

Notice here that the term "German" stands for a language that is related to English but is not a descendant or ancestor of English. Rather, English and German are like cousins that are descended from the sister languages Old German and Anglo-Saxon; they belong together in the western branch of Germanic.

Some members of the Germanic language family are known only through written texts; this is true of Gothic, the only representative of the East Germanic group of which we have extensive knowledge.

> **By the Way:**
>
> In older scholarship, and even today in some dictionaries, you will find the term "Teutonic" in place of what is more generally called "Germanic," and occasionally the currently accepted term "Proto-Germanic" appears as "Primitive Teutonic." You will sometimes need to know this term when you are looking words up in a dictionary.

From the time of its first documentation in texts dating from the eighth century, English has been influenced by other languages. For about two centuries (the tenth and eleventh centuries), the English had to share their land with Viking settlers who spoke Old Norse, a North Germanic language that is the ancestor of Swedish, Danish, Icelandic, and Norwegian. In 1066 the Normans conquered England and became the ruling class. The Normans, who inhabited the north of France, were themselves of Viking descent, but they had adopted the French language a few generations earlier. Consequently French was the administrative language of England for the next three centuries. During the Renaissance of the fifteenth and sixteenth centuries, a time of the revival of classical learning, many words from (or based on) Latin and Greek entered English to form the backbone of the scientific and philosophical vocabulary.

Today, the English vocabulary consists of a mixture of words from these sources. Modern English is a Germanic language whose Anglo-Saxon roots are heavily overlaid with Norse, French, Latin, and Greek words. Not only the vocabulary but the grammar of English may also have been affected by its interactions with other cultures. English is a highly analytic language. This means that it indicates relationships among words in a sentence by the order of words and by putting words together in combinations rather than by adding suffixes to the words themselves. In this respect, English differs from, for example, Latin and Russian, which are inflected rather than analytic languages. Some linguists believe that the very simple word structure of English is the result of a history of bilingualism (between Anglo-Saxons and Normans, between Anglo-Saxons and Danes) in earlier periods of the language.

> ### By the Way:
> There are several good histories of English if you would like to pursue this topic in more detail. One of the best is Celia Millward's *A Biography of the English Language* (New York: Holt, Rinehart and Winston, 1988). And don't forget encyclopedias and Internet reference works.

1.2 A Complex Language

Like any language spoken by large and diverse modern societies, English exists in countless varieties. In this book, we are studying English grammar. But the term "English grammar" immediately raises a difficult question of what, or perhaps whose, grammar.

Variation in Speech and Writing

Speech is influenced by many factors in our social environment, such as

- immediate family members
- peer group members considered worthy of emulation
- classes on grammar and style taught in our early years of schooling
- popular books and articles on the English language, including columns by people like William Safire and "Miss Grammar"
- role models of various kinds, such as movie stars, TV personalities (including network newscasters), and other public figures
- schoolteachers and college professors

While your speech may be continually changing in small ways to reflect the influence of these models, the environment of your childhood years will largely determine such things as your regional accent and whether you speak an ethnically marked variety such as African American English or English with a component of Spanish.

Remember that this is true of everyone—we are *all* brought up in a region, and in a sense *everyone* has an ethnic accent. But we are also led to believe that some regional and ethnic accents are less desirable than others, and often this element of desirability may be confused with that of correctness. For very complicated reasons, for example, we may feel that someone who speaks with a white, urban, educated, midwestern accent, such as NBC's Tom Brokaw, is speaking more "correctly" than someone who was raised in a small town in the Deep South.

Perhaps because it is perceived as a neutral accent, not clearly identified with a particular region, ethnic group, or social class, the English of educated national newscasters like Tom Brokaw (sometimes called "Network English") is as close as American English comes to a standard spoken variety.

Register

Variation in speech is found across different individuals, according to level of education, social class, ethnic group, and regional dialect. It also exists simultaneously in one and the same individual. The activity in which you are engaged at a particular time will typically be accompanied by a particular kind of speech. If you are putting up a garage with your friends, you will not talk the same way as you would if you were delivering a eulogy or being fitted for new glasses.

The difference between the following two sentences

[1] George Ellis *was* promoted to vice president for sales for the southeast region

[2] George Ellis *got* promoted to vice president for sales for the southeast region

is not one of grammaticality, since both "was" and "got" are grammatically correct here, but of the *formality* of what is said or written. The first of these might be appropriate for a speech to the board of directors, the second for a more casual office conversation or a personal letter.

The people we happen to be speaking with—our audience—will influence our speech. We have an infinite variety of audiences to go with all our talking activities: in an office or a library, for example, or an aerobic exercise class, a church fund-raising committee, a softball team, a support group for alcoholics, a small claims court, a sailing club. In these different capacities you will find that you unconsciously adjust your speech to the kinds of people and situations you come into contact with.

By the Way:

An important dimension of language variety is that of male and female differences. You may wish to read some of the work of Deborah Tannen on "gendered" styles of speech, such as her books *Talking from Nine to Five* (New York: Avon, 1995) and *You Just Don't Understand!* (New York: Ballantine, 1991).

A variety of speech that is adapted to a particular level of formality is known as a **speech register**, or simply as a **register**. We may speak in a formal register when, for example, chairing a large meeting. We may speak in an informal register, when, say, buying gasoline. The more formal a register is, the more carefully thought-out the words are. Informal registers are typically less planned and more spontaneous. Registers are like a spectrum, with one merging into the next. The registers at the formal end of this spectrum are often referred to as **high registers**, and those at the informal end as **low registers**.

Formality, in both speaking and writing, is largely a question of the relationship between the writer and the audience: how familiar do I want to be with readers or listeners? For example, the appropriateness of contractions like *won't, didn't,* and so on is heavily dependent on register. In the most formal (highest) registers, these contractions would be inappropriate. A printed invitation that included a warning to guests not to park their cars on the street is more likely to be phrased with the words *parking is not allowed* than *parking isn't allowed.* In spoken and more casual registers the use of the contractions is normal, and they are increasingly found in academic writing.

By the Way:

A more fine-grained division of registers has been proposed:

(1) *Frozen or Oratorical* The register of written literature, spoken poetry, ceremonies, and so on.

(2) *Deliberative or Formal* The register of formal writing and of spoken addresses to audiences who do not talk back.

(3) *Consultative* The register of formal conversations in which words are chosen carefully. It is the typical register of business transactions, for example.

(4) *Casual* The register of informal conversation, for example among students or co-workers. It suggests an absence of social barriers.

(5) *Intimate* Similar to Casual, but suggesting in addition some special tie, such as kinship or close friendship, that permits confidences to be exchanged.

See Dwight Bolinger, *Aspects of Language*, 2nd ed. (New York: Harcourt Brace Jovanovich, 1975), 359. The five levels described derive from the work of Martin Joos.

Writing is generally in a more formal register than speaking, because writing tends to be planned in advance and even revised before it goes public, and because it is typically directed at an unfamiliar audience that cannot talk back.

But writing, too, is done in different registers; letters to friends and notes on the refrigerator door are quite different from eviction notices and manuals for toasters. The interactive written communications of electronic mail and Internet chat are eroding some of the distinctive differences between speaking and writing.

A Standard English?

Given all this diversity of spoken language, isn't there *one* variety that can be singled out as being correct and so desirable that everyone would want to emulate it on all occasions?

The answer is clearly no, for if there were such a uniquely correct, universally respected variety, everyone would long ago have adopted it, and there would be no diversity. Correctness means conforming to what is called a "norm." But there is more than one norm, and so there is more than one correctness.

You may consider your local dialect to be incorrect English, but your immediate family and childhood playmates may not share this view and might—with full justice—even be quite offended by it. They would also find it a little bizarre if you were to change your way of speaking in a way that you felt was "more correct." They might feel that you were putting on airs and considered yourself too good for them. The norms of speech, in other words, often pull us two ways and lead us to convenient compromises; I speak one way when I'm away at college and another way when I come home for the summer.

Just as there is no single standard of correctness for spoken English, there is also no single "grammar" of spoken English that we can hold up as a model to be emulated by everyone. Different social groups have different grammars:

- The sentence *This shirt needs pressed* is grammatical in some parts of the country and ungrammatical in others.
- In many regional dialects, there are plural forms of the pronoun *you.* Speakers of these dialects (they are not restricted to the South) use *you* to address one person only, but to address more than one person they use special forms such as *you-all* (*y'all*), *you-uns* (*yins*), *yous*, and others.
- *Ain't* would be identified by most people as incorrect. Yet *ain't* should not be seen as ungrammatical—only as suffering from a class stigma.

This relativistic view of correctness and grammaticality in language might seem to make the task of learning English grammar a quite hopeless one. If there is no single standard, why should we learn anything at all? Or what value is there in studying just one, rather than one hundred thousand varieties of, English grammar?

Fortunately, there is nonetheless one widely accepted uniform variety of English grammar that we can and should learn. This is the formal written language, whose norms have to a large extent settled into a fixed form. We will refer to this variety of English (that is, the formal standard written language) as Standard Written English. Standard Written English provides us with a more or less stable, more or less uniform set of norms for writing. Standard Written English is stable in that it changes only very slowly, and usually in the face of resistance from professional writers. It is uniform in that it varies only slightly among different cultures in the English-speaking world (there are minor differences, for example, between British and North American English).

The conventions of writing provide a kind of anchor, a court of appeal on questions of correctness and grammaticality. But we must be careful not to apply the standards of the written language to those of speaking, and not to imagine that the norms of writing can provide us with a standard for speaking as well.

The grammar of what we will call Standard Written English is not "English grammar" in its entirety. Studying Written English will not provide anyone with an ability to speak correctly or even to use English correctly on all occasions.

But the study of the grammar of Standard Written English will familiarize you in an explicit way with the conventions for writing acceptable sentences in a formal style of writing commonly used in business, administrative, academic, and other kinds of professional writing.

1.3 Written Language

Since the written form of English is the only form that can claim any universality and uniformity, it is important to grasp some ideas about the nature of written language.

The Historical Background of Writing

When and how people first began to write their language is not known. However, it is certain that by about 3000 B.C.E. the Sumerians, who lived in what is now Iraq, were writing down their language using a fully fledged writing system. The invention spread and changed its form as it did so. In the West, writing went through several stages of development before finally settling down into the alphabets of ancient Greece and Rome.

There are several different types of writing system, of which the alphabet is only one type. An alphabet is a collection of symbols that aims to represent the individual sounds of a language. Most alphabets are (directly or indirectly) descended from the Greek alphabet that came into use around 700 B.C.E. Some of the Greek-based alphabets are

- the Greek alphabet itself
- the Roman alphabet, in which English, all the other Germanic languages, and numerous other languages are written
- the Runic alphabet, used by the ancient Germanic tribes for magic and ritual inscriptions
- the Cyrillic alphabet, used for Russian, Bulgarian, and a few other languages
- the Armenian alphabet

The type of writing system used for a language has nothing to do with the linguistic family that language belongs to. For example, some Slavic languages use the Cyrillic alphabet and others the Roman alphabet.

The Roman alphabet came to the English with Christian missionaries, who used it at first to write Latin texts. Beginning in about 700 C.E., it was adapted to write English, and with the advent of printing, which was brought to England by William Caxton in 1476, the spelling of English words became more or less fixed. It remained fixed right up to the present day, in spite of quite drastic shifts in the spoken language, with the result that as we approach the twenty-first century, we are still writing words in a way that reflects how they were pronounced in the fifteenth century.

By the Way:

There are several good surveys of writing. Two recent works are

- Florian Coulmas, *Writing Systems of the World* (Oxford: Blackwell, 1988).
- Geoffrey Sampson, *Writing Systems: A Linguistic Introduction* (London: Hutchinson, 1989).

The Uniformity of Present-Day Written English

In English, then, the written and spoken languages diverged considerably.

Most of the variety and diversity of the English language today resides in speaking. Written English is for practical purposes uniform across all styles and varieties. How we "read off" spoken English from the written language will depend on our own dialect, but the way we write down our words does not depend on our dialect.

The word which we write as *butter,* for example, has numerous different pronunciations in the English-speaking world. According to where you learned to speak, the vowel is pronounced like the [u] in *run* or like the [oo] in *book;* the [r] is pronounced or dropped; the double letters [tt] are said as a glottal stop [bu'er], or like the [d] in *den,* or like the [t] in *ten.*

Yet *everywhere in the English-speaking world* the combination of letters b-u-t-t-e-r is accepted as the standard way of identifying this word in writing. More importantly, while not everyone would agree that [bu'er] is an incorrect way of saying this word, we do agree that there is one way, and only one way, to write it. In a widespread and culturally diverse language like English, where words are pronounced a wide variety of ways, uniform spelling guarantees communication among different users of the language.

By the Way:

Differences exist between North American and British spellings, but these differences are few in number and very trivial. The most obvious are the dropping of "u" in £*labour,* $*labor,* £*colour,* $*color,* and the spelling of the suffix $*-ize,* £*-ise* as in $*realize,* £*realise.* (When it is necessary to mark a form as British or American, we will use the currency symbols £ and $ respectively.)

The Relationship of Writing to Speech

There are essentially two ways of thinking about the relationship between written words and speech.

The first is to see speaking and writing as two codes that can be converted into one other. If we were to adopt this view, it would follow that my own particular dialect of English must be somehow changed so that it conforms to the written language before I can write it down. Suppose, for example, I pronounce a certain word, normally written *test,* as [tess]. If speech is converted into writing, it would follow that when I want to write this word, I will have to make sure I mentally put in a [t] before I write it as *test.* And if I see the written word *test,* I will somehow have to realize that I must ignore the last [t] before I read it out loud.

In either case, I may feel that the [t] really ought to be there, that the form is correct if it has a [t] and incorrect if it doesn't. Differences of this kind between written and spoken English are often responsible for the feeling experienced by many people that they speak incorrectly. Yet such differences have always existed in English. No speaker of English nowadays pronounces the word *knight* as if it had an initial [k] and a guttural sound where there is now a [gh], although in Chaucer's time (the fourteenth century) this is how the word was said. So it is quite wrong to think that there must always be a perfect match between letters and sounds. A standard system of writing can *at the most* fix only one variety of the language; thus there will always be speakers whose language is not perfectly represented in writing, and if, as is the case with English, the writing system is several centuries old, there will be no speakers at all who have a perfect match between sounds and letters.

So perhaps the idea that writing and speech are interdependent, and that writing *represents* speech, is a wrong one. We need a second way of thinking about the relationship between speech and writing. In this second view, speech and writing are more distinct from one another. They are not simply written and spoken versions of the same language, but are to a large extent *two different languages,* and, although there may be large areas of overlap, they have their own grammatical conventions and rules. We should not use writing as a standard by which to judge the correctness of speaking, nor should we use speaking to judge the correctness of writing.

The view that speaking and writing are better viewed as different languages, while it should not be taken too far, does help us explain a number of facts about writing that will be useful to bear in mind as we go along.

One is the point that was made earlier, that writing cannot serve as a final court of appeal for spoken correctness. I cannot, for example, accuse someone of mispronouncing the word *left* as [leff] on the grounds that the [t] is there in writing. I would instead have to have some other reason for criticizing that pronunciation—for example, by pointing out that a majority of present-day society as a whole values the pronunciation with final [t] more highly, and by suggesting that in certain contexts, and at the present point in time, the person's career and other life interests are better served by saying [left] than by saying [leff]. Future generations may find the pronunciation with final [t] to be affected and without value.

Another reason for finding it more practical to think of writing as a distinct code, rather than one that is linked closely to speech, is the point made earlier—to a large extent the *grammar* of writing is different from that of speech. These grammatical differences, it is true, are largely due to the formal register that we were talking about, and to the more planned, thought-out nature of writing. But they are real differences. Wallace Chafe and Jane Danielewicz have studied written and spoken texts to arrive at a list of grammatical features that are characteristic of each kind of text.[1] Some of these features are presented in the box below. (You may not be familiar with all the terms used right now, but refer back to this box at the end of the course.)

Together, Chafe and Danielewicz suggest, these features derive from the fact that writing usually aims to present us with an *integrated* text, a text with a certain tightness of argument and a unified theme.

By the Way:

Some Grammatical Features Characteristic of Writing

- nominalizations
- adjectives placed before a noun
- present participles used as adjectives
- present participles placed after a noun
- past participles placed before a noun
- excessive use of prepositional phrases
- complement clauses
- restrictive relative clauses
- clauses introduced by subordinating conjunctions
- pluperfect verb forms
- subjunctive verbs
- adjectives placed immediately after a noun
- *no* used as an adjective
- reflexive-emphatic (*himself*, etc.) placed after a noun
- passive voice
- abstract nouns used as subjects

Similarly, certain grammatical features are characteristic of spoken styles. Speech, Chafe and Danielewicz suggest, typically does not aim to create an integrated text, as writing does, but to gain the attention and interest of others in face-to-face encounters. They term this aspect of speech **involvement**. Some of the grammatical features of spoken language that they have found are pre-

---

[1]Wallace Chafe and J. Danielewicz, "Properties of spoken and written language," in *Comprehending Oral and Written Language*, ed. R. Horowitz and S. J. Samuels (New York: Academic Press, 1987).

sented in the next box. Here again you may not know all the terms that are used, but you can return to the box later in the course.

> ### By the Way:
>
> **Some Grammatical Features Characteristic of Speaking**
>
> - disfluencies (stops and starts)
> - "colloquial" vocabulary (*maybe* for *perhaps*)
> - indefinite *this* (*this guy walks over and . . .*)
> - pronoun referring to event or state
> - pronoun with no established referent
> - vague verb agreement
> - trailing conjunction (*and . . .*)
> - contractions (*we'd*)
> - ego involvement
> - lively involvement with topic (evaluation)

Much of the task of developing a mature writing style involves eliminating features of the second box (speaking) from your writing and developing your ability to use the features of the first box (writing). An important beginning consists in acquiring an understanding of the principles of English sentence structure and a standard terminology for talking about them.

Genre

Another important variable that determines the kind of English we use is what is called **genre**. A genre is a kind or class of text. Novels, short stories, poems, business letters, company reports, concert programs, lab reports, office memos, wedding invitations, obituaries, and holiday letters are examples of written genres. Lectures and sermons too, although they are spoken out loud, have all of the features of written language other than graphic form. In each of these, certain uses of English would be considered normal while others would sound strange or funny.

For the most part, what is special about genres is not so much grammar but the choice of words and the kinds of things talked about. Some genres have their own grammatical peculiarities, however. Recipes are commonly written as a series of imperatives. Scientific writing avoids first- and second-person reference (the pronouns *I/me/we/us/you*) and often uses the passive voice. In some religious traditions, prayers make use of the special pronouns *thou* and *thee*. Moreover, genre is closely linked to register, in that some genres (such as a sermon) are intrinsically more formal than others (such as a stand-up comedy routine).

1.4 "Grammar"

Grammar does not enjoy a positive reputation. This is unfortunate, because professional writing demands not just an ability to write good sentences, but a certain awareness of what you are doing (that is, a way of talking about what makes some sentences good and others bad). A vocabulary for talking about sentences will help you to identify mistakes—deviations from the written standard—in your own writing and to explain to others the mistakes they make, will assist you in making decisions about how to put together and punctuate a sentence, and in general will increase your understanding about structure in language.

An explicit knowledge of this kind is needed by the professional writer in much the same way that a professional driver needs to know something about the mechanical workings of motor vehicles.

Kinds of Grammar

Most adults have not thought about grammar since grade school. They may have a vague memory of a few terms like "noun" and "subject" and are perhaps aware of a few rules of thumb, most of them misleading, such as "don't use *like*," "avoid the passive," and "don't end a sentence with a preposition." The attitude that may accompany these memories is of a subject that is simplistic and elementary, one that adults have outgrown.

Grade-school memories and attitudes might be a barrier to studying sentence structure in a very intense way and with unfamiliar methods such as are taught in this course. It might help to think of this task as having the same relationship to grade-school "grammar" as advanced mathematics does to simple arithmetic. Grammar, like many other subjects, can be studied at a variety of levels, from simple anecdotes to a hugely complex discipline (called linguistics) to which entire journals, professorial chairs, and libraries full of books are devoted.

In this course, we will approach grammar from a position somewhere between these two extremes. We will aim for a comprehensive and practical grasp of the main syntactic constructions of English that goes far beyond the primary-school level, but we will not be studying what linguists call formal syntax, with its detailed, logic-based theories and symbolisms. Our emphasis will rather be on identifying and describing types of grammatical constructions and pointing out errors often associated with these constructions.

Grammar and Written Usage

Although Written English is quite uniform, it is nonetheless true that there is no official body in the English-speaking world that is authorized to set a single standard of grammatical correctness. There are various public institutions such as schools, dictionaries, and voluminous reference grammars, but it is important to recognize that ultimately what regulates correctness is **usage**—and usage itself may be established in rather arbitrary ways. While there is a broad consensus on most aspects of grammar, disagreement among authorities in details is not at all rare, as in the following example involving *fewer* and *less*.

A well-known rule of English grammar states that *fewer* should be used for plural objects and *less* for singular ones referring to a mass, undifferentiated object. So we should write *less honey* but *fewer plums,* and avoid using *less* with plural nouns—that is, we should avoid *less plums.* A number of writers have pointed out, however, that *fewer* is being replaced by *less (There were less empty seats at the concert this week).* The degree to which the newer usage is accepted can be seen from the following quotation:

> [A]lthough the preference follows the rule as stated [that is, *fewer* with plural and *less* with singular nouns], *less* is often found with plurals even in formal contexts, and two other critics consider this usage acceptable. Webster and Webster's New World give *fewer* as a synonym of *less*; Harper, American Heritage, Random House, and the American College and Standard College dictionaries follow the rule. The consensus favors the rule, though strong forces are working against it.
> —Roy Copperud, *American Usage and Style: The Consensus*
> (New York: Van Nostrand Reinhold, 1980), 147

Even in Standard Written English, then, grammatical correctness is not an undisputed fact but is more a question of a *consensus* involving the actual practice of established writers: rules laid down by the creators of dictionaries and style manuals, the usages mandated by publishing houses, newspapers, and magazine publishers to their employees, and, increasingly, language mavens like William Safire, whose syndicated weekly column "On Language" often contains astute observations on the trends and shifts in usage (not to mention baseless prescriptions!).

The Boundary between Grammar and Style

Judgments about language are of many different kinds, not all of which are normally thought of as "grammatical" ones. For example, we may be concerned with different pronunciations of the same word, such as *nuclear* (often heard as [nucular], perhaps on the basis of *molecular*). Or we may be concerned with other kinds of judgments, such as choosing a gender-neutral word like *chair* in place of *chairman*. At a different level, we may be considering questions of **style**.

The border between grammar and style is especially hard to draw, since there are no real guidelines which will tell us whether a problematic sentence is wrong for purely grammatical or purely stylistic reasons. Broadly speaking, an ungrammatical sentence can't exist, whereas a stylistically wrong sentence is possible, but awkward in some way, or ineffective, or ambiguous, or inappropriate. But the line is blurred. We don't have precise enough definitions of "grammar" and "style" to say whether in particular cases sentences are stylistically or grammatically suspect. Sometimes our judgments about sentences are as much esthetic (based on a feeling for elegance, tastefulness, and generally being pleasing) as they are strictly grammatical. The question of the English passive is of this nature, for example. Some grammarians would forbid sentences like *The proposal was discussed extensively by the subcommittee* and insist instead on *The subcommittee discussed the proposal extensively.* But, as we will see, there are perfectly legitimate uses for the passive, and its appropriateness is a stylistic question, not a grammatical one.

And surprisingly often we cannot simply correct a sentence's grammar and let it stand, but must instead rewrite it, or even rewrite the entire paragraph, to avoid an awkward construction. So grammar serves stylistic ends, and the two are not easily separated.

1.5 Conclusion: Convention and Change

Consider the following:

- Someone says: "She was plainly inferring that I should resign." The listener mentally corrects the speaker by changing "inferring" to "implying," but is too polite to say anything.
- A reporter writes: "The attorneys whom the police said had removed the evidence were indicted." A reader winces at the "whom" and writes an irate letter to the editor.
- A student writes: "None of these methods have worked." Her teacher corrects the "have" to "has."
- A scholar writes: "The political factors which led Pitt to this decision have often been debated." An editor changes the "which" to "that." The scholar, on reading the proofs, angrily changes the emendation back to "which."

In all of these events, someone is perceived to have made a mistake and another person has, perhaps silently, corrected it. For the person noting the mistake, more than the mere correction of an error has happened: something that was wrong about the world has been set right again.

As we have said, most speakers of English believe that English grammar is analogous to arithmetic. Grammatical mistakes often have the same air of wrongness as arithmetical ones, and grammatical facts seem as unarguable as arithmetic ones. Eight times three won't equal twenty-two for me or for my great-grandchildren, so why should it be any more correct to say "none . . . have" now than it was fifty years ago?

But grammar is not the same as arithmetic. Grammatical judgments do not have the same timeless certainty as arithmetical ones. Knowledge of grammar is more like the social knowledge of how to behave in certain situations. That is to say, grammar is a set of *conventions,* somewhat like clothing and etiquette.

Changes in conventions spread slowly through the society, but eventually not adopting them comes to be considered old-fashioned and stuffy, and may even be economically ill advised.

The same is true of grammar. The student mentioned above who wrote "None of these methods have worked" was in the company of plenty of present-day good writers who use a plural verb with "none of . . . " An older and more conservative generation would write "None of these methods has worked." But sooner or later it will universally be seen as pedantic to insist on the singular verb "has" in the face of what is obviously a plural subject. When we are unsure about the correctness of a given phrase or sentence, it is possible that usage is changing. The name of the game is not to be the first to adopt the new, nor the last to abandon the old.

Uncertainty about the correctness of a phrase may also come about simply from a lack of understanding of the grammar of the sentence we want to use. The reporter who wrote "The attorneys whom the police claimed had removed the evidence were indicted" was probably confusing this sentence with a very similar kind of sentence in which "whom" would be correct, namely: "The attorneys whom the police claimed to have removed the evidence were indicted." In these instances, most would agree that the sentences produced are intelligible, even though they violate somebody's idea of good grammar.

On the other hand, it is also possible for a sentence to be grammatically correct but to be simply incomprehensible, or fatally ambiguous, or even to say something quite different from the author's intentions. A knowledge of grammar might have saved a writer some embarrassment in the following instance. A letter to a nationally known newspaper contained the following sentence: "A society that denies individuals access based on race or gender is an inherently unstable society."

The author clearly did not realize that her words could be understood in diametrically opposite ways, according to whether gender and race are interpreted as the basis for *access* or the basis for *denial of access*—that is, according to whether the phrase "based on race or gender" goes with "access" or "denies." The two senses are paraphrasable as follows:

[a] A society in which access by reason of race or gender is denied is an inherently unstable society.

[b] A society in which access is denied because of race or gender is an inherently unstable society.

A writer with some expertise in grammar might, for example, have noticed that the object of the verb "denies" could be either "access" or "access based on race or gender," and that the phrase "based on race or gender" could be either a modifier of "access" or an adverbial phrase modifying "denies." It could be argued that sentences of this kind are worse than ungrammatical ones whose meaning is unambiguous—though of course neither is as good as a sentence that is both grammatical and unambiguous.

Careful writing, then, requires an explicit knowledge of the conventions of grammar. For better or for worse, we live in a world in which a rather small number of good writers (and speakers) are called on to interpret a complex environment for those who must live in it. Those who use Standard Written English professionally therefore need to be familiar with the grammatical conventions and to be able to talk about them in a standard terminology.

EXERCISES

Exercise 1.1

(Some items for class discussion) Some of the following statements reflect misunderstandings or are inadequate as they stand. Change or amplify them so that they reflect the discussion in Chapter 1.

1. Swedish and Icelandic are Germanic languages. (Can you be more specific than this?)

2. The older Germanic languages evolved into the present-day spoken Germanic languages. (Give examples. Did any of the older Germanic languages fail to survive into the present day?)

3. "The German for 11 and 12 is *elf* and *zwölf* (from which the English was presumably derived)."—Leonard Gillman, cited in the *New York Times*, Aug. 6, 1995, 7E. (Give Dr. Gillman, an eminent mathematician, some help with his linguistics!)

4. Old Norse, Gothic, and Anglo-Saxon are all early representatives of the Proto-Germanic language family. (How is the term "Proto-Germanic" being misused here?)

5. Proto-Germanic is the hypothetical ancestor language of the Germanic language family, reconstructed on the basis of linguistic evidence taken from all the languages of the family.

6. Roman, Greek, and Cyrillic are the names of alphabets.

7. The Slavic languages are written in the Cyrillic alphabet. (Of which Slavic languages is this not true?)

8. *Ain't* is a dialect form of *isn't*. (Is *ain't* really a dialect—a regionally restricted—form?)

9. Writing is a graphic representation of speech. (Refer to the section in 1.3 on the relationship of writing to speech.)

10. Studying English grammar will help us speak more correctly. (In discussing this statement, don't forget to talk about the implications of the notion of "speaking correctly"!)

Exercise 1.2

Numerous other language families have been studied. One of these is the Romance family, whose members include French, Italian, Spanish, and Portuguese. Go to an encyclopedia or other source, find other examples of Romance languages, and construct a family tree similar to the one we gave for Germanic in Chapter 1. The proto-language for the Germanic family (Proto-Germanic) does not exist in actual documents; in what important respect is the proto-language for the Romance family different?

Exercise 1.3

Both the Germanic and the Romance families are in turn members of a wider family known as Indo-European. What can you find out about the Indo-European family? Which other well-known languages does it include?

Exercise 1.4

Find out about the family relationships of some of the following languages: Turkish, Finnish, Swahili, Indonesian, Chinese, Navaho, Arabic, Cree, Japanese, Korean, Aztec.

Exercise 1.5

Construct a visual timeline for the history of English, starting from 400 C.E. and ending in about 1700, that will include important events and figures in the language's past, such as the arrival of Germanic tribes on the shores of England, Alfred the Great, the epic poem *Beowulf*, the Viking settlements, the Norman Conquest, and others. Don't forget more recent events like the colonization of North America and the importation of Africans in the slave trade.

Exercise 1.6

There are a number of books that discuss the different conventions of English grammar as prescribed by various publishing houses and other authorities. Roy Copperud's *American Usage and Style: The Consensus* (New York: Van Nostrand Reinhold, 1980) is convenient and quite comprehensive for disputed usages. Go to one or more of these books, find examples of the following, and report on them to the class.

1. *burglarize*
2. the use of the last comma in *bread, butter, milk(,) and cheese*
3. *different from/than/to*
4. *due to*
5. *finalize*
6. *It's me* (*him, them*, etc.)
7. *like* as a conjunction ("The car doesn't pick up speed *like* it should.")
8. agreement of the verb after *none of* ("None of us is/are . . . ")

9. *slow* as an adverb ("go slow/slowly")

10. split infinitive

Exercise 1.7

The *American Heritage Dictionary* has usage notes for many entries. A panel of educators, editors, and public figures was polled for their reactions to controversial aspects of English grammar and word usage. Look up the following entries. If possible, find the 1969 and 1993 editions and compare the entries.[2] Ask a variety of people you know about how they use these forms.

1. *agenda* used as a singular noun ("The agenda was approved.")

2. *anxious to* used in the sense of "eager to" ("I am anxious to meet her.")

3. *badly* used after *feel* ("We felt badly about his misfortune.")

4. *between* rather than *among* with more than two objects ("The family arranged it between themselves.")

5. *comprise:* "be comprised of" used in place of "comprise" ("The United States is comprised of the forty-eight continental states, Alaska, and Hawaii.")

6. *criteria* used as a singular noun (". . . by this criteria . . .")

7. *data* used as a singular noun ("The data shows conclusively . . .")

8. *disinterested* used in place of *uninterested* ("He is disinterested in the literature of this period.")

9. *hopefully* used in the sense of "it is to be hoped that" ("Hopefully the situation will change.")

10. *phenomena* used as a singular noun ("This phenomena is . . .")

Exercise 1.8

Which of the following terms did you encounter during your early schooling in grammar?

noun	helping verb
noun phrase	auxiliary
linking verb	syntax
adverb	complement
adjective	morpheme
preposition	phrasal verb
two-word verb	modifier

Give examples of the ones you remember. Look up the others in the index to this book. We will be returning to most of them later on.

---

[2]From Craig Sirles, "Linguistic prescription and social proscription: Lexicography and the changing face of American English," unpublished paper read at the Modern Language Association, 1994.

Exercise 1.9

Identify the genre. What word choices and grammatical forms provide the best clues?

1. He is best remembered for his performance as a streetsweeper in the 1955 Broadway musical *Starlit Nights*. *obituary*

2. Profits were up slightly in the third quarter, but not enough to recoup the severe losses resulting from the natural disasters earlier in the year. *financial report*

3. We beseech thee, O Lord, to preserve and defend those we love. *prayer*

4. For the third night running, UN relief convoys have been turned back by heavy shelling. *news report*

5. After a reception in the Tivoli Hotel, the couple will fly to Majorca for their honeymoon. *wedding announcement*

6. The alleged suspect was apprehended while attempting to conceal himself in a freight elevator. *police report*

7. Stir into the melted butter one tbsp. refined flour and heat until almost brown. Add the sauce slowly to the flour mixture. *recipe*

8. Anyway, gotta go now, but Jack sends his love, and we'll see you next month in San Diego, I hope. *letter, personal*

9. If a document you are working on is part of a longer document, you can use the Number From option under Footnotes in the Document command to set a start number. Be sure to turn off the Restart Each Section option if necessary.

10. Gone to class. Back 9:30. Don't forget to take dog out. Spaghetti sauce in fridge. Love, J. *note*

Exercise 1.10

Convert all the sentences into a more formal register, such as, for example, an office memo or a published report. What changes in *content* do you find yourself wanting to make when you adapt them? Is there any material you might prefer not to express at all in the formal register?

1. I wouldn't park back of that building if I was you.

2. Hate to hafta tell you this, but you know Chuck Kovak? The Big Enchilada of the whole outfit? Keeled over last night. Heart attack. Never knew what hit him. They got him to the ER, but he'd already croaked. I heard he was out on a binge with his drinking buddies.

3. If there's anything in the way of paperclips, stationery, notepads, that kind of thing, you need, just get ahold of Bud Rethke, he's the office manager around here.

4. We just added a few drops of that stuff and the whole kaboodle started to bubble and seethe like you wouldn't believe.

5. The whole area of the building catty-corner across the courtyard from us is gonna be off limits to us folks 'coz they're tearing everything down to build a snazzy new headquarters for the big cheeses.

2

WORDS

2.0 Parts of Speech

We begin the study of English grammar with some elementary concepts and techniques.

The entry point into the grammar of English is through the **categories** of words—the ways of classifying words that have proved the most useful in analyzing the language. Categories are what were once (and often still are) called "parts of speech," what you learned as nouns, verbs, adjectives, etc.

In studying grammar we will have to discuss some of the problems of assigning words to categories when categories are considered from a more precise grammatical point of view.

2.1 The Meanings of Categories

Traditional ways of defining categories often involved finding a common meaning for all members of the same category. Thus verbs were action or doing words, nouns were names of places, persons, or things. Adjectives were describing words. Such definitions share a common problem. If a certain word that obviously belongs to the category does not fit the meaning, the meaning must somehow be extended to accommodate it. Thus if *occurrence* or *injustice,* which are obviously nouns, are not apparently thinglike, that must be because we have an inadequate conception of *thing.* And if *seemed,* a verb, does not suggest an action, we must expand our notion of actions in order to include it.

Meaning-based definitions are therefore circular. But it is not clear that other kinds of definitions are superior. There are, in fact, many unresolved problems with the system of categories currently in use, and grammarians disagree both about the categories themselves (how many there are, what labels to give them) and about what criteria to use for assigning a word to one category or another. The best one can say is that we have to start somewhere. In order to construct a system such as a grammatical description, we must always make some initial assumptions, and the validity of these assumptions will depend on how useful they turn out to be in practice.

2.2 The Categories

Because there is no fixed agreement on how to define categories, the number of categories varies according to criteria adopted by different grammarians.

By the Way:

Our system of categories is very ancient. It goes back to the Roman rhetoricians, who in turn got it from the Greeks. Something very similar to the present-day system of categories was in use by the time of the Greek-speaking grammarian Dionysius Thrax (ca. 100 B.C.E.). Dionysius Thrax assumed the following: noun, verb, participle, article, pronoun, preposition, adverb, and conjunction. An accessible discussion can be found in R. H. Robins, *A Short History of Linguistics*, 2nd ed. (London: Longman, 1979).

There is also some variation from language to language. A number of languages appear to have no class of adjective distinct from nouns or verbs. For certain Native American languages, we find linguists even disputing the necessity of a noun-verb distinction.

Furthermore, it is a matter of judgment in some cases whether a class of words represents a category all to itself or is a subcategory of a larger class. This is true, for example, of auxiliaries and participles, included by some under the category of verb, but separated by others into one or two more categories.

In English, the category a word belongs to is not usually apparent in isolation. This means we often cannot identify the category just by looking at the word. Obvious exceptions to this are words that have a suffix associated with a particular category, such as *-ful*, which forms adjectives, and *-ation*, which is characteristic of nouns. But very many nouns could in isolation just as easily be verbs. Here are a few: *watch, look, nail, delay, drive, shoe, carpet, paper, ink, book*. In fact, it is a challenging exercise to think up nouns that cannot, under any circumstances, be used as verbs.

The major categories that will be assumed in this book are:

- noun
- pronoun
- verb
- adjective
- adverb
- preposition
- determiner
- conjunction

Nouns, verbs, adjectives, and adverbs are sometimes referred to as **lexical** categories. This term stems from the fact that nouns, verbs, adjectives, and adverbs are the categories that supply the bulk of lexical, or word-based, meaning to a sentence. Pronouns, prepositions, determiners, and conjunctions are **grammatical** categories, in that they give structure to sentences rather than supplying meaning. Thus a set of words consisting entirely of lexical categories, such as:

    *Schoolteacher play banjo tomorrow grandmother grandfather

while strange-sounding, is meaningful in a way that

    *that will the for his and

(consisting entirely of grammatical categories) is not. We will discuss the categories in order, noting some of their salient features, with a view to returning to them for a more detailed discussion in the context of their grammar in later chapters.

By the Way:

An asterisk * in front of a sentence signals that the sentence is incorrect.

2.3 Nouns and Pronouns

Nouns and **pronouns**, which will be treated together, are **referring** forms. They mention the entities in our environment, including our own discourse, that are talked about and to which qualities and actions are attributed.

Examples of nouns: *hammer, octogenarian, word, salmon, hay, injustice, delay, face, knot, day, pronouncement, beauty.*

Examples of pronouns: *I, you, she, us, them, that, someone, what, himself.*

Both nouns and pronouns may refer not just to tangible things, but to less substantial entities like words that have been spoken:

[1] That was an uncalled-for remark ("That" is a pronoun referring to spoken words)

[2] The echo repeated Bill's question ("Question" is a noun referring to what Bill said)

We cannot therefore define nouns or pronouns merely as labels for objects, but must have some other reason for grouping them together. Probably the best way to think of nouns and pronouns is as *potential topics*. A potential topic is whatever can be mentioned, talked about, and referred to. Some examples:

- You see a beautiful picture and refer to its *beauty* with a noun.
- You hear an account of a judge treating an accused person unfairly and comment to a friend about the *injustice* that is being committed.
- You become angry when something that is due is postponed and inquire about the *delay*.
- You see a crowd leaving a cinema and refer to the people as *they*.
- You see someone being helped by a Boy Scout and refer to the Boy Scout as *he*.

In these situations, a quality, an event, or an entity is made into a topic so that it can be talked about. The noun "beauty" allows us to make a topic of the picture's quality; the adjective "beautiful" cannot serve this purpose. The noun "injustice" similarly gives us a starting point for discussing the unfair treatment of the accused. "The enemy has attacked" *reports* something that happened, but if we wish to refer to the event as a topic, we must say "the attack." And so on.

In general, then, we can say that *we must convert actions, states, things, people, and qualities into nouns and pronouns before we can mention them or talk about them.*

Nouns and pronouns may change their form according to whether they are singular or plural (number) and according to the relationship they bear to other elements of the sentence (case).

2.4 Verbs and Auxiliaries

Verbs serve to report actions and states and to introduce predicates. A predicate is something that is said *about* something. Examples of verbs: *walk, cook, agitate, think, resemble, provoke, postpone, pronounce, seem, sway, possess*.

The Meanings of Verbs

We saw that nouns and pronouns function to *mention* or *refer to* topics. The verb is a pivotal category that functions as the center of a group of words that **predicate** or attribute a quality or an action to the topic noun or pronoun. The meanings of individual verbs fall into a number of types.

Some verbs report events—that is, things that happen:

[3] The second car *swerved* to *avoid* the bicycle and *struck* a pedestrian

Others describe states:

[4] The lovely island of Capri *lies* in the Bay of Naples west of Sorrento

Still others link a topic noun with a quality of some kind (the so-called "linking verb"):

[5] Your cat *seemed* a little depressed this evening

Here "a little depressed" says something about the cat, and "seemed" links the cat with the quality "a little depressed."

These three different kinds of meanings (event, state, and link) are logically connected. The following examples illustrate how a verb could have some characteristics of two of these meanings at the same time:

[6] Charles and Camilla *were floating* on a mattress in the swimming pool

"Float" is partly like an event, since Charles and Camilla could be said to be doing something, namely floating, and partly like a state, since floating is at the same time a state something is in.

[7] Lefty *turned* pale when Dalgleish mentioned the candlesticks

"Turned" links "Lefty" to the attribute "pale," but is at the same time an event, since something happens.

[8] Memorial Park *looks* incredibly eerie on a moonlit night

"Looks" has characteristics of a state and at the same time attributes the quality "incredibly eerie" to "Memorial Park."

So although the three kinds of verbs may not have one general meaning in common, they fade into one another as a group.

The Forms of Verbs

In addition to having shared general meanings, verbs are capable of showing tense; that is, they may indicate present or past time. Often the tense appears not on the verb itself but on an auxiliary verb, such as *can* or *have*. However, unlike nouns or any other category, a verb can indicate present time or past time without any help from another word. The verbs in the following sentences are all in the past tense; the corresponding present tense is placed in parentheses beside each one:

[9] Leslie *cooked* (cooks) the most delicate crepes

[10] They *kept* (keep) the dinosaurs on a remote island

[11] We *drank* (drink) a toast to the retiring dean

[12] I *hit* (hit) the ball right out of the park

[13] Robin *went* (goes) to a mah-jongg game every Thursday

Verbs that report events, describe states, or link a subject with a quality are known as **lexical** verbs. Lexical verbs are distinct from auxiliary verbs, which add an indication of time or manner to a lexical verb.

Auxiliary Verbs

As we have noted, most of the time English verbs do not appear alone as they do in these five sentences, but are accompanied by various kinds of **auxiliaries**. Auxiliary verbs or auxiliaries, as they are more commonly known, are verbs that accompany a lexical verb and supply extra information about the verb's context, such as obligation (*must*), futurity (*will*), an ongoing perspective (*is* with the suffix *-ing* on the verb), recent completion (*have* with the suffix *-ed* or *-en* on the verb), and others.

In practice—that is to say, in actual texts—tense is more commonly shown on the auxiliary than on the verb itself. When tense is shown on an auxiliary, the verb is in a **non-tensed** form. The verb "grow," for example, appears in one of its non-tensed forms in each of the following sentences:

[14] We are growing geraniums in our window box

[15] The sunflowers have grown as high as the house

[16] They can grow rice and millet in their fields

The non-tensed form chosen depends on the auxiliary. The auxiliary "be" is followed by a verb with the suffix *-ing*, as in [14] "growing." The auxiliary "have" is followed by a verb with a suffix that may take one of several different forms; in example [15] it is *-n* ("grown").

A small number of auxiliaries, exemplified by "can" in [16], are followed by the simple base form of the main verb; that is, the verb is not preceded by the word *to*, nor does the verb have a suffix. This set of auxiliaries contributes the meaning of **modality**, which adds meanings of possibility and obligation to the verb. These auxiliaries are therefore called **modal auxiliaries,** or simply **modals**. The meanings of the modals are illustrated in:

[17] You *should* apologize to the judge immediately (obligation)

[18] We *may* get a tornado later in the day (possibility)

[19] *Can* you help me with the piano tomorrow? (willingness)

Note the sense, common to all of them, that no statement of certainty is made, but that in each case an action is presented as a possibility or a future obligation or appeal.

2.5 Adjectives

The next category we will deal with, the **adjective**, serves to attribute some quality to a noun or pronoun. Examples of adjectives: *green, angry, far-fetched, irreconcilable, cute, fast, quick, slow, tempestuous.*

Among the most important positions in the sentence occupied by adjectives are (1) immediately before a noun, and (2) after a linking verb. The first kind are known as **attributive adjectives,** the second as **predicative adjectives.** Examples of attributive adjectives:

[20] Scottie served us one of her *succulent* quiches

[21] The crisis was building up to an *explosive* situation

[22] The *economic* advantages of reinvesting were obvious

And of predicative adjectives:

[23] The milk had turned *sour*

[24] Dr. Goodshoe's qualifications were *impressive*

[25] The workers seemed *angry* this morning

2.6 Adverbs

Adverbs are, from the point of view of their grammatical functions, a mixed class. They are also the hardest to define and to identify. Two of their most important uses are to add meaning to a verb and to qualify an adjective.

In the following three examples, adverbs add something to the meaning of a verb:

[26] Bill looked at me *strangely*

[27] The train chugged *slowly* through the pine forests

[28] They ate their sandwiches *ravenously*

The next three examples show adverbs modifying adjectives:

[29] *Unusually* low temperatures had ruined the artichoke crop

[30] The jaws with their rows of pointed teeth looked *terrifyingly* real

[31] They admired the staircase with its *ingeniously* carved railing

Many, but by no means all, adverbs are derived from adjectives by adding the suffix -*ly*: *warmly, hurriedly.* An important exception is *fast,* which is both an adjective and an adverb:

[32] He likes to drive *fast* cars (attributive adjective)

[33] The new version of MS-DOS is incredibly *fast* (predicative adjective)

[34] Time goes by *fast* during the summer (adverb)

Conversely, not every word that ends in -*ly* is an adverb. Note especially adjectives such as *kindly, cowardly, gentlemanly,* and *friendly,* which cannot add another -*ly* to make them into adverbs. So we cannot write **He clapped me on the shoulder friendlily* but . . . *in a friendly manner.* A helpful rule, although it does have exceptions, is that -*ly* makes adjectives when added to nouns and adverbs when added to adjectives.

An important subcategory of adverbs is one that denotes the direction or place of a verb or the location of an entire statement. Consider the following:

[35] *Outside,* heavy snowflakes were drifting down

[36] Billie and Jeanie went *outside* to see the spaceship

[37] The wagons trundled *westward*

"Outside" and "westward" are adverbs that denote the setting of a sentence or the direction of an action. In their focus on space and direction, these kinds of adverbs have much in common with the next category, the preposition.

2.7 Prepositions

Prepositions are words that begin **a prepositional phrase.** A prepositional phrase can be defined for the time being as a preposition followed by a noun or pronoun. The obvious circularity of this definition is unavoidable; recall that none of our categories can actually be *defined* other than by giving examples of their use. Being a relatively small class of words, prepositions are actually easier to recognize than adverbs. There is, however, as we will see, some overlap between the classes of adverb and preposition.

The noun or pronoun in a prepositional phrase is known as the **complement** of the preposition, or the **prepositional complement.**

Examples of prepositions are *in, of, up, down, for, by, with, from, to.* In the following sentences prepositional phrases are italicized:

[38] A strange creature emerged *from the vehicle*

[39] I am dedicating the free love pamphlet *to my father*

[40] He was chasing the unfortunate reporter *with an umbrella*

[41] Aunt Agatha had always wanted to do Niagara Falls *in a barrel*

A number of prepositions are spatial; that is to say, they refer to a location: *above, below, against, behind, opposite.*

"Marooned" Prepositions

Many prepositions in English have the peculiarity that they can appear without a following noun or pronoun, in a function that is very similar to that of an adverb:

[42] Billie fell *down*

[43] All the children from the orphanage came *along*

Such prepositions are said to be **marooned**, because they are, so to speak, stranded and all alone. An interesting ambiguity may arise if a marooned preposition is placed in front of a noun, where it may seem to be forming a prepositional phrase with the noun:

[44] Some drunk in a red Lexus ran down our dog

In sentences of this kind, "down" is separate from "our dog," as can be seen from the fact that it can be moved around the noun:

[45]′ Some drunk in a red Lexus ran our dog down

Movable (marooned) prepositions of this kind should be distinguished from prepositions that are part of a prepositional phrase that includes a noun or pronoun, as in

[46] A small boy ran down the hill

In cases like [46], no alternative form is possible in which the preposition is moved to the other side of the noun:

[47]′ *A small boy ran the hill down

REMINDER!

An asterisk * in front of a sentence signals that the sentence is incorrect!

The Boundary between Preposition and Adverb

The boundary between the categories preposition and adverb is not always distinct. Consider, for example, the word "ashore" in

[48] They sent a landing party ashore

It is clearly an adverb, since it cannot combine with a noun or pronoun to make a prepositional phrase (*ashore the island*). Yet "ashore" is similar in some ways to a marooned preposition like "down" in

[49] We sent another messenger down

[50] We sent another messenger down the mountain

For example, "ashore" can be moved next to the verb just like "down":

[51] They sent ashore a platoon of fully armed marines

[52] We sent down another messenger

Some grammarians prefer to assign the marooned prepositions to a special category known as particles. (We have not adopted this analysis here.) The term "preposition" would then be restricted to prepositions that occur with a noun or pronoun. In terms of the above examples, there would thus be three rather than two categories:

[53] They sent a landing party ashore (adverb)

[54] We sent a messenger down (particle)

[55] We sent a messenger down the mountain (preposition)

2.8 Determiners

Nouns rarely appear alone. Usually they are accompanied by various words that are said to determine them.

The name **determiner** differs from the other category names in that it is not really a single part of speech, but rather a blanket term for a variety of kinds of words that come before a noun and indicate its quantity, its presumed degree of familiarity (definiteness), and its location with respect to the speaker. The determiners include articles (*the* and *a*), demonstratives (such as *this* and *that*), and quantifiers, such as *all* and *some*. The class of determiners also includes numerals (*one, seven, twenty-nine, fourth*) and possessives such as *my, your.*

Articles

In keeping with the traditional terminology, we distinguish the **definite article,** which is *the,* from the **indefinite article,** which is *a* or, before a vowel, *an.* The definite article suggests that the writer assumes the noun is already familiar to the reader in some way. The indefinite article implies that the noun it determines is new to the discourse and unfamiliar to the reader. The following examples illustrate these meanings:

[56] A passing motorist pulled us out of the ditch

[57] The president of Acme Industries gave an inspiring speech

[58] The sky on the eastern horizon was streaked with pink

[59] We arrived late because the road was blocked by a fallen tree

Notice that the sources of familiarity suggested by the definite article *the* are quite varied. In [56] "the ditch" has clearly been mentioned before; in [57] "the president of Acme Industries" is familiar because an outfit like Acme Industries is expected to have a president, even though we may never have met her; in [58] "the sky" and "the eastern horizon" are permanently present in our natural environment; in [59] "the road" may not have been mentioned before, but may simply be implied by an act of driving or walking.

The use of the indefinite article with the nouns "motorist" in [56], "speech" in [57], and "tree" in [59], by contrast, suggest that these nouns have not been mentioned before, and that there is no obvious way their presence can be inferred from the discourse environment.

Demonstratives

Demonstratives point to location near to or distant from the speaker. *That, those* are the distant, or **distal**, demonstratives, and *this, these* are the near, or **proximal**, ones. Unlike other determiners, the demonstratives show a difference of singular and plural according to the following noun: *this bottle/these bottles; that bluebird/those bluebirds.* Demonstratives have some resemblances to pronouns, and in fact become pronouns when no noun follows: ***those are my parents and two sisters; this is my favorite tune.***

Quantifiers

Quantifiers say something about the quantity or distribution of the noun. Some common quantifiers are *all, each, every, some,* as in

[60] *All* the passengers cheered when the plane landed

[61] We managed to rescue *some* of the pumpkins

[62] *Each* child carried a small green-and-red flag

2.9 Conjunctions (Subordinators and Coordinators)

Conjunctions are grammatical words that link sentences or clauses together. A **clause** is a sentence that forms part of a larger sentence. For example, in

[63] The Dow Jones is down again *and* they are predicting more rain

there are two clauses ("The Dow Jones is down again" and "they are predicting more rain") joined by the conjunction "and."

Subordinating Conjunctions

Subordinating conjunctions are also known as **subordinators**, and are so called because they introduce a clause that is *part of* another sentence, this wider sentence being known as the **main**, or **matrix**, **clause**. In the following sentences, the subordinating conjunction is italicized; notice that, as in [65], the subordinate clause can sometimes precede the main or matrix clause:

[64] I fixed the halyard to the mainsail *before* Maeve lowered the centerboard

[65] *Because* the notary's stamp was illegible, they declared the contract invalid

Some other examples of subordinating conjunctions are *while, because, after, before.* A number of subordinating conjunctions are identical to prepositions (for example, *before, after, since*).

One particular type of subordinator is known as a **complementizer**. A complementizer links a new clause, known as the complement clause, to a specific word or phrase in another clause. For example, in

[66] She claims that Ephraim is unreliable

the complementizer "that" links the verb "claims" to the clause "Ephraim is unreliable." In

[67] The charge that he had libeled the First Citizen was dismissed

"that" links the noun "charge" to the clause "he had libeled the First Citizen." Further discussion of the quite complex differences among types of subordinators will be postponed until Chapter 14.

Coordinating Conjunctions

Coordinating conjunctions, or **coordinators**, join together words and sentences that have equal status. That is, the statements they make or the words they join are presented as being equally important, as in:

[68] The battery is dead, *or* perhaps the fuse is blown

[69] Our firm's headquarters are in Dallas, *and* many of our employees come from the Dallas–Fort Worth area

[70] We have nearly a full tank, *but* Pottsville is 400 miles away

[71] Beatrice *and* Muhammed were dancing the two-step

[72] Hank *or* Big Mike can bring the refrigerator down the stairs

A coordinated clause may not change places with its partner:

[73]′ *Or perhaps the fuse is blown, the battery is dead

[74]′ *And many of our employees come from the Dallas–Fort Worth area, our firm's headquarters are in Dallas

The coordinators are *and, or, but,* and *for.* Some coordinators can link smaller groups of words such as nouns and adjectives (as, for example, *cinnamon and orange, pipes or cigars, wealthy and attractive but already married*).

2.10 Summary

In this chapter, we have aimed to make a few introductory remarks about each of the categories that form the starting point of any investigation of grammar. Nouns and verbs serve to state topics and to present predicates about those topics, respectively. Determiners tell us about the familiarity, quantity, and distribution of nouns. Auxiliary verbs, or auxiliaries, are special verbs that give us information about the tense (time) and certain other aspects of the lexical verb's use. Adjectives and adverbs are modifiers: adjectives modify nouns, and adverbs modify verbs and adjectives. Prepositions stand before nouns to form prepositional phrases, which have a variety of grammatical uses; prepositions may be "marooned"; that is, they may stand alone without a noun or pronoun complement. Conjunctions (subordinate and coordinate) and complementizers join clauses together.

EXERCISES

Exercise 2.1

Each of the items 1–4 below consists of a set of words and a pair of category names. For each item, place the words in one of three columns according to whether they belong unambiguously in one of the categories (columns I and II), or could plausibly belong to *either* of the categories named (column III). For each of the words in column III, make up two sentences exemplifying its use in each category. Here are some examples from item (1) by way of illustration:

I. NOUN	II. VERB	III. EITHER NOUN OR VERB
photo	misjudge	alarm

"alarm" as noun: We left the building when the alarm sounded.
"alarm" as verb: The earthquake warnings alarmed the population.

1. *Noun and verb:* cat, squirrel, misjudge, violin, photo, arm, wrist, unlock, thumb, entertainment, carry, alarm

2. *Adjective and verb:* large, smooth, amaze, dry, calm, drunk, silence, renew, thin, mellow, red, force

3. *Adjective and adverb:* deadly, heavy, poor, poorly, good, well, faster, early, late, soon

4. *Preposition and conjunction:* and, although, during, since, while, except, because, of, but, after, near, until

Exercise 2.2

In each of the following sentences, one item is italicized. Identify its category (part of speech).

1. There was not enough *oxygen* in the fish tank.

2. The children had been *flying* kites in the park.

3. He had gone to the movies *with* some of his friends.

4. He was wearing a pink blazer *and* a green tie.

5. The eighteenth century was a *time* of intense reflection on the human condition.

6. An *ingeniously* contrived arrangement of string and tin cans guarded the entrance.

7. *They* were coming for us at eight o'clock.

8. Someone asked me to hand *over* my passport.

9. The books *were* fascinating.

10. All the guests *were* leaving.

Exercise 2.3

In the following sentences, underline the word or words that belong to the category or have the function indicated in parentheses after the sentence.

1. The toolshed behind the parking lot looked cluttered. (adjective)

2. I looked up the word in an old dictionary. (complement of preposition)

3. The "fast" train to Boston was quite slow. (adverb)

4. Besides Marty and me, a couple of flashy-looking guys, each with two bodyguards, were in the elevator. (coordinating conjunction)

5. Gary had a battered Mercedes that had seen better days. (auxiliary verb)

6. I will have another of those delicious Campari sodas, please. (demonstrative)

7. Apparently Fred had been hallucinating again. (verb)

8. These marginal sects are unlikely to influence the election. (article)

9. Since they have vented the nuclear reactors again, we will have to cancel our outdoor barbecue. (subordinating conjunction)

10. The editor maintains that that "that" that I used should be "which." (demonstrative)

3

PHRASES

3.0 Phrases

The serious study of grammar (that is, any study that takes you past a few elementary concepts like "adjective" and "noun") demands a grasp of some fairly abstract ideas about the structure of sentences. Among the most important of these is the notion **phrase**.

In the everyday, lay use of the term, a phrase is a group of words that are commonly used together, as in, say, *economic refugee* or *at this point in time*. In grammar (as in music), the word "phrase" is a technical term with a more precise meaning. It refers to a set of words that belong together because they function as a grammatical unit in the sentence.

3.1 The Notion of "Phrase" in Grammar

Take the following sentence:

[1] The Nationalists lost the election

The first step in analyzing such a sentence is to say that it consists of two phrases, one acting as a subject ("the Nationalists") and one acting as a predicate ("lost the election"). So "the Nationalists" is one phrase, and "lost the election" is another. Phrases may consist of only one word, as for example in

[2] People cheered

Here the subject phrase is the single word "people," and the predicate phrase is the single word "cheered." Another example:

[3] Oranges were once an exotic fruit

This time the subject phrase is again a single word, "oranges," and the predicate phrase is much longer ("were once an exotic fruit").

3.2 The Analysis of Declarative Statements

The kinds of sentences that most easily lend themselves to division into a subject and a predicate are what are called **Declarative Statements,** sentences that make a simple declaration about the world. Here are some examples of declarative statements:

[4] The school bus leaves before breakfast

[5] A swarm of bees drifted over the meadow

[6] Sunspots are interfering with our radio reception

[7] The children next door have been eating wax crayons

[8] The members of the orchestra were tuning their instruments

[9] You should remember your manners

[10] The languages of the Caucasus belong to several different families

[11] Captain Scott and his party perished in a blizzard

In the simplest kind of declarative statement, like the ones just listed in [4]–[11], there is a phrase, the **subject,** which stands at the beginning of the sentence and which announces a topic for the sentence. The subjects of these eight sentences are: "the school bus," "a swarm of bees," "sunspots," "the children next door," "the members of the orchestra," "you," "the languages of the Caucasus," "Captain Scott and his party." Notice that the length of these subjects varies from a single word in "you" or "many" to several words in "the members of the orchestra," "Captain Scott and his party."

The subject is, as we have noted, a phrase. The words it is composed of form a group that functions as a unit—as a subject. No matter how large the subject is, the words which comprise it will always be a phrase. And if a subject consists of a single word, that single word is itself a phrase. For the moment we will practice identifying subjects in declarative statements by asking, quite simply, "What or who is this statement *about?*"

If the subject is the topic of the sentence (what the sentence is about), the **predicate** is what is said about the subject. In the simpler declarative statement kind of sentence, the predicate is that part of the sentence that is left over when the subject is set aside. But you should be warned that this subtractive definition of the predicate will not suffice for any but the simplest kind of sentence.

Going back to the example sentences above, we can mark off the predicates by drawing a vertical line between the subject or topic and the rest of the sentence:

The languages of the Caucasus I belong to several different families

At the same time, we can verify to ourselves that "belong to several different families" is indeed what is said about "the languages of the Caucasus." Similarly, in

> Captain Scott and his party | perished in a blizzard

"Captain Scott and his party" is what the sentence is about, and "perished in a blizzard" is what is said about them.

In all of these sentences, the predicate is also a phrase. The predicate phrase is a group of words that says something about the subject.

3.3 Diagramming: Some Introductory Concepts

In the previous section, we separated the two phrases (the subject and the predicate) in declarative statement sentences with a vertical line. But vertical lines have their limitations both as graphic devices (they do not permit us to label elements) and as analytic tools (there may be not only divisions, but sub-divisions, and sub-subdivisions in a sentence). Eventually we will want to introduce more detail into the analysis of a sentence, and a series of vertical lines is too limited a device to reveal all the complexity of sentence structure.

Consider the following two alternatives:

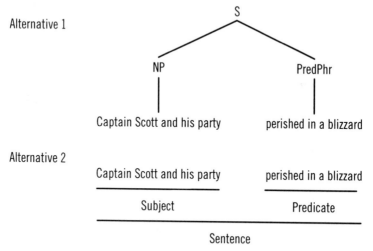

Diagram 3A.   Two Possible Ways of Analyzing a Sentence

These two alternatives show two different ways of presenting phrases. One of them is a **tree diagram**, with branches. Each branch culminates in a phrase. The other is a simple or multiple underlining of the phrases. We will refer to this as an **underlining diagram**. Each unbroken underline signals that the words written over it form a phrase—that is, that they belong together grammatically.

Alternative 1, the tree diagram, names the two parts as a noun phrase (NP) and a predicate phrase (PredPhr), and tells us they are part of the same sentence (S). In Alternative 1, each phrase is the end of a branch whose common root is the sentence.

Alternative 2, the underlining diagram, says, in effect: There are two phrases, "Captain Scott and his party" and "perished in a blizzard," which are respectively the subject and the predicate of the sentence. These two phrases are in turn combined into the phrase "sentence."

We will be making considerable use of these two ways of representing phrases. In fact, soon we will combine them into a single graph (diagram) of a sentence. This graph will have in its upper part (the tree part above the line with the written sentence) *category* names like NP and PredPhr and in its lower part (the underlining part below the written sentence) *function* names like "Subject" and "Predicate." Looking ahead a bit, so that you understand why these two different ways of representing sentences are being introduced, we will want to analyze this sentence in something like the following way:

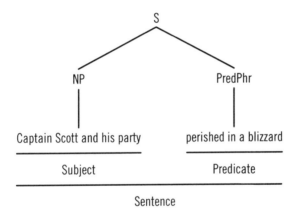

Diagram 3B.   Combining tree and underlining diagrams.

We can read this diagram off by saying that the sentence "Captain Scott and his party perished in a blizzard" consists of a noun phrase, "Captain Scott and his party," functioning as a subject, and a predicate phrase, "perished in a blizzard," functioning as a predicate.

Phrases, then, have two aspects which must both be represented, and which you must be careful to keep apart in your mind. One part—the tree part—consists of **forms** with labels for categories like "Verb," "Noun," and "Adjective," and phrase labels like "Noun Phrase" and "Predicate Phrase." The other part, the set of underlinings, consists of **functions**, with names like "Subject" and "Predicate."

Because the diagram combines the form part and the function part into a single diagram, this kind of diagram is known as a **form-function diagram.**

Note that in a form-function diagram,

- every identifiable function in a sentence is a phrase, and
- every phrase in a sentence has an identifiable function.

We need to keep forms and functions separate because some kinds of phrases may be capable of having several different functions in a sentence. Noun phrases are a good example. In each of the following three sentences, the noun phrase "these stones" functions differently:

[12] These stones will make a nice rock garden (subject)

[13] We will place these stones in a circle (object)

[14] You can make an arrow on the ground with these stones (complement of preposition)

In [12], the noun phrase "these stones" is the subject of the verb "will make." In [13], "these stones" is said to be the **object** of the verb "place," because it is the thing affected by the action of placing. In [14], "these stones" follows the preposition "with"; as we saw in Chapter 2, the noun phrase that follows a preposition is known as the **complement** of the preposition. We will return to these and other grammatical concepts later; they are introduced here to illustrate the point that one form can have more than one function.

Just as certain kinds of phrases can have more than one function, so some functions can be served by more than one form. For example, the function of **modifying** (describing or limiting in some way) can be performed by several kinds of phrases, as in the following, where the modifier is italicized:

[15] a *sharp* knife (adjective)

[16] the knife *in the drawer* (prepositional phrase)

[17] a *fruit* knife (noun)

Here the noun "knife" is modified in [15] by an adjective, in [16] by a prepositional phrase, a phrase consisting of a preposition and a noun phrase, and in [17] by a noun.

In our study of English grammar, we will explore many of the different kinds of phrase/function pairs that are needed in the construction (and analysis) of English sentences.

3.4 Summary

You have now been introduced to the concept of a *phrase*. You have seen that the term "phrase" is not a casual expression, but a central term and a crucial concept in the study of grammar. It is in effect a technical term, and therefore its meaning must be understood in a special way.

A phrase has two aspects, its *form* and the *function* that this form serves.

You have learned about the two major functions of phrases in declarative statement sentences, the *subject* and the *predicate*.

You have also been introduced to ways of representing phrases graphically. A phrase is represented graphically in one of two ways. It is a branch in a *tree diagram*. In this case, what is being represented is the *form* of the phrase. Or it is a group of words with an unbroken underline in an *underlining diagram*. In this case, we are representing the *function* of the phrase. The two methods of representing a sentence are combined in the *form-function diagram*.

3.5 Form-Function Diagrams

We will conclude this section with some examples of form-function diagrams applied to different kinds of phrases, and exercises which will have you practice drawing some kinds of trees for yourself. The examples are a little simplified and should not be taken as permanent models of these phrases. As we proceed in the book, more complete versions of the trees will be presented. For now, these examples will introduce you to the technique of form-function diagramming, and to some of the concepts and terminology that go along with it.

As an initial example, consider a noun phrase consisting of an article (Art) and a noun (N), such as "the dinosaur." Since the phrase is a noun phrase, the topmost point of the tree diagram will be labeled "Noun Phrase," or just "NP" for short:

Diagram 3C.   Starting a form-function diagram.

The function part of the diagram must now be filled out. Assuming that this particular NP is the subject of a sentence, the long underline that goes the entire length of the phrase will be identified as "Subject":

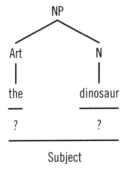

Diagram 3D.   Filling in functions.

The NP might, of course, have some other function, such as complement of a preposition or object of the verb. The one we are most familiar with at present is subject, and so for the purposes of this demonstration we will assume that it is functioning as the subject of a sentence. (For example, it might be part of the sentence "The dinosaur looked menacingly at the tourists.") We now need to fill out the functions of the individual words where the question marks are: under "the," identified as an article, and under "dinosaur," identified as a noun.

Articles serve to identify more closely, or "determine," the noun phrase they precede. Under the word "the," then, we will write "determiner."

The most important word in the phrase, in this case "dinosaur," is known as the **head of the phrase**. We will discuss further uses of the crucial notion "head of a phrase" later in this chapter. The head of a phrase carries the function of the entire phrase. If we know the function of the whole phrase, we automatically know the function of the head, for it is the same. In other words:

> **The head of a phrase always has the same function as the entire phrase.**

What this means here is that, since we have stipulated that "the dinosaur" is the subject of its sentence, the function of the word "dinosaur" without "the" is also "subject."

We are now in a position to draw the tree for the noun phrase "the dinosaur":

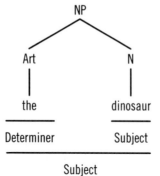

Diagram 3E.   Completing the diagram.

A second example of a noun phrase will include an adjectival phrase "very fierce." An adjectival phrase (AdjPhr) consists of an adjective (Adj) accompanied by an adverb (Adv) that modifies the adjective in some way. This form-function diagram is analogous to the NP diagram; it looks as follows:

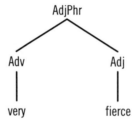

Diagram 3F.   Diagramming an adjectival phrase.

When we put this structure inside the form part of the previous tree, we get the following:

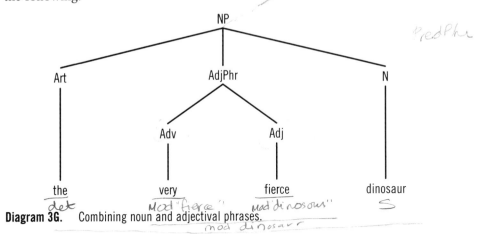

PredPhr

the *det* very *Mod "fierce"* fierce *Mod "dinosaur"* dinosaur *S*

Mod dinosaur

Subj

Diagram 3G. Combining noun and adjectival phrases.

A complete list of form-function terms and abbreviations appears at the end of this book. Here are the ones we have used up to now:

SOME TERMS AND ABBREVIATIONS USED IN FORM-FUNCTION DIAGRAMS	
Forms	
Noun	N
Verb	V
Adjective	Adj
Adverb	Adv
Article	Art
Pronoun	Pron
Noun Phrase	NP
Predicate Phrase	PredPhr
Prepositional Phrase	PrepPhr
Adjectival Phrase	AdjPhr
Functions	
Determiner	Det
Predicate	Pred
Sentence	S
Subject	Subj

The function part of the diagram has the same sort of complexity. Successive underlinings of the phrases-within-a-phrase will have to show that "very" modifies "fierce," and that "very fierce" in turn modifies "dinosaur."

Since "very" modifies "fierce," "fierce" must be the head of the phrase "very fierce." Therefore "fierce" must itself be a modifier of "dinosaur." (Remember, this is because of the principle that the head of a phrase has the same function as the entire phrase.)

In very complex trees, it is often necessary to distinguish the different kinds of modifiers; we can always do this by adding an explanation of what is being modified, as is done in the complete form-function diagram that follows:

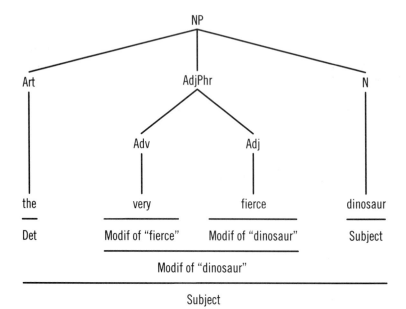

Diagram 3H.   The completed form-function diagram.

This may seem like a lot of structure for a very simple phrase, but of course we will eventually be dealing with far more complex phrases and sentences, and the principles will be the same. Notice, however, that in this diagram we have shown the following (you may wish to verify each of these claims with a pencil in hand):

- "The" determines "dinosaur," but "the" does not determine "very fierce."
- "Very" modifies "fierce," but does not itself modify "dinosaur."
- The words "very fierce" form a phrase that in its entirety modifies "dinosaur."
- The words "the very fierce" do not form a phrase, and these words do not have a function as a group. (There is no underline that goes under these three words other than the one that goes under all four words.)

• The two words "fierce dinosaur" likewise do not have a unitary function other than the one that goes with all four words.

Form-function diagrams are a powerful way of revealing the structure of phrases and sentences.

3.6 The Triangle Convention for Abbreviating a Tree   =7 triangulating

In drawing a tree diagram, we may have different purposes in mind according to which part of the tree we want to focus attention on. Perhaps, for example, in diagramming the sentence

[18] That "completely harmless" beer contains a lethal dose of strychnine

we may not be interested in the internal structure of the predicate, but only in the modifiers in the subject NP. The **triangle convention** allows us to bypass the predicate structure by representing the sentence as follows:

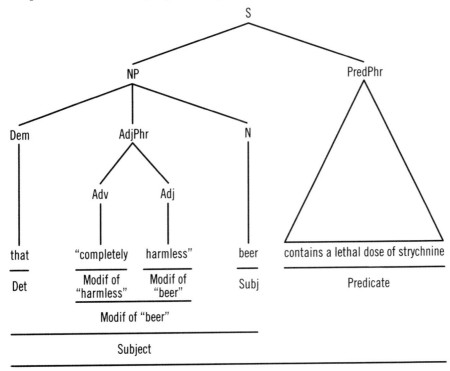

Diagram 3I.   Using the triangle convention.

Notice that the predicate phrase (PredPhr) is not analyzed with respect to its internal structure but is represented by an empty triangle. Here the triangle labeled "PredPhr" ignores all details and simply identifies "contains a lethal dose of strychnine" as an undifferentiated predicate phrase. Any phrase can be abbreviated in this way, such as:

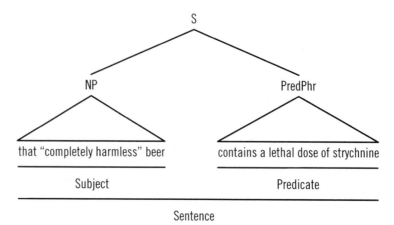

Diagram 3J.   Using the triangle convention for noun phrases.

This convention is widely used and will appear often in this book, especially when the details of a certain area of the tree contain complications that are irrelevant to the point being made in the text.

3.7 The Notion of "Head of a Phrase"

When we discussed the adjectival phrase "very fierce" in "the very fierce dinosaur," the notion "head of a phrase" was introduced. We noted there that the phrase "very fierce" as a whole functioned as a modifier to the noun "dinosaur," and that also the single adjective "fierce" was likewise a modifier of "dinosaur." The adjective "fierce" is the **head** of the adjectival phrase "very fierce," and, as we noted, the head of a phrase has the same function as the entire phrase.

The head of a phrase is the focal element in the phrase about which other elements, known as **dependents,** cluster. The name of a phrase (noun phrase, adjectival phrase, etc.) usually tells us what category the head will belong to. For the moment, a few examples of the typical analysis of parts of phrases as head and dependent will be mentioned.

(1) Noun phrase. The head of the phrase is a noun or a pronoun, though there may be a problem of analysis if, as sometimes happens, the noun phrase has more than one noun. Along with the predicate phrase, the noun phrase is one of the two richest types of phrase. The dependents of a noun phrase may include adjectives and adjectival phrases, determiners, prepositional phrases, other noun phrases, and in fact any word or phrase that can form part of a modifying phrase. Thus noun phrases can be of considerable length.

(2) **Prepositional phrase.** The preposition should be analyzed as the head. The noun phrase that is the complement of the preposition is the dependent. This means that the preposition will have whatever function is assigned to the prepositional phrase. Prepositional phrases may also consist of a single preposition without a complement ("marooned" prepositions). The functions of prepositional phrases (and, hence, of prepositions) are quite diverse.

> **REMINDER!**
>
> The *complement* of a preposition is the noun phrase that follows it. In "after the storm," "the storm" is the complement of the preposition "after."

(3) **Adjectival phrase.** An adjectival phrase has an adjective as its head. If there are dependents, these very often consist of adverbs that intensify the adjective, such as *extremely* in *extremely hot.* A small number of adjectives may take complements (**fond** *of his German Shepherd,* for instance), and adjectival phrases can include an element of comparison (*larger* **than a pizza pie***)* that is a dependent.

(4) **Adverbial phrase.** An adverbial phrase has an adverb as its head. The possibilities for dependents are not great, but other adverbs can intensify an adverb: "very" in "very rapidly," "unusually" in "unusually quickly." Like adjectival phrases, adverbial phrases can have comparative elements inside them, for example, "more swiftly than a speeding bullet."

(5) **Predicate phrase.** The head of the predicate phrase is the verb. The predicate phrase is potentially the most complex of the phrases, since it comprises the entire predicate of the sentence. The predicate phrase thus includes the verb with its auxiliaries (known as the verb phrase; see the following paragraph), and any noun phrases, adverbial phrases, and prepositional phrases that are part of the predicate. Since the function of the predicate phrase is to be the predicate of the sentence, the predicate phrase in a simple declarative statement is assigned the function "predicate."

(6) **Verb phrase.** The verb phrase consists of the verb together with any auxiliaries, negative markers such as *not* and *never,* and certain adverbs, such as *yet, then, always,* and others whose position is within the verb phrase.

The head of the verb phrase is the main verb. The main verb is the verbal form that carries the principal meaning of the verb phrase—*leaking* in *could have been leaking.* The main verb is also known as the **lexical verb** (see 2.4).

The verb phrase itself functions as the head of the predicate phrase and is therefore assigned the function "predicate" (since the head of any phrase carries the function of the entire phrase). In turn, the main verb is the head of the verb phrase, and so it, too, is assigned the function of predicate.

(7) Determiner phrase. The determiner phrase is a word or group of words that precedes a noun (and any adjectives modifying it) and functions as a "determiner" of the noun. In its longest expansion, the determiner phrase includes (1) pre-determiners like *some of, a few of;* (2) the head of the determiner phrase, which may be an article such as *the,* a demonstrative such as *that,* or a possessive such as *my, Henry's;* and (3) a post-determiner, such as *many* in *some of my many friends.*

3.8 Some Important Terms

- **Node** In Diagram 3H, the tree we drew for "the very fierce dinosaur," the labels NP, Art, AdjPhr, N, Adv, and Adj mark places where new lines start. These points are known as *nodes*. Nodes that branch into two or more lines are, not surprisingly, *branching nodes*.
- **Dominates** Any node that is higher in the tree than another one and leads to it by a direct downward path is said to *dominate* the lower node; so in Diagram 3H, NP "dominates" Art, AdjPhr, N, Adv, and Adj; and AdjPhr dominates Adv and Adj.
- **Immediately dominates** A node that is just above another node and connected to it, with no other nodes intervening, is said to *immediately dominate* that node. In Diagram 3H, the node labeled NP immediately dominates Art, AdjPhr, and N, but not Adv and Adj. The node labeled AdjPhr immediately dominates Adv and Adj.

These terms and relationships are essential to explaining and discussing grammar. The more familiar you are with them, the easier it will be to follow the analyses. The following diagram of the noun phrase "an excruciatingly boring movie" illustrates the relationships we have just discussed:

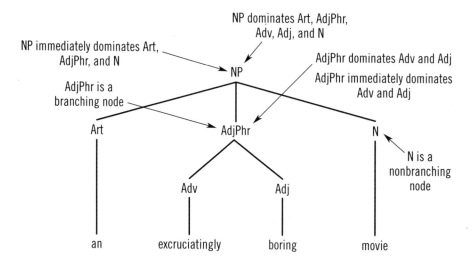

Diagram 3K.   Relationships in a tree diagram.

EXERCISES

Exercise 3.1

Underline the noun phrases which are the subjects of the following sentences.

1. Some of the nation's leading economists agreed with the committee's conclusions.
2. The Lorentz transformations are a system of equations.
3. These equations link the coordinates of events in different inertial frames.
4. The nineteenth-century Dutch physicist H. A. Lorentz devised the equations.
5. The subject-predicate division perhaps reflects the dualism of western thought.
6. Temperatures in the polar regions can be dangerously low.
7. A sudden and dangerous downturn in the economy startled the bankers.
8. The unexpected failure of the electric fences had made the dinosaur park a scary place to picnic.
9. Our annual shipment of men's and women's winter clothing will be arriving tomorrow.
10. We almost never went swimming in the polluted lake.

Exercise 3.2.

Parts a and b may be ignored if you are confident that you understand the principle.

a. Go back to Exercise 3.1 and draw for each sentence a *form* diagram (tree diagram) similar to Diagram 3A, Alternative 1. Use the triangle convention to abbreviate the tree.

b. Then do the same using the underlining convention, with the *function* labels Subject and Predicate, as in Alternative 2.

c. Finally, for each sentence, combine the two diagrams into a unified form-function diagram.

Exercise 3.3

For each of the following NPs, draw a complete form-function diagram starting with S as the highest node. Assume in each case that the NP is the subject of the sentence.

1. terrifying images
2. they
3. undrinkable Belgian beer
4. the barely perceptible outline
5. the lifeboats

6. an almost unbelievably ingenious contraption

7. you

8. a valuable antique vase

9. the very highly prestigious award

10. shiny new stethoscopes

11. a long, very boring lecture

12. water

Exercise 3.4

Draw form-function diagrams of the following sentences, using the triangle convention to abbreviate the phrases identified in parentheses.

1. The sun was already sinking in the western sky. (Predicate)

2. That incredibly scary movie was playing. (Predicate, Adjectival Phrase)

3. Jenny, Cheryl, Tracy, Marvin, and Justin have already left. (Subject, Predicate)

4. One of those policemen that stopped us yesterday was at the mall. (Subject, Predicate)

5. That short attorney is going to be defending us. (Predicate)

6. I have noticed your reluctance to join the Marine Corps. (Predicate)

Exercise 3.5

The following diagram has a set of true/false questions after it. Inspect the diagram carefully and answer the questions with T or F.

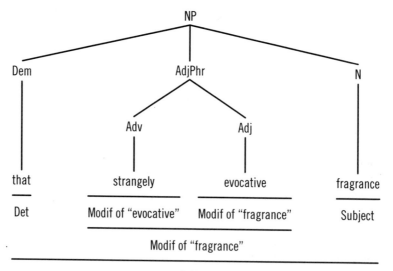

1. Dem (demonstrative) is a nonbranching node. _____

2. NP dominates AdjPhr and Dem. _____

3. The Determiner is a Demonstrative. _____

4. AdjPhr dominates Adj and Dem. _____

5. NP immediately dominates Dem. _____

6. "Strangely evocative fragrance" is a subject. _____

7. "That strangely evocative" is a phrase modifying "fragrance." _____

8. AdjPhr is a branching node. _____

9. "Strangely" modifies "evocative fragrance." _____

10. AdjPhr immediately dominates Adv and Adj. _____

Appendix: Some Tips on Drawing Form-Function Diagrams

Some of the preceding exercises, and further exercises in subsequent chapters, ask you to draw form-function diagrams. Form-function diagrams can be simple or of considerable complexity. It's a good idea to get into the habit of planning a diagram with some care before you start drawing.

It is advisable to use legal-size paper, that is, 8.5" × 14". Your page should be positioned so that the longer dimension is horizontal. The form-function diagram will have the target sentence (the one you are analyzing) across the horizontal middle of the page. Use a fresh sheet for each diagram, no matter how small the tree. Except for your own rough drafts, *don't draw diagrams on both sides of a page!* The imprint of the lines on the reverse page is certain to make your diagram unreadable.

To start with, use a pencil and sketch lightly, as you will almost certainly have to do some erasing. There will always be last-minute details and corrections.

Eventually, when the diagram is the way you want it, you should use a ruler to draw the straight lines. Lines should in any case be straight; curved lines lead to confusion. This means placing the labels (nodes) in advance so that they do not interfere with one another when the appropriate straight lines are drawn.

Begin with the form part (the tree). Do not write the target sentence in until you have decided on a general map of the tree. You may need to place long gaps between certain words and to compress others closely together, but you won't know this until your plan for the tree has been developed. When the target sentence is written in, *it must—somehow—all go on one line.*

Get a preliminary sense of where the phrase boundaries are and of how wide the major phrases are. Get used to using your space to its maximum. Plan the diagram so that lines pass through empty space without crowding or barely missing the labels and other lines.

Lines should *always be straight* and *must never cross another line.*

However, a long line that does not branch can be bent like an elbow joint, as follows, if it is necessary to avoid impinging on another line:

The tree should have a more or less symmetrical appearance. If more than one line branches from a node, the lines should be splayed out like a fan, the outermost lines forming a triangle whose top is the node. If a node does not branch, make the line descending from it vertical.

Lines will terminate in the words of the target sentence. This means that some of the lines will be longer than others; compare the line joining Art to "an" with the line joining Adj to "boring" in Diagram 3K above.

You may wish to experiment with a graphics program to produce printed diagrams. MacPaint is quite good. Successful diagrams have also been made with desktop publishing software such as PageMaker.

4

SENTENCES AND THEIR PARTS

4.0 Sentence Types

In this chapter we will leave the question of phrases and categories for the time being and consider a broader question, that of **sentence types.**

4.1 Sentences

The sentence is a basic unit of grammar for Written English. Definitions of the sentence have often occupied grammarians. Earlier generations tried to explain the concept of a sentence by reference to "a complete thought." But it is extremely difficult to imagine what a complete thought might be unless one already has a notion of "sentence," and therefore definitions of this kind get caught up in an unproductive circularity. Probably the best way to think of a sentence would ultimately be in terms of an intermediate level of discourse between "word" or "phrase" and "paragraph."

4.2 The Classification of Sentence Types

Sentences fall into several distinct types, according to both their form and their discourse function.

Declarative Statements

The more formal registers and genres of Standard Written English consist almost exclusively of **declarative statements,** with clearly identifiable subjects and predicates. (Most of the sentences in this book, both the ones in the text itself and the ones cited as examples, are declarative statements. For example, every sentence in this paragraph is a declarative statement.) The declarative statement is therefore a fundamental kind of sentence, at least in the written language, and is treated as such by grammarians. Declarative statements do not ask questions, give commands, or directly express desires. Rather, they make assertions about events and states of affairs.

Declarative statements are *subject-predicate* sentences. This means that they make a declaration in the predicate about a topic which is the grammatical subject. The following are some further examples of declarative statements:

[1] I was amazed at Gerry's forthrightness

[2] Most of the native animals of Australia are marsupials

[3] Its right fender struck a mailbox

[4] The best course of action would have been to ignore him

[5] A glow on the eastern horizon already heralded the dawn

Other kinds of sentence exist also, in which the subject-predicate structure is either absent or not so easily seen. We will now consider some of them.

Imperatives

One type of sentence that lacks the characteristic subject-predicate structure of declarative statements is that which is used to give orders. The following is an example of an **imperative** sentence:

[6] Wash your hands thoroughly after you have handled the adhesive!

In the examples of imperative sentences, we will here use the exclamation point (!) to signal that an imperative is meant, rather than a sentence fragment (see below) or some other sentence type that resembles an imperative. The use of the exclamation point is not obligatory, however; in fact, it normally signals that an abrupt or insistent command is being issued.

Imperative sentences are often assumed to have an understood subject, *you,* and there are some good reasons for this view. One is that there is a particularly emphatic type of imperative in which the *you* is retained:

[7] You leave that poor little dog alone!

Another is that in sentences like

[8] Help yourself to some more figs!

the word "yourself" contains a reference to a missing subject *you* in exactly the same way that in

[9] We helped ourselves to some more figs

"ourselves" contains a reference to the subject "we." If imperatives do in fact contain a hidden subject *you,* they might be classified as a special form of statement and analyzed with a subject-predicate form.

On the other hand, there are some mysterious things about imperatives as well. The negative of an imperative is known as a **prohibition**. Prohibitions begin with "don't," as in:

[10] Don't tell Clive about the orchids!

However, the emphatic form of [10] is not

[11] *You don't tell Clive about the orchids!

but instead

[12] Don't you tell Clive about the orchids!

Perhaps, then, the *you* that appears in some imperative sentences should not be regarded as the subject of the imperative, but as the addressee. In this case, we would have to see imperatives and declarative statements as two quite distinct types of sentence, and the imperative would not be analyzable in terms of a subject-predicate structure.

There is one sentence type that is actually a declarative statement but bears some resemblance to the imperative. This is the sentence with a generic "you" whose verb is in the present tense, such as

[13] You put the batteries in end to end, with the plus signs all pointing to the right

In writing, sentences like [13] are barely distinguishable from ones like [7]:

[7] You leave that poor little dog alone!

But when spoken out loud, the difference is unmistakable. In [13], the "you" is unstressed ("ya **put**"), while in [7] it is given an extra emphasis ("**you!**"). In terms of discourse functions also, the two sentences are quite different. Sentence [13] is informational (what you or anyone else must do for a certain effect), whereas [7] is a command urging a specific person to start doing something they are not now doing.

Finally, notice that while imperatives are used to give commands, it is possible to have the effect of a command without using the form of the imperative. Thus the following are not imperatives but declaratives:

[14] You should water the cacti once a week

[15] I order you to leave the room immediately

In [14] and [15] there are subjects ("you," "I"), and they cannot be omitted. The corresponding true imperatives, of course, would be:

[14]′ Water the cacti once a week!

[15]′ Leave the room immediately!

Interrogatives

The **interrogative** is the type of sentence used for asking a question. Interrogatives, although perhaps more frequent in written prose than imperatives, also present difficulties when we try to identify subjects and predicates. The problem here, however, is that typically questions are formed by inverting the position of the subject with part of the predicate. For example, from the statement

[16] Senator Midgeswitch will lead the parade

a corresponding question can be formed:

[17] Will Senator Midgeswitch lead the parade?

The exchange of the subject and an auxiliary verb is often called **inversion**. If we were to try to analyze sentences with inversion in the same way as declarative statements, we would have to find a point between the subject and the predicate to draw our dividing line, such as:

[18] Will Senator Midgeswitch I lead the parade?

Clearly, this analysis will lead to problems, since "will" is part of the predicate, not part of the subject, yet the dividing line places "will" in with the subject noun phrase "Senator Midgeswitch."

Incidentally, sentences like [18] provide us with a useful rule of thumb for identifying the subject of a sentence. The subject, we can see, is that entire group of words that must change places with "will" and other auxiliaries when statements are converted into questions. Therefore "Senator Midgeswitch" is the subject of the sentence.

There is more than one type of interrogative. The two most important are classified according to the characteristic kinds of replies they elicit. Sentences like "Will Senator Midgeswitch lead the parade?" can be appropriately answered with *yes* or *no*. Because the typical reply to this kind of question is limited to these responses, the kind of question that can be answered with *yes* or *no* is called a **closed interrogative**.

By the Way:

Note that closed interrogatives *can* be answered with *yes* or *no*, but they do not have to be. I could appropriately answer [18] with *He will* or with *I'm afraid Senator Midgeswitch is sick today and can't come.*

The other type of question cannot be appropriately answered with *yes* or *no*, but requires some further information to be supplied. An example would be:

[19] When will the meeting begin?

Obviously *yes* or *no* as an answer could only signify that the person giving the answer has misunderstood. This kind of interrogative, therefore, which calls for a judgment as to how much information to give, is called an **open interrogative**. Open interrogatives center around a ***wh*-word**, such as *when, what, why, who,* or *how* (which doesn't contain *wh-* but can be thought of as an honorary *wh*-word).

The word order of the open interrogative is the same as that of a statement if the *wh*-word is the subject:

[20] Who stole my teddy bear? *(question)*

[21] Jackie stole my teddy bear *(statement)*

However, if the *wh*-word is not the subject, inversion—the switching around of the *wh*-word and the subject—takes place, with the *wh*-word now appearing at the beginning of the sentence:

[22] Why has the yellow light come on? ("The yellow light" is the subject)

[23] What are the architects proposing? ("The architects" is the subject)

The full grammar of interrogatives is quite complex, and since we are here concerned basically with declarative statements, we will not be treating this topic in full.

Other Sentence Types

The main sentence types are the declarative statement, the imperative, and the interrogative. Of these, the declarative statement is by far the most significant. In most written genres, and in the more formal registers, it is virtually the only sentence type found. Exceptions are recipes, where the imperative is overwhelmingly the most common sentence type, and prayers, where imperatives and other minority sentence types (precatives and hortatives; see below) predominate. Most of the analysis of English grammar centers around the declarative, therefore. But there are a few other types of sentence, not all of which are "sentences" in the established sense of the word.

Sentence fragments. One of these types does not qualify to be a sentence at all, but must be considered nonetheless, since it can often be used to good effect in writing. This is the **sentence fragment**.

The sentence fragment consists of part of a sentence, but may lack the subject-predicate structure and is not recognizably an imperative or other sentence type. It is used as a device to surprise the reader with a new item of information, or to underline (emphasize) something, or to dramatize words, as in advertising and newspaper headlines or political slogans, or to suggest the unuttered thoughts of a character.

Whether to consider an incomplete sentence as an effective sentence fragment or as an attempted sentence that went wrong is not always a simple decision. Good writers can use sentence fragments very effectively. Sentence fragments can be used in fictional narratives to suggest a character's spontaneous thoughts, for example, or the author's comments on a situation:

[24] He saw the attorney coming up the steps, and a sense of relief washed over him. Good old Thornburg. Always on time, always reliable.

Sentence fragments often appear in advertising copy, accompanied by pictures and other images, and they are normal in headlines. In the lower registers of speech (informal or casual speech), sentence fragments are common. (Indeed, the application of the notion of "sentence" to normal spoken language is questionable.) Outside of these contexts, sentence fragments in the body of a text should be regarded with suspicion. To write one where it may not be appropriate is to risk its being seen as an error, no matter how good your intentions.

Exclamative and precative sentences. Exclamative sentences, beginning with *if only . . . , what (a) . . . !*, and *how . . . !*, proclaim dramatically expressed surprise or desire:

[25] If only we could get rid of the frogs!

[26] What big eyes you have!

[27] How long your teeth are!

The first kind, the *if only* sentences, have the form of a subordinate clause continuing, perhaps, with something like . . . *we would be happy*, although of course sentences like [25] are not to be considered grammatically incomplete. On the other hand, the [26] type beginning with *what . . . !* is more typical of spoken language, and often consists of a bare noun phrase:

[28] What a lovely necklace!

One subtype of exclamatives is known as the **precative** (that is, involving a prayer). The precative is a rarely used sentence type largely restricted to ceremonial, ritual, or proverbial contexts:

[29] May you have calm seas and a prosperous voyage!

[30] God save the king!

[31] From ghoulies and ghosties and long-leggity beasties may the good Lord deliver us!

Such sentences typically start with or imply the auxiliary verb *may*, which is either expressed, as in [29] and [31], or implied, as in [30]. Where some of them apparently have a subject-predicate structure, as in [30], it is questionable whether it is worth analyzing them as such, since often the expression is a fixed one, without any grammatical options. The invoked subject of a precative is almost always a supernatural entity (*The saints preserve us!*, *The devil take you!, Jesus help me!*) of the kind that is notoriously infrequent in professional writing contexts. Note in these sentences the peculiarity that the verb lacks the otherwise expected *-s* suffix with a singular subject:

[32] *God saves the king!

> **REMINDER!**
>
> **The asterisk * alerts us to a sentence that is ungrammatical in the intended sense. So [32] is ungrammatical if it is intended as a precative sentence.**

Verbless interrogatives with *wh-*. Another minority sentence type that does not have a subject-predicate structure is that which consists of a *wh*-word, or a *wh*-word with *about,* and a noun phrase, without a verb:

[33] How about another serving of bread pudding?

[34] What about the workers?

[35] Why all the fuss?

These are interrogatives that often function to elicit a very broad range of unspecific answers. Sentences like [34] and [35] in fact resemble exclamatives in not really functioning to ask a bona fide question, but in rhetorically drawing the listener's attention to an already known state of affairs.

Hortatives. Sentences beginning with *let's* and its more formal register version *let us* are known as **hortatives**, because they encourage or spur on the person being addressed.

> **REMINDER!**
>
> **You may remember the terms "register" and "formal register" from Chapter 1. The term "register" refers to the degree of formality of an utterance or a piece of writing.**

Historically, *let's* is an imperative verb *let* followed by the pronoun *us,* and *let's* still requires some reference jointly to a *you* and to an *I* or *we:*

[36] Let's put sugar in his gas tank!

[37] Let us remember those who fought and fell on this sacred spot

Switching *let's* and *let us* in these two sentences vividly reveals the dependence of the two forms on register.

4.3 Ellipsis

The term **ellipsis** refers to the omission of a word or words that can be supplied. While ellipsis rarely makes its appearance in the simple kind of declarative sentence, it increasingly becomes a factor as the sentences we consider become more complex. In a conjoined sentence such as the following, for example,

[38] The giraffes fastened their seat belts, extinguished their smoking materials, and returned their seat backs and tray tables to the upright position

there are three verbs ("fastened," "extinguished," and "returned") but only one subject ("the giraffes"). It is simple and intuitive to think of the second and third occurrences of "the giraffes" as having been erased. This erasure is known as ellipsis. Similarly, in sentences like

[39] Sanford washed, peeled, and boiled the potatoes

it is useful to assume that the words "Sanford," "and," and "the potatoes" have undergone ellipsis:

[39]′ Sanford washed (the potatoes), (and) (Sanford) peeled (the potatoes), and (Sanford) boiled the potatoes

The understood subject or addressee of imperatives mentioned above could also be seen as an instance of ellipsis. Thus

[40] Take Jumpy off the dining room table this instant!

is understood as

[40]′ (You) take Jumpy off the dining room table this instant!

The diagramming of sentences in which there has been ellipsis is not as difficult as might be imagined. Usually ellipsis affects an entire phrase such as the subject, and the diagram simply lacks this phrase. Beyond what has been said here, the topic of ellipsis will not be treated as a whole, but it will come up during the discussion of individual constructions in subsequent chapters.

4.4 Diagramming Sentences

What corresponds in the function part of the diagram to the topmost node S of the form diagram? Up to now, we have simply been calling this function "Sentence" (see, for example, some of the diagrams in Chapter 3). But this suggests that the sentence is a special phrase whose form and function are identical. We are now in a position to improve on this practice by writing under the lowest underline the name of the sentence type being analyzed. Almost always this sentence type will be the declarative statement, and we can identify its function as "Declaration." The revised version of the diagram of sentence [18] in 3.6 will thus be:

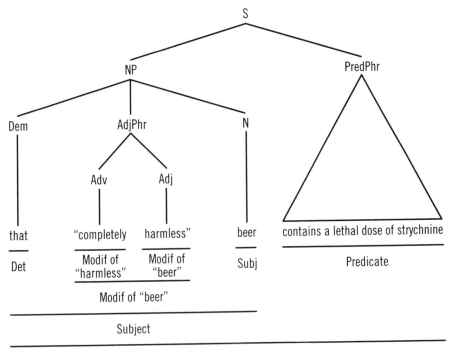

EXERCISES

Exercise 4.1

a. Convert the following statements into (closed) questions, and in doing so identify the NP that is the subject of the sentence. Underline the *whole subject* (i.e., the whole phrase that inverted with the auxiliary).

b. At the same time, identify the *auxiliary verb* with which the subject NP switches places.

c. In some of the sentences, you will have to use a trial-and-error procedure to find the exact beginning of the subject noun phrase. Put parentheses around any words that precede the subject in these sentences.

1. That little kid from Kalamazoo with a blue ribbon in her hair will explain her theory to all these important scientists.

2. A bottle of the best Highland single-malt Scotch whiskey would make a nice present.

3. They don't sell tickets to nonmembers. *Do they sell*

4. The day after tomorrow you could please help me get the piano up the steps.

5. The Buccaneers have reached the quarter-finals.

6. If it doesn't rain tomorrow, they are having a barbecue in the state park.

7. When the workers come, they should fix the TV as well as take away the dishwasher.

8. A course in basket-weaving does count for credit under the Creative Activity requirement.

9. After sunset astronomers will be able to see the new comet.

10. Just one of these new super-high density disks can hold the entire manuscript.

11. If the electric fence were down, the dinosaurs would be able to reach the compound.

12. The new recruits are being trained properly.

13. Next year that professor of statistics who lost his shirt in Las Vegas might be spending his vacation in Orlando.

14. That battered old 1943 Ford with the silver hubcaps will make it up this steep hill.

Exercise 4.2

(For class discussion) In this exercise you are asked to make a stylistic judgment to distinguish between attempted sentences that are poorly constructed and effectively used sentence fragments. Identify those "sentences" that are grammatically incomplete but that still seem to be appropriate (if hackneyed!) in the context of the whole example. Comment on the registers and genres that seem especially hospitable to sentence fragments.

1. It happened one warm June evening. An evening heavy with the fragrance of jasmine and honeysuckle. The sort of evening that made you wish you were young again.

2. Before turning on the ignition, press the gas pedal right to the floor and hold it down. For a few seconds.

3. Now Jack was gaining on him, and the finish line seemed miles away. He summoned up every last ounce of strength. Twenty more yards.

4. Face on Mars "Portrait of Julius Caesar"—NASA Expert

5. The homeless man looked at him pitifully, but Salford ignored him and walked resolutely past. Didn't do any good to encourage them. No good at all. Obstructing the public sidewalks like that, harrassing responsible, hard-working citizens.

6. You wait until the kettle is boiling its head off. Then you pour the water onto the tea leaves. Right on top of them. While the water is still actually boiling.

7. The gala opening ceremony was canceled. Because of the tornado warning.

8. The aftershave with the fragrance that speaks to *her*. Cool. Bracing. And now with all-new doctor-recommended polypromethalone skin toner!

9. The shipment is being held up for no good reason, and I suggest contacting the customs people in London. Immediately.

10. Down with capitalist exploiters and other enemies of the people!

Exercise 4.3

Identify the following sentences from the point of view of their form as declaratives, interrogatives (open or closed), imperatives, sentence fragments, verbless interrogatives, exclamatives, or hortatives.

1. The covered casserole should be baked for 25 minutes at 375°F. *D*

2. Must I remove the plunger before tightening the wing nut? *Closed Inter.*

3. Because of my asthma. *Frag*

4. How long will you remain in Ulan Bator? *Open Inter*

5. Let's push the buttons for all 71 floors and then get out of the elevator! *hort.*

6. So help me God! *exclam.*

7. What about the third-quarter losses? *Verbless inter.*

8. Who put a piece of barbed wire in Buster Bottomley's bed? *open inter*

9. When the sauce has thickened, spoon it carefully over the scallops and orange slices. *Imp.*

10. "World War II Bomber Found on Moon"—NASA Officials *Frag*

11. Heaven forbid that he should wash the dishes for once! *Excl.*

12. What if Ms. Dulwitz sees us putting the toadstools in the stew? *Verbless inter*

13. Don't you worry about Cobber Doogan! *Imp*

14. Would that it would rain for a week! *exclam*

15. You must apologize to Aunt Agatha about the chewing gum. *Imp/Dec*

16. What to Do If Skweezit Does Not Boot. *Frag*

17. Mr. Van Hefflin knows all the regulations by heart. *Dec.*

18. Remember the time we sent a mouse up in the elevator to Niedermeyer's office? *Closed inter*

19. Avoid those guys in double-breasted suits standing next to the car! *Imp*

20. How much is that army-issue bazooka in the window? *open inter.*

5

OBJECTS AND ADJUNCTS

5.0 Elements of the Predicate

We have seen that a simple declarative sentence can be analyzed into two major divisions, a subject represented by a noun phrase, and a predicate represented by a predicate phrase. In this chapter we will look a little more closely at the components of the predicate, and at some looser, less-structured elements of the sentence. It is with these latter that we will begin.

5.1 Elements That Precede the Core Sentence

We can think of the subject and predicate of a simple declarative sentence as the **core** of the sentence. To this core can be added, at either end, various kinds of phrases that add circumstances about or comments on the core sentence. These phrases have different forms and functions, but we will refer to them informally as **precore phrases** and **postcore phrases**.

Pre-Adjuncts

One kind of precore phrase is that which frames the sentence by telling us a circumstance that is true of the entire sentence. Here is an example:

[1] In my opinion, this painting is a forgery

The subject-predicate structure here is plainly

This painting | is a forgery

This is the core sentence, whose subject is "this painting." The prepositional phrase "in my opinion" is not part of the subject. On the other hand, it is also not part of the predicate; it does not say anything about the painting. Instead it presents a circumstance that provides a comment on, or a setting for, the sentence as a whole.

A phrase of this kind, which provides a general circumstance for the entire sentence and is placed at the beginning of the sentence, is called a **pre-adjunct**. The term "pre-adjunct" refers to the *function* of the phrase. In *form* a pre-adjunct may consist of different kinds of phrases. Pre-adjuncts provide a frame for the core sentence and are not connected in meaning to any particular part of the sentence.

In the following examples, each sentence starts with a pre-adjunct, which can be either a prepositional phrase [2]–[4] or an adverb [5]–[7]:

[2] *In my opinion,* this picture is not worth the canvas it is painted on

[3] *With respect to the ozone level,* considerably more research on the impact of industrial pollution on the atmosphere is needed

[4] *With all due respect,* Mr. Forsythe is not the most capable office manager in the world

[5] *Frankly,* your sudden change of mind troubles me

[6] *Ironically,* the president himself once proposed this same regulation

[7] *Sadly,* many of our younger people cannot speak the traditional language of the tribe

Pre-adjuncts can be seen as an intrusion of the writer, who is expressing an attitude toward the sentence ("frankly"), or telling the reader what the next topic of the text will be ("with respect to the ozone level").

Adverbials

Another kind of phrase that can precede the core sentence is an **adverbial**. Like the term "pre-adjunct," the term "adverbial" refers to the function of the phrase. Adverbials, like pre-adjuncts, can consist of simple adverbs or prepositional phrases. Noun phrases can function as adverbials of time in fixed expressions like *last July, Monday afternoons.* Adverbials express a time at which an action takes place, a place where an action occurs, or the manner in which an action was carried out. In sentences [8]–[12], adverbials are italicized:

[8] *On the plane to Pittsburgh,* James explained his new theory to me

[9] *During the night* a spaceship landed on our patio

[10] *In a brusque tone of voice,* he asked me my business

[11] *Every Monday* Sarah had to lecture on English grammar

[12] *Carefully* we unwrapped the parcel

In [8]–[10], prepositional phrases are functioning as adverbials of place [8], time [9], and manner [10]. In [11], a noun phrase ("every Monday") functions as an adverbial of time, and in [12] an adverb functions as an adverbial of manner.

> **REMINDER!**
>
> We must distinguish always between the grammatical *form* that a phrase has, and the *function* this form serves in the sentence. If we remember this, it will not be surprising that a noun phrase like "every Monday" or a prepositional phrase like "during the night" can function as an adverbial.

Diagramming Precore Phrases

In the diagram of the basic sentence, the precore phrase will appear joined to the topmost node S. Examine the following carefully. As usual, the triangle convention for abbreviating parts of a tree is used here.

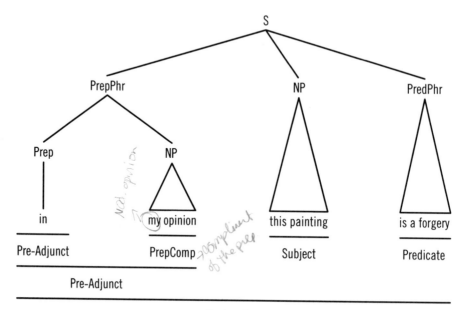

Diagram 5A.   Diagramming precore phrases.

Here, as usual, NP stands for "noun phrase," PrepPhr is "prepositional phrase," and PredPhr is "predicate phrase."

> ### By the Way:
>
> We will frequently present specimen diagrams of the grammatical constructions that are analyzed. You should be aware that *you are not expected to be able to diagram all the sentences that are used as examples in the text.* Many example sentences are given in order to illustrate just one phrase; the remainder of the sentence may be too complex to lend itself to diagramming at this stage. The sentences that are given for diagramming purposes, both in the text and in the exercises, are specially constructed for their simplicity, and even in these the triangle convention may be used in order to cover structural details that have not yet been introduced.

In the next example, the precore phrase is again a prepositional phrase, but this time it functions as an adverbial:

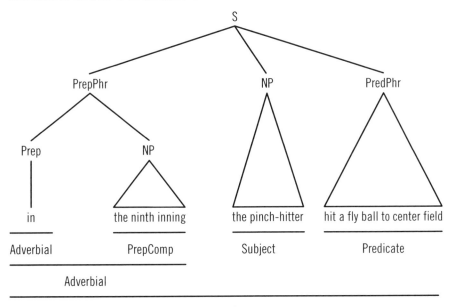

Diagram 5B. Diagramming adverbials.

Study the diagram carefully, making sure you understand every node label, every use of the triangle convention, and every underlined function. Notice how every node above the target sentence has a corresponding underline below it with a function label. To check your understanding, try writing out all the function labels (there are six) in a column. Beside each function label, write the node that corresponds to it in the tree and, in a third column, the words from the target sentence that each underline represents. Then turn the page to see if you got it right.

FUNCTION	NODE LABEL	UNDERLINED PHRASE
Declaration	S	In the ninth inning the pinch-hitter hit a fly ball to center field
Subject	NP	the pinch-hitter
Predicate	PredPhr	hit a fly ball to center field
Adverbial	PrepPhr	in the ninth inning
Adverbial	Prep	in
Complement of Preposition	NP	the ninth inning

The Punctuation of Precore Phrases

The punctuation of precore phrases requires a note. In principle, the precore phrase may be followed by a comma. However, an overuse of commas can make a text very tedious to read, and the comma may be omitted if the phrase is a single word or a short prepositional phrase. It is especially advisable to be stingy with commas in precore phrases if there is already a profusion of commas in the text. But be careful not to confuse the precore phrase with the subject itself, which is *never* set off from the predicate by a comma:

[13] *During the daytime, the noise and fumes coming from the sugar processing plant, are quite obnoxious to tourists

Here a comma after "daytime" is acceptable, but not after "plant."

5.2 Phrases That Follow the Core Sentence

Precore phrases are not difficult to identify. In declarative statements they precede the subject and either state the writer's comment on, or attitude toward, the sentence (pre-adjuncts), or express the time, manner, or place of the action (adverbials).

The same kinds of phrases can occur *after* the core sentence. The equivalent of a pre-adjunct that follows the core sentence is called, not surprisingly, a **post-adjunct.** Examples are italicized in the sentences below:

[14] Owen was killed in action shortly before the armistice, *unfortunately*

[15] I do not think Mr. Evans should be promoted, *with all due respect*

Sentences like [14] and [15] are stylistically awkward. Post-adjuncts often sound like afterthoughts and are usually better formulated as pre-adjuncts.

Adverbials, especially adverbials of time and place, on the other hand, frequently occur in post-sentence position (that is, following the predicate). Here are some examples of post-predicate adverbials:

[16] Bertie built a twenty-foot sailboat *in his basement*

[17] One of the performers was taken ill *during the show*

[18] They revised the document *in great haste*

Like those in [14] and [15], such postcore phrases might just as easily have been placed in pre-sentence position, with very little difference in meaning. (In the last chapter of the book we will look at some of the different ways pre- and postcore phrases are used in discourse.) Sentence [16] is diagrammed as follows:

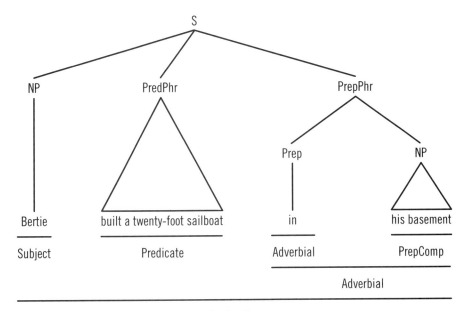

Diagram 5C. Diagramming post-adjuncts.

Adverbial Complements: A Preliminary Look

We will conclude the discussion of adverbials with a brief look at a construction that looks very much like an adverbial, but must be carefully distinguished from it. Consider the following sentence:

[19] That maniac next door rode his motorbike through my shrubbery during the night

In this sentence, "during the night" is a postcore adverbial. On the other hand, "through my shrubbery" is not an adverbial but instead part of the predicate. Even if we omitted "during the night,"

[20] That maniac next door rode his motorbike through my shrubbery

"through my shrubbery" would still not be an adverbial. Yet both "through my shrubbery" and "during the night" are prepositional phrases. So it is evidently not enough for a prepositional phrase to occur at the end of a sentence to identify it as an adverbial. How, then, are we to identify adverbials? Why is "through my shrubbery" not an adverbial?

One very important way we can tell adverbials is by their function. The relationship of an adverbial to the rest of the sentence is to state a circumstance such as a time or place that is valid for the sentence. Thus "during the night" is the time frame within which the entire action of the maniac from next door riding his motorbike through my shrubbery occurs. "Through my shrubbery," however, limits and describes only the act of riding a motorbike. "During the night" is not part of what is predicated of that maniac next door, but is the time during which the person in question performed this activity. Whereas "through my shrubbery" is linked closely to "rode his motorbike," "during the night" is not linked to any particular part of the sentence, but is attached in a rather loose way to the sentence as a whole. It is an add-on to the sentence. In stage terms, "during the night" is part of the scenery, but not part of the action, while "through my shrubbery" is part of the action.

Phrases like "through my shrubbery" are discussed in Chapter 7. Because they extend or complete the verb in some way, they are known as **adverbial complements**. We will not analyze adverbial complements in this chapter, but will simply note them in contrast to adverbials. Adverbial complements have a closer grammatical relationship to the sentence as a whole than do adjuncts; they are in fact part of the predicate, whereas adverbials are more loosely connected to the core subject-predicate sentence.

We can make use of this looseness in a second way to identify adverbials. An adverbial can easily be moved to the front of the sentence:

[21] During the night, that maniac next door rode his motorbike through my shrubbery

If the phrase being moved is an adverbial, this movement does not result in any special emphasis or literary style. When "through my shrubbery"—which, remember, is *not* an adverbial but an adverbial complement—is moved to the front of the sentence, the result is jarring:

[21] *Through my shrubbery that maniac next door rode his motorbike during the night

An adverbial can also be dropped entirely, as in

[22] That maniac next door rode his motorbike through my shrubbery

When an adverbial is dropped, we lose certain additional information, but nothing central to the statement has been lost—the core sentence is not affected by the loss of an adverbial. On the other hand, omitting an adverbial complement such as "through my shrubbery" is not really possible, and this shows us that "through my shrubbery" is not an adverbial:

[23] ?That maniac next door rode his motorbike during the night

The omission of something like "up and down the street" or "through my shrubbery" in [23] results in a strangely incomplete sentence, but perhaps not an incorrect one. Most people feel that this sentence is odd without some indication of a place or direction. (When asked to give an interpretation of the sentence, they often repeat the sentence adding in the extra words such as *around the neighborhood* or *along the highway* needed to make it sound natural!) At the very least, it needs a special interpretation. We have marked it with a question mark rather than a star to acknowledge its questionable status.

It must finally be said that these tests cannot always be applied with 100 percent infallibility, and that how to apply criteria like "looseness," "dispensability," and "movability" will sometimes depend on judgments about likely contexts and on preferences among competing ways of interpreting the sentence.

5.3 Objects

By analyzing sentence adjuncts and adverbials, we are able to isolate the core sentence, and we are now in a position to delve more deeply into the structure of the predicate itself.

We have seen that in the very simplest type of declarative statement there is a subject and a verb:

[24] The crowd cheered

Here the predicate consists of one word, the verb "cheered." It is also possible that the crowd's applause was directed at one target:

[25] The crowd cheered the astronauts

Sentences like [25], in which there is a second noun phrase that is the target of the verb, are known as **transitive sentences,** and the verb in such a sentence is a **transitive verb**. The second noun phrase ("the astronauts" in [25]) is called the **direct object** of the verb. By contrast, a sentence that does not have a direct object, such as [24], is said to be **intransitive.**

A direct object is always a plain noun phrase that is not the complement of a preposition. Therefore, sentences that contain prepositional phrases immediately after the verb, such as *Mary looked after the children* or *The cat stared at the statue,* are not transitive. We return to this point in 7.5.

Transitive and Intransitive Verbs

It might seem that verbs can be divided into two classes: transitive verbs like *examine* and *elect* that must always have a direct object, and intransitive verbs like *look* and *snooze* that may never have one. In actual fact, however, English verbs are remarkably resistant to such a division.

It happens that the verbs *examine, elect, look*, and *snooze* belong to a rather small class of verbs that can only be used transitively or only used intransitively. Most English verbs are not like this, but can be used with or without a direct object according to their meaning in a particular sentence. Let us consider the verb *to smoke.*

By the Way:

It is customary in English grammar to mention a verb by what is called the infinitive. The infinitive consists of the bare form of the verb (the "base form"), without any ending, preceded by the preposition *to.*

We can think of an action like smoking in two ways. In one of them, someone is doing something to an object such as a cigarette or a pipe. In the other way of thinking about smoking, an object such as a cigar, a revolver, or a jacket pocket is emitting smoke. The following sentences give these possibilities:

[26] Mr. Butt was smoking a cigarette

[27] Little Michael smokes already

[28] The chimney was smoking

The ambiguity in the uses of *to smoke* is seen in [27] and [28]. Sentence [26] is clearly transitive: there is a verb ("was smoking") and a direct object ("a cigarette"). In [27], Little Michael habitually smokes *something*, that is, consumes something by smoking it, but we are not being told what. In [28], the "emitting smoke" sense, nothing is being consumed or otherwise affected by the smoking. The only thing that is happening is that smoke is coming out of the chimney. Sentence [28] is clearly intransitive.

Sentences like [27] are intransitive too, but they also have something in common with transitive sentences. In fact they actually exploit a possibility that exists for most English verbs that can take a direct object: the object can be left out if any of the following circumstances occur:

• the direct object is very general:

[29] Fran Zwicker used to *buy* for Nieman-Marcus

[30] Mr. Tataglia *writes* for the *St. Louis Post-Dispatch*

• it is obvious from the context:

[31] Zubin Mehta was *conducting*

[32] Maisie had brought her harp, and when we arrived she was *playing* for the van Hefflins

• the activity is a standard one:

[33] The Zuckermans always *ate* at 6 o'clock, no matter what

[34] Carl *opened* for the Red Sox in the 1970 season

• (for some verbs) the only thing affected by the verb is the subject ("reflexive" and "reciprocal" sentences):

[35] Dan *washed* and *shaved* before the interview

[36] Daphne and Bernard first *met* at an embassy reception

The need for a term for the kind of sentence whose verb is transitive in nature but lacks a direct object has struck many linguists, but there is no standard usage. "Pseudo-intransitive" has been proposed, but is a mouthful. "Understood object sentence" is hardly elegant, but it will suit our purposes here when it becomes necessary to distinguish these two kinds of intransitive sentences. When transitive sentences must be distinguished from intransitive sentences, however, it must be stressed that the only relevant distinction is the presence or absence of a direct object. Sentences without a direct object are intransitive sentences, whether or not there is an understood object.

Diagramming Transitive and Intransitive Sentences

The diagramming of transitive and intransitive sentences calls for a division in the predicate phrase between the verb itself and the direct object NP. Since the verb is often a complex of perhaps several auxiliaries, an adverb, and the verb, it will be referred to as the verb phrase.

> **REMINDER!**
>
> **The verb phrase is discussed in 3.7. The verb phrase is the phrase whose head is the main lexical verb and whose dependents are auxiliaries and certain adverbs.**

Here we have abbreviated it using the triangle convention. The function of the verb phrase is "Predicate," the same as that of the predicate phrase. The reason for this is that the verb phrase is the *head* of the predicate phrase, and, as we have noted several times, the head of any phrase is automatically assigned the same function as that of the entire phrase.

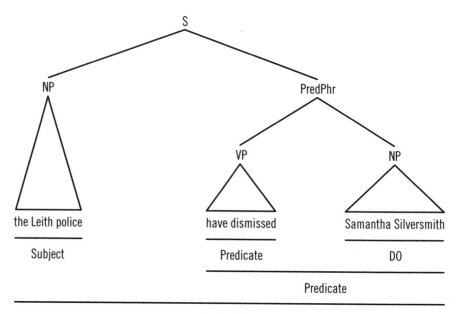

Diagram 5D.   Diagramming transitive sentences.

A simple intransitive sentence, both the truly intransitive and the type with an understood object, is identical to this, only it lacks the second NP node:

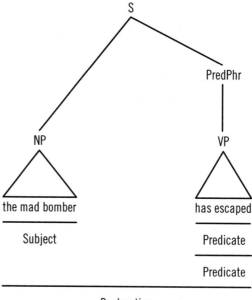

Diagram 5E.   Diagramming intransitive sentences.

The diagram for a simple intransitive sentence requires some comment. Notice that in this particular sentence, the predicate phrase consists solely of the verb phrase itself. This means that the function "predicate" occurs twice for the same phrase: once because it *is* the predicate phrase, and again because it is the *head* of the predicate phrase.

This kind of duplication is *theoretically* necessary whenever a node is non-branching, as the predicate phrase is in this tree.

REMINDER!

- **Node: A node is any point in a tree that has a category label such as NP or PredPhr.**

- **Dominates: A node dominates another node if the first node is higher in the tree than the second and there is a path from the first to the second.**

- **Immediately dominates: A node immediately dominates another node if there are no other nodes on the path between the first node and the second one.**

If you had forgotten any of this, look through Chapter 3 again!

Conventionally, however, such trees are usually pruned so that nonbranching nodes are eliminated, and duplication of the function label is minimized. We would prune away the lower function label so that the tree looks as follows:

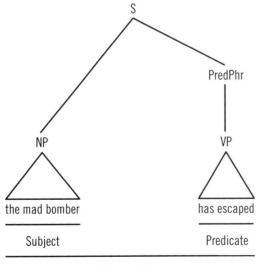

Diagram 5F.   Pruning form-function diagrams.

Pruning is only a graphic convenience, however. It does not change the general principle that wherever the tree above the target sentence has a node, the function diagram below the target sentence will always have a corresponding function label, even if this means that function labels below the sentence must be duplicated.

Second Objects

In two types of sentence, there is a second noun phrase in the predicate. Consider the following two sentences, representing the two different types:

[37] They elected Mr. Satyaswami mayor

[38] Someone handed Lefty Pinkerton a wad of banknotes

In the type represented by [37] there is a direct object, "Mr. Satyaswami," followed by a second noun phrase that **qualifies** the direct object. "Mr. Satyaswami" and "mayor" do not refer to two different entities; they are one and the same. "Mayor" is said to be a **complement** of "Mr. Satyaswami." The word "complement" refers to an element that "completes" or extends the sense of another element in a construction.

By the Way:

Notice that while Mr. Satyaswami was no doubt flattered to be elected mayor, "mayor" is a complement, not a compliment, of Mr. Satyaswami. If you think of a complement as something that *completes* something else, you will not be tempted to misspell it.

In the type represented by [38] there is also a second noun phrase. Yet here the second noun phrase does not complement the first one, in the sense of further describing it, but adds a new item. Here the first noun phrase ("Lefty Pinkerton") is said to be the **indirect object** of the verb "handed," and the wad of banknotes is the direct object.

The sentence type that has an indirect object can always be distinguished from that with a complement, in that the complement always refers to the same entity (person or thing) as the first noun phrase, whereas an indirect object and the direct object must refer to two distinct entities. The order of a direct object noun phrase and its complement is almost always DO - Comp, while the order of indirect and direct objects is always IO - DO.

The complement of a direct object NP is known as an **object complement**. Object complements, when they consist of a noun phrase, characteristically refer to epithets assigned to people, roles that people play, and positions that they hold. Object complements may also be adjectival phrases, as in

[39] This thundery weather is turning the milk *sour*

[40] The new tax forms make the citizens *very angry*

The indirect object of a verb is typically a person. When there is an indirect object, the direct object is typically an inanimate thing. This is because typically only people are active recipients of things, and only inanimate things can be passed to and fro among people. When humans are the direct object of a sentence in which there is an indirect object, they are always being considered as things. In the next example, it is suggested that the children are the spoils of a legal war:

[41] The family court awarded Mrs. Richardson the children

In [41] it would be more usual to say:

[41]′ The family court awarded the children to Mrs. Richardson

(or better still "awarded Mrs. Richardson custody of the children"). In fact, many grammarians would regard the [41]′ sentence (with the direct object following the verb and the recipient expressed as a prepositional phrase *to+NP)* as also being an indirect object sentence. This analysis, however, would cause a number of difficulties later when we come to consider the grammar of prepositional phrases in more detail. (It becomes impossible to differentiate these prepositional "indirect objects" from other kinds of adverbial complements.) For this reason we here restrict the term "indirect object" to those instances where

• the sentence also has a direct object;
• the human recipient NP immediately follows the verb; and
• the human recipient NP does not have a preposition.

The prepositional phrase in sentences like [41]′ is then to be analyzed as an adverbial complement.

Diagramming Different Types of Transitive Sentences

The diagramming of transitive sentences is quite straightforward. Direct and indirect objects and object complements are all part of the predicate phrase. The verb itself, of course, is also part of the predicate phrase; it is in fact the head of the predicate phrase. Examples of several types follow:

> **R E M I N D E R !**
>
> **Remember, when reading the diagrams: NP = "noun phrase," VP = "verb phrase," IO = "indirect object," DO = "direct object," and OC = "object complement."**

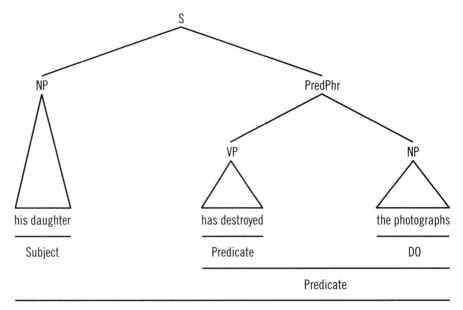

Diagram 5G.   Diagramming direct object sentences.

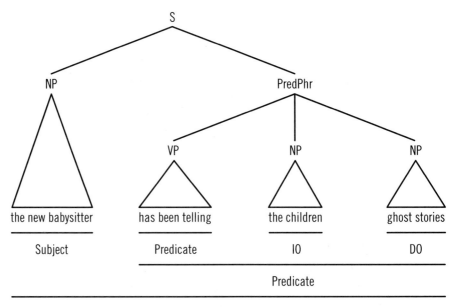

Diagram 5H.   Diagramming indirect object sentences.

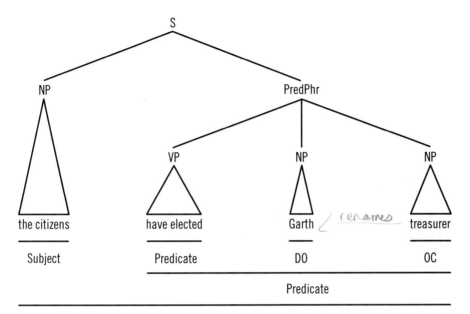

Diagram 5I. Diagramming object complement sentences.

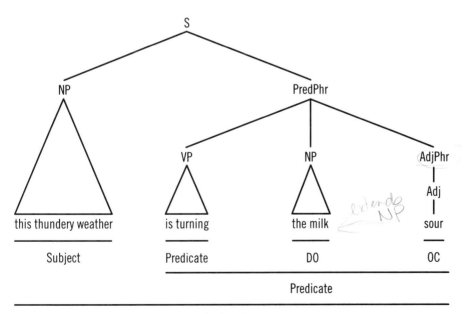

Diagram 5J. Diagramming adjectival phrases as object complements.

It is worth pointing out that in Diagrams 5H, 5I, and 5J the two NPs in the predicate, taken together, do not make a phrase. Consider tree 5I. Here the two NPs "Garth" and "treasurer" do not constitute a meaningful group of words. It is only when the verb phrase is added, "have elected," that we get a meaningful group "have elected Garth treasurer."

Two facts about the structure of the diagram go hand in hand with this observation:

(1)   No node dominates "Garth" and "treasurer" that does not also dominate the verb "have elected." (The node that dominates "have elected," "Garth," and "treasurer" is the one labeled PredPhr.)

(2)   There is no underline linking "Garth" and "treasurer" that does not also link these to the verb. (The underline that links "have elected," "Garth," and "treasurer" is, of course, the lower one with the label "Predicate.")

5.4 A Formal Definition of the Term "Phrase"

We are now in a position to define one more relationship in a tree. Look at the predicate phrase part of Diagram 5I:

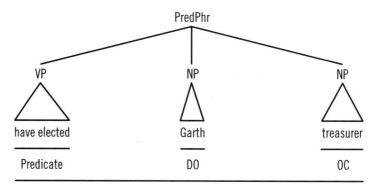

Diagram 5K.   Exhaustive domination.

The node PredPhr (predicate phrase) is said to **exhaustively dominate** the words "have elected," "Garth," and "treasurer." One node exhaustively dominates a set of words *if it does not dominate any other words in addition* to those in the set. (The set of words does not have to be *immediately* dominated by the single node.) Using this notion, we can reformulate the definition of a phrase as follows:

A phrase is any set of words that is exhaustively dominated by a single node.

By this definition, then, "Garth treasurer" is not a phrase, since the only node that dominates these two words (PredPhr) also dominates other words, namely "have elected." Notice that this definition of phrase means that single words can, and ultimately do, constitute phrases, for the individual words of a sentence are themselves always exhaustively dominated by single nodes such as "Article," "Noun," and so on. Finally, recall that *only a phrase can have a function.* A set of words that is not exhaustively dominated by a single node will also not have a single exclusive underline identifying its function. This is why the words "Garth treasurer" in Diagram 5I do not have their own underline with a function label under it.

5.5 Subject Complements

Some verbs are said to be **linking** verbs. Linking verbs are not transitive. That is, they do not have a direct object, but they serve to join a noun phrase to another phrase that tells us something about the noun phrase.

> **R E M I N D E R !**
>
> **Linking verbs were introduced in Chapter 2. Take another look at this chapter if you have forgotten what a linking verb is, or are having difficulty distinguishing linking verbs from transitive verbs!**
>   **The most important linking verb is *to be*, which is discussed in the next chapter. Here are some of the forms of this verb:**
>
> | | |
> |---|---|
> | *I am* | *we/they are* |
> | *you are* | |
> | *he/she/it is* | |
> | *I was* | *we/you/they were* |
>
> **Some other linking verbs are *to become*, *to turn*, and *to look*.**

Sentences that contain a linking verb are said to have a **subject complement** in the predicate. Usually, the subject complement is an adjective:

[42] John is *tall*

[43] Ms. Higginbottom seems *unhappy*

[44] The milk has turned *sour*

However, if the linking verb is *to be* or *to become,* the subject complement may be a noun phrase:

[45] Ms. Higginbottom has become *vice president*

[46] The Pirates will be *league champions*

Subject complements often lack the definite or indefinite article *the/a,* because they do not refer to a new person but to the role assumed by the subject.

Prepositional phrases and adverbs denoting a time or place may also function as subject complements. In this case the linking verb is always *to be*:

[47] All the committee members were *in the room*

[48] The auction is *today*

[49] Our guests are *here*

The diagramming of subject complement (SC) sentences is as follows. With an adjective as SC:

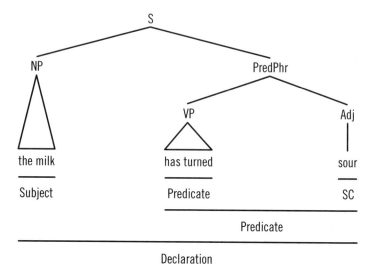

Diagram 5L.   Adjectives as subject complements.

And with a noun phrase as subject complement:

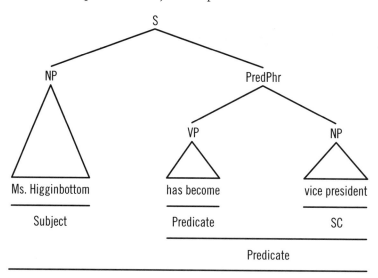

Diagram 5M.   Noun phrases as subject complements.

5.6 Sentence Patterns

Every simple declarative sentence in English belongs to one of a rather small number of **basic sentence patterns.** In this book we follow a standard analysis of English that assumes seven such patterns. So far we have encountered the following five:

(1)   Intransitive

(2)   Subject complement

(3)   Simple transitive

(4)   Transitive with indirect object

(5)   Transitive with object complement

Using the abbreviations S (subject), V (verb), SC (subject complement), DO (direct object), IO (indirect object), and OC (object complement), the sentence patterns encountered up to now can be represented by the following formulas:

(1)   S-V

Example: *The dynamite exploded.*

(2)   S-V-SC

Example: *The pages of the manuscript had turned yellow.*

(3)   S-V-DO

Example: *The intense heat buckled the railroad tracks.*

(4)   S-V-IO-DO

Example: *The owners paid the star performers enormous salaries.*

(5)   S-V-DO-OC

Example: *The inflation made many people poor.*

The basic sentence patterns (1)–(5) are based on what we earlier called core sentences—that is, sentences with a subject-predicate structure and no pre- or postcore phrases. Of course, any of these basic sentence types can be further accompanied by one or more of the pre- and postcore phrases introduced in the first part of this chapter.

EXERCISES

Exercise 5.1

Here are some examples of sentences that contain precore phrases. Identify these phrases as *pre-adjuncts* or *adverbials,* and state whether they express the writer's attitude, introduce a new topic, or state a time, place, manner, or circumstance for the sentence.

1. Astonishingly, Dr. Kromm accuses me of misusing my sources.
2. With a flourish, Mr. Samsonov produced a Lithuanian-English dictionary.
3. The night before last a number of strange lights appeared in the sky.
4. During the chamber music concert, Mr. Leary ate candies with noisy wrappers.
5. As regards your memo of September 20, I will raise this matter with the board at their next meeting.
6. With considerable vigor, Lee hit a fly ball to center field.
7. Tomorrow morning we will investigate those funny noises.
8. Brusquely, the border guard asked to see our passports.
9. Concerning your inquiry about costume jewelry, we are sending you a catalog by express mail.
10. Yesterday our plan seemed flawless.

Exercise 5.2

Draw diagrams for some or all of the sentences in Exercise 5.1, making use of the triangle convention to avoid detail. Display the information given in your diagrams in the form of three columns, as in the box in section 5.1.

Exercise 5.3

Write beside each of the following sentences the formula selected from (1)–(5) below that sums up its basic structure. Some sentences have multiple possibilities (indicated by a number in parentheses after the sentence).

(1) S-V

   Example: *The dynamite exploded.*
(2) S-V-SC

   Example: *The pages of the manuscript had turned yellow.*
(3) S-V-DO

   Example: *The intense heat buckled the railroad tracks.*
(4) S-V-IO-DO

   Example: *The owners paid the star performers enormous salaries.*
(5) S-V-DO-OC

   Example: *The inflation made many people poor.*

1. At the shopping mall Lisa bought a fancy key ring.
2. The asparagus were already cooking.
3. The king made Little Mattie Grove a knight of the Round Table.
4. The colors were fascinating.
5. Mr. Hollingsworth often used to get angry.
6. Little Mattie Grove made the king one of his fine rabbit pies.
7. In the workshop, a skilled carpenter was finishing a table.
8. Bill tore his pajamas.
9. Mr. Bridges was cooking.
10. The tunnel was dark.
11. The jury has awarded Mr. Hodgkins first prize in the oil painting category.
12. One of the speakers called the king a fink.
13. The volcano erupted violently.
14. The rainy weather made hiking a messy affair.
15. The firm promoted John last year.
16. Chris cooked us some wonderful crepes last night.
17. Many of the sailors went mad.
18. The weather had brightened up by the next day.
19. Jane found Rupert a delightful companion. (2)
20. Mr. O'Herlihy left his wife a total wreck. (2)

Exercise 5.4

Which of the following sentences are transitive? For those that are, identify (underline or write out) the noun phrase that is the direct object of the transitive verb. Make sure that you identify the entire direct object and only the direct object!

1. Julie has copied all my linguistics files onto her hard drive. transitive
2. Mr. Dranek looked at me as if I came from another planet. intransitive
3. The guys from Red Alert were snoozing in the bottom of the boat. intransitive
4. The survivors had improvised a fuel tank out of an old gas can. transitive
5. We examined each box carefully. transitive
6. Day care centers look after the children of the employees. transitive
7. The voters elect a new president every eight years. transitive
8. The groom smoked incessantly. intransitive
9. Max was cooking up one of his special breakfasts. transitive
10. The crew from Sweeps Clean was pulling into the driveway. intransitive

Exercise 5.5

Adverbials, unlike adverbial complements, can be moved to the front of the sentence or omitted without changing the verb's meaning. Adverbial complements *complete* the sense of the verb; they are often found after verbs in which movement in a direction is involved, and with verbs that easily combine with prepositional phrases. Using these criteria, determine whether the final prepositional phrase in the following sentences is an adverbial or an adverbial complement (these are the only two possibilities in this set of sentences). Always assume the most natural and least forced interpretation of the sentence.

1. Bernadette dropped a quarter in the wishing well.
2. Billy took his medicine in the bathroom.
3. Billy took his medicine into the bathroom.
4. Brutus and his gang attacked Caesar in the Forum.
5. Cassius stabbed Caesar in the chest.
6. Mr. Whitfield spilled his coffee on the rug.
7. The younger children were playing Monopoly on the rug.
8. A telegram arrived for you during the night.
9. Mr. Harris always receives his guests in the living room.
10. Ms. Thurman invited her friends to a sumptuous party.

Exercise 5.6

In the following sentences, all of which are intransitive, identify any that have understood objects.

1. We listened carefully.
2. Ms. Higgins cooks for twelve people every day.
3. The maharajah died in his sleep that night.
4. Harvey had to fetch and carry for the new office manager.
5. The beans have to soak for four hours.
6. You wash and I'll dry.
7. The water was already boiling.
8. The children were sleeping.
9. In my opinion, he drinks excessively.
10. After the game, Jenny showered and changed.

Exercise 5.7

Indirect objects and direct objects refer to different entities (things and people); direct objects and object complements refer to the same entity. Using this criterion of same/different reference, identify the IO-DO sentences and the DO-OC ones.

1. Marlys was telling the children a ghost story. *IO DO*
2. They elected Mr. Fitzpatrick recorder of deeds for the county. *DO OC*
3. The chamber of commerce has declared Betsylou Strawberry Queen of Berkshire County. *DO OC*
4. The Duchess threw Alice a pink flamingo. *IO DO*
5. Jack and Mo are cooking the orphans a wonderful breakfast.
6. We have named Siegmund chair of the Pollution Committee. *IO DO*
7. Someone has sold Mr. Braithwaite a used mandolin.
8. The local citizens called our quarter of town "Little Italy."
9. Janet poured old Miss Madder a stiff vodka.
10. Mattie sent the dean of Arts and Sciences a box of chocolates. *IO DO*

Exercise 5.8

Verify from the sentences in Exercise 5.7 that the indirect object sentences obey the three restrictions discussed in section 5.3.

Exercise 5.9

This question practices the recent discussion of diagramming and reviews the earlier material in Chapter 2.

In the following abstract diagrams, the nodes in (1) and (2) are labeled with meaningless letters. In (3), the underline labels are equally meaningless colors. Answer the questions beside each diagram with T or F:

1.

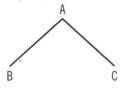

i. A dominates B. _____
ii. C and B exhaustively dominate A. _____
iii. A immediately dominates B and C. _____
iv. A is a branching node. _____

2.

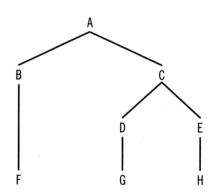

i. F, G, and H together are a phrase.   _____

ii. A dominates E and F.   _____

iii. G and H are exhaustively dominated by C.   _____

iv. F and G together are a phrase.   _____

v. B is a branching node.   _____

3.

A					
B		C		D	
E	F	H	K	L	M
Indigo	Violet	Pink	Black	Beige	Whit
Purple		Red	Blue	Brown	
Green			Yellow		
Orange					

i. Brown is a phrase.   _____

ii. A immediately dominates H.   _____

iii. Yellow is a phrase.   _____

iv. B functions as a Purple.   _____

v. K, L, and M are a D functioning as a Yellow.   _____

vi. Brown is a D.   _____

vii. A exhaustively dominates E, F, K, L, and M.   _____

viii. Green is a phrase.   _____

  ix. D immediately and exhaustively dominates K, L, and M.   _____

   x. A immediately dominates C and D.   _____

Exercise 5.10

Diagram sentences 2, 8, and 9 in Exercise 5.7. Use the triangle convention to abbreviate the NPs.

Exercise 5.11

(For class discussion) The principle that the indirect object is a human recipient does not always hold up. Obviously, we use the names of household animals as indirect objects (as in *It's time to give Fido his dinner*). But there are also expressions like

1. They gave the wall a coat of paint
2. The player gave the football a kick

Can you think of other kinds of examples in which the indirect object is not the recipient of a transfer? How do sentences like (1) and (2) differ from other kinds of sentences with indirect objects? What kinds of verbs occur in them?

THE VERB PHRASE

6.0 The Verb Phrase

In this chapter we will survey some of the more basic functional distinctions found in the English verb phrase.

A verb phrase (see Chapter 3) is a phrase having a lexical verb as its head. A lexical verb (see Chapter 2) is a word that carries the main meaning of the verb phrase, as distinct from an auxiliary or adverb that supports or amplifies the meaning of the verb. Thus in

[1] They *would always insist* on immediate payment

the verb phrase (the words in italics) is "would always insist." Within it, "would" is an auxiliary, "always" is an adverb, and "insist" is the lexical verb and head of the verb phrase.

6.1 Forms of the Verb

It is useful to distinguish six forms of the verb: a base form and five further forms. These five other forms are potentially distinct from one another, although the differences among them do not show up in every verb; for many verbs, two or more of the five forms are the same.

The verb *to take* will show the distinctions:

(1) Base form   take
(2) -ing form   taking
(3) -en form   taken
(4) General present   take

(5) -s Present   takes

(6) Past tense   took

Note that the form called the general present is the same as the base form. This is true of all English verbs except *to be,* whose base form is *be* and which has special forms for the general present. The verb *to be* is also unique in that it distinguishes three different forms for the present: *am* (first-person singular), *is* (third-person singular), and *are* (second-person singular/plural, and first- and third-person plural).

REMINDER!

It is customary to distinguish three *persons*, first, second, and third, and two *numbers*, singular and plural. This gives the following set of forms for the pronouns:

First-Person Singular:	*I*
First-Person Plural:	*we*
Second-Person Singular:	*you*
Second-Person Plural:	*you*
Third-Person Singular:	*he/she/it*
Third-Person Plural:	*they*

The verb forms are divided into two groups. Consider the forms of *to take* listed above. Forms 4–6 show independent tense, while 1–3 show tense only through an auxiliary. For example, *took* can only be past tense, but *taking* can be past or present, according to the auxiliary: *is taking* or *was taking*. For this reason, forms 4–6 are referred to as **tensed**, and 1–3 are said to be **non-tensed**. (The tensed forms are also often known as **finite**, as opposed to the non-tensed **nonfinite** forms.)

In the following table, a sample of English verbs (*be, move, drive, have, shut, keep, go,* and *eat)* is displayed:

NON-TENSED VERB FORMS			TENSED VERB FORMS		
Base form	**-ing form**	**-en form**	**General present**	**-s present**	**Past tense**
be	being	been	am/are	is	was/were
move	moving	moved	move	moves	moved
drive	driving	driven	drive	drives	drove
have	having	had	have	has	had
shut	shutting	shut	shut	shuts	shut
keep	keeping	kept	keep	keeps	kept
go	going	gone	go	goes	went
eat	eating	eaten	eat	eats	ate

Some remarks about these forms:

(1) The base form of a verb is a non-tensed form that occurs after certain aux-iliaries such as *must* and *will* and in a few other environments. As has been pointed out, a distinction between the base form and the general present is found only in *to be*, a verb which is also exceptional in many other ways.

(2) The *-en* form of the verb is used together with the auxiliary *have* to form what is called the *perfect*, which is discussed in more detail below. The perfect is exemplified in sentences like *You have woken up the baby*. The name "*-en* form" is taken from the characteristic shape of the suffix, even though the suffix *may not have this shape for every verb*. In particular, notice that for many verbs, such as *move*, *have*, *shut*, *keep*, the *-en* form is identical with the past tense—and does not have the shape *-en!* These verbs are traditional-ly known as "weak" verbs; see the box.

(3) The general present is a tensed form. It consists of the present tense of the verb other than the third-person singular (the *-s* present).

By the Way:

In some books on English grammar, verbs are divided into two classes, known as "weak verbs" and "strong verbs." The important difference once lay in the formation of the past tense: weak verbs used a suffix *-t* or *-d;* strong verbs had no suffix but made use of a vowel change in the past tense instead. In present-day English, weak verbs are those whose past tense has the same shape as their *-en* form, and strong verbs are those whose *-en* form and past tense are different in shape. Because of later changes, many modern "weak" verbs show a vowel change in the past tense, and some have even lost the *-t/-d* suffix. For this reason, the distinction between weak and strong is mainly of historical interest and has little relevance to Modern English.

No difference in meaning, such as tense, is involved between the general present and the *-s* present. The difference between the general present and the *-s* present has to do solely with the nature of the verb's subject. If the subject is third-person singular, the present tense of the verb must have the *-s* present; for all other persons in the present tense the general present is used:

[2] Frank *keeps* racing pigeons in his attic

[3] They *advertise* in all the major newspapers and magazines.

This distribution is known as **agreement**: the verb is said to "agree with" its subject. Third-person singular subjects include third-person singular pronouns such as *he, she, it,* and singular noun phrases such as:

- the governor of Mississippi
- the judge
- my French-English dictionary
- a juicy papaya
- the debate over these controversial issues

Note that in this last example the noun phrase may include any number of plural nouns, but in current usage as long as the head noun is singular (and the tense of the verb is present), the verb must be in the -s form. One of the commonest of all grammatical errors, committed even by good writers, is to allow the verb to agree with a more recently mentioned plural dependent noun rather than with the more remote singular head noun: *The debate over these controversial issues, many of which go back more than a century, have not diminished. The head noun here is debate, not issues, and so the auxiliary should have the -s present form, not the general present form.

The -ing Form as Gerund

One important use of the -ing suffix is to make a **gerund**. The gerund is a verb that has been converted into a noun so that it can serve as a subject or in some other capacity restricted to noun phrases. The gerund is identical to the -ing form of the verb; thus, from drink we have drinking, from believe, believing, and so on. In the following sentences, gerunds are given in italics:

[4] *Flying* is an expensive way to travel

[5] *Parking* can be more difficult than *driving*

[6] Susan prefers *rafting* to *kayaking*

Gerunds differ from ordinary nouns in that they can also behave like verbs. Gerunds can have subjects and direct and indirect objects:

[7] *Riding a bicycle* in Pittsburgh is arduous and dangerous

[8] *Gerald's opening the letter* scandalized his roommates

[9] We were touched by *Mary giving the beggar* her ice cream money

Notice in [8] that the subject of a gerund is in the possessive case ("Gerald's"). Even in formal writing, however, this convention is sometimes disregarded, as in [9].

The -ing Form as Modifier

The -ing form can also be used as *modifier of a noun*. It is possible to distinguish adjectival -ing forms that have become pure adjectives from those that retain a sense of being verbs. In

[10] *A passing* motorist telephoned the fire department

[11] We could see the light of *burning* torches on the hillside

the verbal sense of the adjective is quite strong; "passing" and "burning" could not themselves be modified by an adverb like "very" in the way that is possible for many other adjectives. On the other hand, in

[12] Some scientists had developed a very *interesting* theory

"interesting" is clearly an adjective, and hence "very" is appropriate.

As we will see when we come to discuss adjectives in more detail, English does not readily tolerate lengthy adjective phrases in front of the noun. The *-ing* form can modify a noun even when it is part of a longer attribute, but in such cases it must follow the noun it modifies:

[13] A reporter *investigating the incident* followed the taxi

[14] He pointed to a computer printout *lying on the desk*

The use of the *-ing* form as a modifier will be taken up in Chapter 13.

6.2 Tense and Aspect

English sentences invariably contain a verb or auxiliary that shows the **tense** of the sentence. Tense refers to the time of the action, whether it is in the present or past time with respect to the speaker. Sentences also show what is called **aspect**. Aspect refers to the way the action is depicted in relation to the context of the sentence.

Tense

The three tensed forms of the English verb, consisting of the general present, the *-s* present, and the past, show only two tenses, present and past, with the present being represented by two forms. The two tenses—present and past—are basic. Every English sentence must contain a reference to one of them either in the lexical verb or in an auxiliary. The future tense (discussed later in this chapter) can be expressed in English, but it is not so basic, and has a number of different forms with slightly different shades of meaning. One of these makes use of the auxiliary *will*, as in *Alicia will pay the bill.*

The present tense. The present tense in English ordinarily refers to an action or state of affairs that is *generally true.*

While the time within which the general present is valid includes the present, the general present does not refer to actions that are actually current; this meaning is reserved for the **progressive.**

The progressive includes sentences like "He is making the announcement right now" (where "makes" would be wrong, even though the action is in the present tense). There are a few exceptions, such as play-by-play sports commentaries (see example 1d below), in which by convention the present tense is used to report current happenings, but this is not usual. Here are some examples of the present tense:

(1) *-s* present:

   (a) Mahler's tone poem *explores* the tragic depths of the human psyche

   (b) The strange tower in his back yard *interferes* with our view of the sunset

   (c) She *takes* vitamin pills every morning

   (d) He *pops* it up, and Figueroa *makes* an easy catch, and the side *retires*

(2) general present:

   (a) We *publish* pamphlets on such topics as Freemasonry and Moral Rearmament

   (b) They *distribute* them through an anonymous agency

   (c) They *deliver* our mail at the side door

The past tense. The past tense can be used to report states or single events in the past, as well as to refer to states of affairs that were generally true in the past:

[15] Chaliapin *sang* an aria from *Evgenii Onegin*

[16] He *bequeathed* his gun collection to the Salvation Army

[17] During the Jurassic Age, thick forests *covered* this entire area

Notice, however, that an alternative to "covered" in [17] would be *used to cover*. The *used to* form is discussed below.

The past tense has a number of different forms, depending on the verb. The vast majority of verbs in English form their past tense by adding the suffix *-(e)d* to the base form, as in *look:looked, boil:boiled, judge:judged, shout:shouted, devour:devoured*, and so on. In fact, *-(e)d* is the default form for the past tense of verbs—any new verb that comes into the language, such as *to fax, to e-mail, to program, to fast-forward*, makes its past tense in *-(e)d*. It is often described as the regular past tense, beside which other forms of the past tense are irregular.

The spelling rules for the suffix show a few variations according to the last letter of the base form; thus, *like:liked* is spelled with *-d* rather than *-ed* because the last letter of the base form is already [e]. If the base form ends in a single consonant, this consonant is doubled. For example, *bat* (as in "to bat three times") has the past tense *batted*. This rule keeps the vowel of the base form intact (notice that *bated* would be pronounced quite differently). British and American English differ in the case of verbs whose base form ends in *-l*: £*cancelled*:$*canceled*; also *dial(l)ed, travel(l)ed*, and so on (a rare case in which the American reformed spelling complicates rather than simplifies a spelling rule).

> **REMINDER!**
>
> The British pound sign (£) is used to mark constructions identified as British, and the American dollar sign ($) for those identified as American.

A few verbs have a past tense in *-t* or *-d* but the expected *-e-* is missing. *Send:sent* is one (beside the regular *mend:mended)*. Another is the type *keep:kept, sleep:slept, meet:met, bleed:bled*, in which the vowel changes from *-ee-* to *-e-*. In *hit:hit* and *shut:shut*, where the base form already ends in *-t*, the past tense for all persons is identical with the general present: *Nowadays we always shut the shop at 4 o'clock* (present), versus *In those days we always shut the shop at 4 o'clock* (past).

A few verbs are variable: *dream:dreamed* or *dreamt; burn:burned* or *burnt; smell:smelled* or *smelt.* There is perhaps a difference between British and American English here, Americans preferring the *-ed* form, British the *-t* form in the past tense of *dream, burn*, and *smell.* (But the *-en* form of *burn* used as an adjective is generally *burnt:* "They served us burnt toast.")

Plead (in the judicial sense of "plead not guilty") has the alternative past tenses *pleaded* (the older form) and *pled*, a new form made, presumably, by analogy to *bleed:bled, breed:bred*. *To dive* is another verb with alternative forms. *She dives: she dived* has tended to be reshaped by analogy to the strong verb *to drive: she drives: she drove* and is now for many speakers—and writers—*she dives: she dove* (though the logical extension of this to **she has diven* is not used).

An important and frequently used set of verbs have no trace of a *-t/-d* suffix in the past tense, but instead form their past tense with a vowel change. There are several subgroups according to the vowel difference between the present and the past tense:

PRESENT	PAST	*-EN* FORM
drive	drove	driven
steal	stole	stolen
sing	sang	sung

These verbs are what were once referred to as strong verbs, because they show no trace of a *-t/-d* suffix in their past tense. They thus contrast with those grammatical wimps the weak verbs, which flop back on a suffix. See the box earlier in this chapter for details.

> **By the Way:**
>
> Most large dictionaries and reference grammars have lists of English verb forms. The variety of forms can only be suggested here, not listed exhaustively.

Aspect

In addition to an indication of the time of the sentence, present or past, the verb phrase may show what is called aspect—the way an action is viewed in relation to the discourse. (The term "discourse" refers to the wider environment of a sentence, such as a spoken conversation or a written passage.) There are many aspects, but the two most important are those known as the **progressive** and the **perfect**.

The progressive aspect. Most verbs can combine with the auxiliary verb *to be* and the *-ing* form in what is called the progressive aspect:

[18] A police inspector *is listening* to their story

[19] The whole village *was gossipping* about the diary

The progressive aspect presents an action as continuing and ongoing with respect to the time being talked about.

It should be emphasized that the actual duration of a progressive action is irrelevant; it may last for eons or microseconds. What counts is the relationship of the action to the circumstances of the discourse. Almost always, the progressive implies an activity that is a background to some other action, even if, as in [18] and [19] above, this second action is not explicitly stated:

[20] Maestro Mozzarello always shakes hands with the soloist while the audience *is applauding*

[21] At the moment of Kennedy's assassination, I *was playing* pool in Garavelli's saloon

In both these sentences, the focus is on an event, and the progressive aspect is used to indicate another action that accompanies that event. The *tense* of the progressive aspect may be present, as in [18] and [20], or past, as in [19] and [21], since an action can be ongoing and backgrounded at any time. Tense is therefore indicated in the auxiliary, which in these examples is *to be*. If the tense is the present, the verb will have one of the forms *am, is, are*. If the tense is the past, the verb will be *was* or *were*.

The perfect aspect. The perfect aspect is formed with the auxiliary *have* and the *-en* form of the verb:

[22] The twins *have put* wax crayons in the turkey stuffing

[23] The governor of Transylvania *has died*

It suggests a terminal which closes off an action or series of actions, and by implication focuses on the *resulting state* or *situation*. Notice how, in [22], although the speaker is certainly telling us what the twins did, the focus is on the disastrous state of affairs that resulted; and similarly in [23] it is the death of the governor, rather than the event of his dying, that is being brought to everyone's attention.

Typically, the perfect sets the stage for a new state of affairs. It is as if you are seeing a single still frame of a film and this frame is the last frame in a (possibly not seen) sequence of events. Not surprisingly, the perfect is useful when delivering hot news, as in example [23], or recounting a series of actions in previous episodes of, say, a soap opera, to bring viewers up to date on a new episode:

[24] Sanford *has proposed* to Marylou, but does not know that she *has already agreed* to marry soft-cheese magnate Desmond Detmuller. Meanwhile, Blazer *has discovered* that she is pregnant . . .

The perfect, then, focuses on the result of an action rather than the action itself. It refers to a state that results from an event; the perfect does not directly report the event itself, but rather the resultant state. This is the difference between

[25] The governor of Transylvania died

and

[26] The governor of Transylvania has died

The first of these sentences, [25], is a report of something that happened. The second sentence, [26], is an announcement of a state of affairs that has *current relevance*; it is a report, so to speak, of the result of the event of dying given for the benefit of current listeners. It always makes reference to one time and one time only: the time being talked about in the utterance (whether this is present or past). For this reason, the perfect, when it refers to a single occasion, is incompatible with a time-at-which expression. We can say

[27]′ The governor of Transylvania died at 1 o'clock this morning

but not

[28]′ *The governor of Transylvania has died at 1 o'clock this morning

Similarly, because the perfect reports states rather than actions, it cannot appear with manner adverbs:

[29]′ *The governor of Transylvania has died suddenly and violently

However, the perfect is compatible with time-during-which expressions, such as *duration* up to the present state:

[30] We have been living in Philadelphia for six years

and when there is some insistence on a repeated set of actions brought up to the time of the sentence:

[31] John has gotten up at 5 o'clock since he was a teenager

(Notice how *?John has gotten up at 5 o'clock today,* without any indication of repetition, sounds strange, or at least in need of a present state interpretation: *. . . and so he is very tired.)*

Tense and aspect combined. Because aspect is distinct from tense, the aspects and the tenses can occur in all combinations. Both the progressive and the perfect can be either present or past. When the writer projects a resultant state back into the past, for example, a past perfect appears, using the past tense of the auxiliary *have,* which is *had:*

[32] Apparently someone *had left* the water running in the bathroom

[33] The speaker *had prepared* her remarks thoroughly

Similarly, the progressive can be located either in the present or in the past and will show the present or the past forms of the auxiliary *be:*

[34] The department chair *is attending* a funeral in Cincinnati

[35] The plaintiffs *were consulting* their attorneys

Moreover, the two aspects can combine with one another:

[36] Two FBI agents *had been listening* at the door

[37] Rhonda *has been commuting* between New York and Atlanta for the past two years

The meaning of such combinations is that an action that is continuous (*listen, commute*) is surveyed from the point of view of its current state.

6.3 Modality

In addition to tense and aspect, the verb phrase also can contain an indication of what is called **modality**. Modality comprises a set of rather imprecise meanings such as obligation, permission, probability, futurity, and other meanings suggesting uncertainty and lack of definiteness in the action. Modality is mainly expressed by way of the **modal auxiliaries,** a small and fixed set of auxiliaries:

can	could
may	might
will	would
shall	should
must	—

But there is one special form of modality, known as the **subjunctive,** whose use, though very restricted, is still important, and which will be discussed below.

As was noted in Chapter 2, the pairs of modal forms line up historically as present and past tenses; the ancestors of the right-hand column were, in Old English, past tenses, while the forms in the left-hand column go back to present tenses in Old English. One of the paradoxes of this historical situation is that the *present* tense of one of the modals, *will*, serves to form the closest thing in English to a future tense:

[38] The ceremony will start at 10 a.m. tomorrow

But it is characteristic of the modals that no single meaning captures any of them. *Will*, for example, in addition to expressing a prediction of the future, can be used in several other distinct senses:

[39] I *will* help you with the piano *(willingness)*

[40] You *will* report to the quartermaster at 0500 hours *(obligation)*

[41] A good pointer *will* always sniff into the wind *(generality)*

[42] The elderly lady on the left of the picture *will* be his mother *(inference)*

A distinction between *permission* and *ability* is still maintained in the standard written language; in higher-register contexts, therefore, it is still advisable to distinguish *can* and *may*, for example:

[43] You *may* have the afternoon off during the World Series

[44] Alton *can* do simultaneous translation between English and Burmese

Most of the modals permit two very general interpretations, known as the **epistemic** interpretation and the **deontic** interpretation. Epistemic has to do with the reliability of the knowledge meant—whether it is certain, probable, likely, possible, and so on. Deontic has to do with giving orders and expressing obligations. In the following, the (a) sentence illustrates the epistemic meaning and the (b) sentence the deontic meaning:

[45] (a) John will easily pass the entrance examination

       (b) You will escort the honorees to the ceremony

[46] (a) The Homeleigh-Brixtons must really be rich

       (b) Patrons of the library must show their membership cards at the front desk

[47] (a) War can break out at any time

       (b) You can (= *may*) leave as soon as you are ready

[48] (a) Hurricane Harvey may touch land in Florida this afternoon

       (b) The members of the wedding party may now take their seats

While general statements about the meanings of the modals are hazardous, we can be more definite about their forms:

• Modals have only one form in the present, the general present form, without *-s*.
• Modals are not followed by the infinitive with *to* or the *-ing* form of the verb.

- A modal is always followed by the base form of the next auxiliary or the base form of the verb, whichever comes next.
- If there is a modal, it is always the first auxiliary in the verb phrase.

The English verb phrase can be summed up by the following formula:

TENSE—MODAL—PERFECT—PROGRESSIVE—VERB

In this formula, tense is never an independent word, but always appears as part of the immediately following word (the verb or one of the auxiliaries). If there is a modal, tense will be distinctive only in the rare cases where there are present and past versions of the modal; recall, for example, the following sentences from Chapter 2:

[49] Today the air is so clear that you *can* see the summit of Mount Fuji (present)

[50] Yesterday the air was so clear that you *could* see the summit of Mount Fuji (past)

In most cases, this distinction of present and past meanings is not found in modals. More commonly, the differences between the so-called present and past forms suggest not tense but different kinds of certainty, degrees of obligation, and so on, as in

[51] You *can* visit your grandmother while you're in Boston

[51]' You *could* visit your grandmother while you're in Boston

[52] According to the weather report, it *may* rain this afternoon

[52]' According to the weather report, it *might* rain this afternoon

Some of the modals have equivalents that use a longer phrase, for example *can = be able to, must = have to*. These phrasal equivalents of the modals are discussed further in 6.7.

We can conclude our discussion of the interaction of tense, aspect, and modal auxiliaries by giving some further examples of the various forms:

[53] The two brothers *sell* kitchen appliances

[54] We *will send* a representative to the meeting

[55] Sheila *has passed* the state bar examination

[56] They *have been organizing* an agricultural workers' union in the fruit orchards

[57] By the end of this year he *will have been practicing* medicine for twenty years

[58] The students *must have drunk* all the beer

The Subjunctive

In addition to the modal auxiliaries, English has preserved from older times a verb form known as the **subjunctive**, whose use is restricted to certain subordinate clauses. There are two forms for the subjunctive, a present and a past. The present subjunctive consists of the base form of the verb. For all verbs except *to be,* it therefore differs from the general present only in the third-person singular. For the verb *to be,* the present subjunctive is *be* for all persons: *I be, you be, he be, we be, they be.*

The present subjunctive is used after a verb of requesting or ordering, and so, except for a few archaic uses, is found only in subordinate clauses. Here are some examples. Remember that, except in the verb *to be,* the subjunctive is only visible in the third-person singular:

[59] I have requested that the minister *resign* immediately

[60] At that point the chair moved that the meeting *adjourn*

[61] The prosecution demanded that he *take* the witness stand

[62] They insisted that you *be* the first to leave

[63] He ordered that they *remain* in custody until the hearing

The past subjunctive is used to talk about hypothetical situations. A special form of the past subjunctive exists only in the verb *to be;* it is *were.* The past subjunctive is used with *if*-clauses to suggest a low degree of expectation on the part of the speaker. It is also used after the verb *to wish.* Since *were* is also the past tense plural of *to be,* the past subjunctive is distinguished from the indicative only in the singular (and even here it is being obliterated). Here are some examples:

[64] If Dr. Goodenough *were* dean, they would never abolish the classics department

[65] I wish I *were* in Hoboken right now

[66] Suppose she *were* to write a letter; could you then visit us?

In both of these types, *was* is commonly used in speaking, but for the higher registers, including writing, the subjunctive *were* is still mandatory. The past subjunctive comes up again later in our discussion of adverbial clauses in Chapter 16.

6.4 The Operator

Operator is a term often used for the first element in a string of auxiliaries. It is this element which always carries the tense of the verb phrase, and it therefore functions somewhat like the signs + and − in arithmetic, to set a value for the string as a whole. In the following examples, the operator is italicized:

[67] Fred *is* worrying about the piranhas

[68] They *have* been spending their vacation in Piddlecombe

[69] They *have* now shelled all the peas

[70] They *can* exchange their free mileage for discounts on long-distance phone calls

[71] The boys *must* have been walking along the railroad trestle

[72] He *should* be studying Chapter 12 now

[73] They *may* already have reached the summit

The notion of "operator" is an important one because of the special role this element has in forming, among other things, negatives and interrogatives. In forming interrogatives, for example, the operator is the element that changes places with the subject:

[67]´ *Is* Fred worrying about the piranhas?

[68]´ *Have* they been spending their vacation in Piddlecombe?

[69]´ *Have* they now shelled all the peas?

[70]´ *Can* they exchange their free mileage for discounts on long-distance phone calls?

The Auxiliary *do*

There is one auxiliary that can also be classified as an operator, but which serves virtually no other function. This is *do*.

Let us first consider the parts of the verb *to do,* which is somewhat irregular:

BASE FORM	*-ING* FORM	*-EN* FORM	GENERAL PRESENT	*-S* PRESENT	PAST TENSE
do	doing	done	do	does	did

The operator *do* has a role in negation:

[74] Rosemary does not permit photographs

and interrogatives:

[75] Does Rosemary permit photographs?

We will return to some of these uses later. In declarative statements, *do* is used to emphasize the verb or to suggest a contrast with a preceding negative:

[76] Rosemary does, however, permit pencil or charcoal sketches

Do as an auxiliary is not used with any of the auxiliaries: the modals, *have,* or *be.* In fact, its most common function is to stand in when an operator is needed but none of the usual auxiliaries that qualify as operators are being used. Thus the following is impossible:

[76]´ *Rosemary does, however, will permit pencil or charcoal sketches

Here "will" already qualifies as an operator, and so no *do* is needed.

6.5 Verb-Auxiliary Homophony

Homophony means two forms that resemble one another but are functionally different. One instance of homophony is the following. The verbs *to have, to be,* and *to do* are identical with the same words used as auxiliaries. It is possible to have two instances of these forms in the same verb phrase, one being an auxiliary and the other the lexical verb, as in these examples:

[77] Alphonse *is being* an idiot again

[78] Dr. Bigglesworth *had had* another letter from the militants

[79] After all, Chang and Murphy *do do* the tax accounts for the entire Southeastern Region

For reasons of stylistic elegance, many writers would look for a way to avoid the repetition of "do" in sentences like [79]. Example [79] is not ungrammatical, however, since the first "do" is an operator and an auxiliary in the general present, while the second "do" is the base form of the lexical verb *to do.*

6.6 Problematical Verb Forms

A typical problem of confusion exists when there are pairs of similar-looking verbs, one of which is regular and the other irregular. One especially troublesome set is *to lie* and *to lay,* because parts of *to lay* are identical with parts of *to lie.* The correct forms are as follows:

BASE FORM	*-ING* FORM	*-EN* FORM	GENERAL PRESENT	*-S* PRESENT	PAST TENSE
lay	laying	laid	lay	lays	laid
lie	lying	lain	lie	lies	lay

The grammatical difference is one of transitivity:

[80] They laid the foundation stone for the new wing (*to lay,* past tense)

[81] The flowers lay on a stone slab (*to lie,* past tense)

The verb *to lay* is transitive—it takes a direct object. On the other hand, *to lie* is intransitive—it cannot take an object. Here are some further sentences illustrating the difference:

[82] They were laying the foundation stone for the new wing

[83] They have laid the foundation stone for the new wing

[84] The representative lays the foundation stone for the new wing

[85] They lay the foundation stone for the new wing

In these four sentences, the verb is *to lay* and the direct object is "the foundation stone for the new wing." Notice that in [85] the verb is in the present tense—"lay" is the general present of the verb *to lay.* In the next group of sentences, the verb is *to lie,* and, it being intransitive, there is no direct object:

[86] The flowers lie on a stone slab

[87] The flower lies on a stone slab

[88] The flowers lay on a stone slab all last week

[89] The flowers were lying on a stone slab

[90] The flowers have lain for six hours on a stone slab (and are now wilted)

In any one of this group, of course, putting *to lay* in place of *to lie* would be an error. A similar confusion is sometimes encountered with *to sit* and *to set,* although here no forms between the two verbs are identical, the meanings are more divergent, and therefore errors are not so frequent. The forms are:

BASE FORM	*-ING* FORM	*-EN* FORM	GENERAL PRESENT	*-S* PRESENT	PAST TENSE
set	setting	set	set	sets	set
sit	sitting	sat	sit	sits	sat

Again the difference is one of transitivity—*to set* is transitive and *to sit* is intransitive. Example sentences would be:

[91] She set the wedding cake down on the sidewalk

[92] One of the visitors sat down on the chewing gum

[93] We have set the date for the final examination

6.7 Other Aspects and Modalities

There is a virtually endless array of secondary tense–aspect forms in the verb phrase, of which we can only consider a few here. Up to now we have been considering forms that adhere to the basic pattern we have identified:

TENSE—MODAL—PERFECT—PROGRESSIVE—VERB

There are a number of other forms that can be considered extensions of this pattern. These other tenses and aspects are followed by a verb or auxiliary with *to* (the infinitive) or with the suffix *-ing.*

Examples of the more important forms are:

(1) *want* followed by the infinitive:

The children *want to play* in the cemetery

(2) *try* followed by the infinitive or *-ing,* with a definite difference in meaning:

(a) Jack *tried to telephone* the police

(b) We *tried turning* the key counterclockwise

To be avoided in written prose is the replacement of *to* by *and* in sentences like (c):

(c) ?You *must try and be* nice to your grandmother

(3)   *keep* and *keep on*, with the verb followed by *-ing*. The difference in meaning is very slight:

(a) They *kept dialing* his number

(b) They *kept on dialing* his number

the (a) sentence suggesting perhaps "on different occasions," the (b) sentence "repeatedly on the same occasion."

(4)   *need* followed by the infinitive. *Need to* is very common, especially in American English. Examples:

(a) You *need to check* the tire pressure regularly

(b) You don't *need to be* concerned about the side effects

(5)   *like* followed by the infinitive or gerund:

(a) He *likes to fish* at Hawkins' Hollow

(b) He *likes fishing* at Hawkins' Hollow

The difference in meaning here, if it exists, is quite subtle.

(6)   *have* followed by the infinitive:

(a) We *had to fill* out several forms

As we saw in 6.3, the modal *must* does not have a past-tense partner, and *had to* stands duty as the past of *must*. But *have to* has its own present:

(b) First you *have to* (or *must*) *fill* out these forms

and the difference between *have to* and *must* in the present is minimal; probably register rather than meaning is involved. Since *must* occurs only in the present, *have to* is useful when other tenses and aspects of *must* are needed:

(c) We *have had to increase* the dosage of the antibiotic

(d) The police *are having to strengthen* their patrols in this district

(e) To counter grade inflation, the faculty *will have to give* fewer As and Bs in lower-level courses

(7)   *be able* followed by the infinitive:

(a) We *may be able to use* the super-high density disks in this machine

Be able to substitutes for the modal *can* in many of its forms, in much the same way that *have to* substitutes for *must*.

(8) *be going* followed by the infinitive:

(a) Bill and Mary *are going to order* some more sushi

Be going to locates an action in future time with respect to the time of the sentence. So

(b) Serge *was going to complain* to the authorities

means that at a time in the past Serge was about to complain. The *going to* tense is sometimes referred to as a **prospective** tense; it is only used when the occurrence in question is already in the works, not when it is merely predicted. The difference is seen vividly in pairs such as

(c) Mary *will have* a baby

(c)´ Mary *is going to have* a baby

(d) I *will die*

(d)´ I *am going to die*

(e) We *will get* some snow later today

(e)´ We *are going to get* some snow later today

In each case, the first sentence is a general prediction that may or may not come true, the second an imminent event. In using the *be going to* form, the speaker suggests that the evidence for the event is already apparent.

(9) *be supposed* with the infinitive is also a frequently encountered construction:

(a) The director of the program *is supposed to chair* the committee

(10) *used* with the infinitive is limited to the past tense:

(a) Sergei *used to pine* for the bright lights of the big city

The *used to* construction is a highly integrated part of the English tense-aspect system. As an indicator of something that *generally and habitually* occurred, it is the closest thing in English to a genuine past-tense counterpart of the general present. It may be called a **generic past:**

(b) Billie *walks* to school every morning, even when it rains

(c) Billie *used to walk* to school every morning, even when it rained

The pronunciation of *used to* and *supposed to* is worth a comment. In all registers and by speakers of all varieties, the *-s* that precedes the suffix *-ed* in the aspect form is voiceless; that is, it is said as if it were spelled with a *-c*: "suppoce," "uce." The *-ed* suffix that appears in the spelling is not pronounced at all. Note the difference between:

(a) Mark is supposed to [suppoce-to] leave tomorrow

(b) Mark is supposed [suppozed] to have left his wife a great deal of money

The (b) sentence means something like "people suppose that Mark left his wife a great deal of money," while the (a) sentence means more or less "Mark is scheduled to leave tomorrow." Similarly with *used*:

(a) Deirdre used to [uce-to] tip the porters generously

(b) That is the knife Deirdre used [uzed] to cut the string

We have here something like the homophony between a main verb and an auxiliary as discussed in 6.5.

EXERCISES

Exercise 6.1

Display the base form, -*ing* form, -*en* form, general present, -*s* present, and past tense of the following verbs (indicate any alternative forms you can think of): go, bear, (to) fell (a tree), buy, shine, strive, speed, lay, spit, hang, creep, steal, let, fall, set, think, bring, beat, speak, run, lie, strike, get, dare, tear

Exercise 6.2

Identify the -*ing* form in each of the following sentences as progressive aspect, modifier, or gerund.

1. John is calling his psychiatrist right now.
2. Anyone wanting to ride The Monster must line up in front of the post.
3. The practice of branding cattle is very cruel.
4. Your son and his friends were plagiarizing term papers.
5. Plagiarizing term papers is a serious offence.
6. Students plagiarizing term papers are always expelled.
7. His career as a wine taster was ruined by his drinking.
8. Fires were already burning when we arrived.
9. Getting up at 6 was an ordeal for Mr. Simmons.
10. Passengers leaving the train were overcome by the fumes.

Exercise 6.3

(For class discussion) What changes would you want to make in the following sentences, and why?

1. We have arrived in Chicago at 8:41 p.m.

2. While Jane drank coffee in the lounge, an announcement was suddenly coming over the loudspeakers.

3. Last night you can see the Northern Lights from our bedroom window.

4. Senator Frogworthy has lain a wreath at the Soldiers' Memorial.

5. I might could replace the spark plugs.

6. Mario hitted the puck behind the Penguins' own goal.

7. Those strange creatures have abducting my mother-in-law.

8. Someone have must taken money from the Rwandan Relief box.

9. Silvester wanted to try and rescue the mountaineers.

10. Nervously, Harvey rung Dr. Tuggem's doorbell.

11. Help me—I shall drown!

12. The loss of weight in a body immersed in a fluid is equaling the weight of fluid it displaces.

13. Mr. Silliman often uses to wish he could be a clown.

14. We require that you are prepared to leave on 24 hours' notice.

15. Now that you have explained your actions, you can leave.

Exercise 6.4

Convert the present tenses into the past tense. Note in doing this exercise that you must be careful not to change any parts of the sentence other than the tense.

Example:

> The city council is going to discuss the new stadium
>
> -> The city council was going to discuss the new stadium.

That is, "is going to discuss" should not be changed to "discussed," "will discuss," or the like, but only to "*was* going to discuss."

1. The bus must come to a complete stop at every railroad crossing.

2. He says he will make an appointment with his therapist.

3. Dr. Nincombe-Poope is supposed to have been checking up on the inmates.

4. Someone has been putting salt water in the ice trays.

5. Hennypenny lays two eggs every day.

6. Every year the Youngstown Twisters beat the Louisville Loopers in the regional frisbee tournament.

7. The graduate students lie around on the beach all weekend.

8. Marvin pleads guilty to the piracy charge.

9. The Martians are watching us through their telescopes.

10. The students at that college have to attend church services every morning.

Exercise 6.5

Diagram the following sentences. See the appendix to this chapter for specimen diagrams and guidelines on diagramming elements of the verb phrase.

1. Last Sunday, Sebastian may have been playing the tuba.
2. Explosions have been rocking the town since early morning.

Appendix: Diagramming the Verb Phrase

The verb phrase is the head of the predicate phrase and consists of the verb itself, any auxiliaries, and any adverbs that are interior to the verb phrase. The following general rules for analyzing the verb phrase apply:

- Forms:

(1)   The lexical or main verb is always the head of the VP and is labeled V.

(2)   Each auxiliary verb is labeled Aux and is immediately dominated by VP.

(3)   The complex auxiliaries *have to, be about to, be going to, used to, be supposed to,* and *be able to* should be analyzed as if they were a single word (see Sample Diagram 2 below).

- Functions:

(4)   The function of the modals and of the complex auxiliaries mentioned in (3) (other than *used to*) is to signal a modality of the next element. Therefore the function should be indicated as "modal of X" (where X is the next adjacent Aux or the verb).

(5)   The functions of the aspect auxiliaries *have, be,* and *used to* are to be indicated as follows

Have:	Perf(ect) of X
Be:	Prog(ressive) of X
Used to:	Gen(eric) Past of X

where X is the *next element to the right* in the VP

(6)   The verb phrase is the head of the predicate phrase. Since the function of the predicate phrase is "Predicate," the function of the entire VP is also "Predicate."

(7)   Similarly, the function of the verb is also "Predicate." It can be seen that the function label "Predicate" may make multiple appearances in the diagram.

1

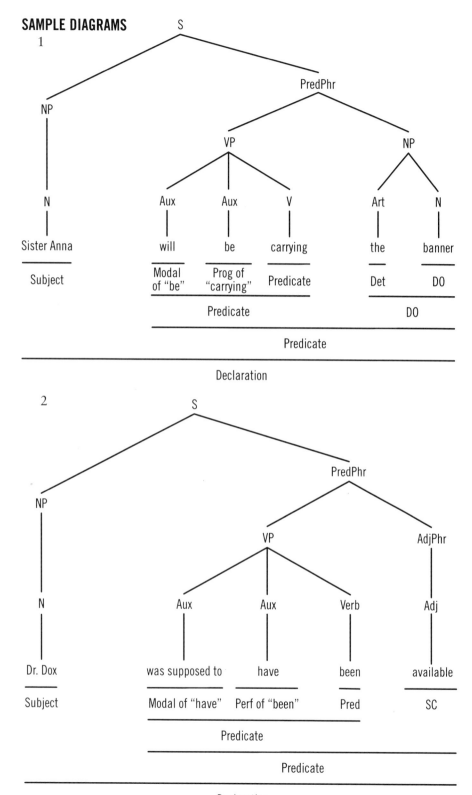

7

PREPOSITIONAL PHRASES AND ADVERBIALS

7.0 Prepositions and Adverbs

We will now examine in more depth the constructions involving prepositions and adverbs—word categories that, as we noted earlier, are often confused because they tend to merge and overlap with one another. The syntax of the preposition and its complement in English is complex, and you will be asked to make some rather subtle distinctions. On the other hand, the extraordinary suppleness of the English sentence, which students of the language often admire, is due to a large extent to the intricate ways in which prepositions, adverbs, and noun phrases interact in the syntax of the language.

We have seen examples of clear distinctions between adverbs and prepositions, for example:

[1] Uniformed officials scurried *importantly* along the corridors (adverb)

[2] Everyone knew there were ghosts *in* the old railroad station (preposition)

There is also a certain amount of overlap between the two classes. Some adverbs are hard to distinguish from marooned prepositions. For example, *home* and *up* are rather similar in their distribution in sentences like

[3] The children went *home*

[4] The doctors gave *up*

[3]′ The adults took the children *home*

[4]′ The doctors gave the patient *up*

There is even disagreement among written grammars of English, for example, over the proper assignment of "home" in sentences like [3] and [3]′. Grammarians that recognize a third category of particle sometimes call "home" a particle, as distinct from an adverb or a preposition. A starting point in distinguishing adverbs from prepositions is the recognition that, unlike adverbs, prepositions can form prepositional phrases.

7.1 Prepositional Phrases

Prepositional phrases have a common structure Prep + NP. Examples of prepositional phrases are

- with you
- against the new amendment to the club's constitution
- by the opposition of the members of the union to the election of a new president

Notice that prepositional phrases can themselves contain prepositional phrases:

by the opposition I of the members I of the union I to the election I of a new president

Here the entire prepositional phrase contains no fewer than five smaller prepositional phrases. We will be studying the analysis of such complex prepositional phrases.

7.2 Forms and Functions of Prepositional Phrases

We will consider first some of the ways that prepositional phrases can function.

Modification of a Noun or Noun Phrase

Prepositional phrases can function in several ways. One of the most frequent is to **modify** a noun, much as an adjective does. When they modify a noun, prepositional phrases always follow the noun:

[5] The board ignored the opposition *of the members*

[6] The creatures *in the spaceship* were trying to communicate

[7] Mike and Teresa O'Reilly own the tavern *by the lake*

Here the prepositional phrases in italics modify a preceding noun, which is the head noun of the NP. A typical NP modified by a prepositional phrase has the following formal structure:

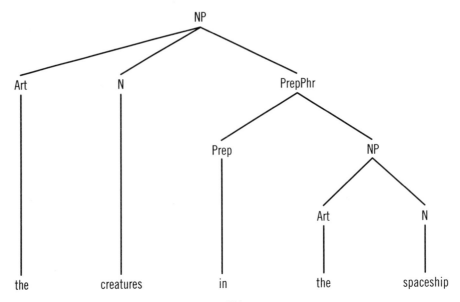

Diagram 7A.   A prepositional phrase modifying a noun.

The form parts of the tree have the following functions:

• The function of the entire PrepPhr in this tree is *modifier of "creatures."*
• The function of the NP "the spaceship" is *complement of preposition* (PrepComp).
• The function of the N "spaceship," which is the head of the NP "the spaceship," is also *complement of preposition.* (Remember that the head of a phrase always has the same function as the entire phrase.)
• In a prepositional phrase, the preposition functions as the head of the phrase. Since the preposition is the head of the prepositional phrase, the function of the preposition is *modifier of "creatures."*

You may wish to complete the drawing by adding the function labels with their underlinings before turning the page.

The above tree will now be repeated, with the function labels written in:

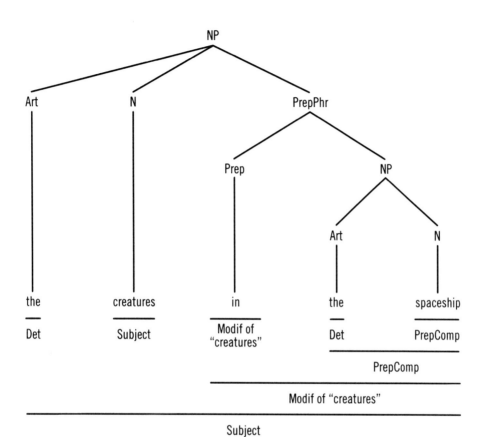

Diagram 7B. Form-function diagram for N modified by PrepPhr.

Diagramming Complex Prepositional Phrase Modifiers

Consider the following tree of the NP "a couple with two children with a duplex on Locust Street."

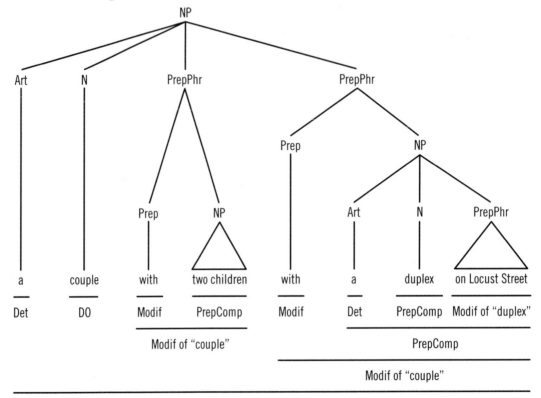

Diagram 7C.   Diagramming complex phrases.

In this tree, the prepositional phrases have an arrangement that reflects their grammatical relationship to one another:

- "With a duplex" does not modify "children" but the head noun of the entire NP, "couple." (We are assuming that this NP is the direct object of its sentence.)
- "On Locust Street" modifies "duplex." It does not modify "children" or "couple."
- "With a duplex on Locust Street" modifies "couple." It does not modify "children."
- "With two children with a duplex on Locust Street" is not a phrase and does not modify "couple."
- The two prepositional phrases "with two children" and "with a duplex on Locust Street" are both equally modifiers of the head noun "couple."

Precore Phrases

A second important way that a prepositional phrase can function is as a **non-core phrase**, a phrase that precedes the subject or follows the predicate. (Noncore phrases are discussed in 5.1.) Some examples of prepositional phrases that are pre- and postcore phrases follow:

[8] *In the morning* they surveyed the damage

[9] *With considerable nervousness*, he gave the news to the ambassador

[10] *Like his predecessor*, the new prime minister was unable to resolve the dispute

[11] *After dinner* Colonel Groznek presented his proposal

[12] The legions encountered fierce German tribes *in the Westphalian forests*

[13] We are going to visit some Indian pueblos *during our summer vacation*

[14] *In actual fact*, the economic fallout from the proposal will be very slight

[15] *For the record*, we have never denied a claim on grounds such as these

Notice that some of these noncore phrases are adjuncts (examples [14] and [15]), and some adverbials (examples [8]–[13].

Adverbial Complements

A third way that a prepositional phrase can function is as an **adverbial complement**. Adverbial complements were introduced briefly in 5.2, and we will now examine them in more detail.

We could start by noting that the general use of the word "complement" is to denote a phrase that *completes* or *extends* a word or phrase. We have seen, for example, prepositional complements, which are NPs that complete a preposition within a prepositional phrase. In the prepositional phrase *with a laptop*, for example, the noun phrase *a laptop* is a prepositional complement. We have also seen subject and object complements, as in

[16] The ringmaster was *furious* (subject complement)

[17] The booing made the ringmaster *furious* (object complement)

Adverbial complements, as their name suggests, complete the sense of a verb. A particularly clear example involves the verb *to put*. It is a transitive verb; that is, it always requires a direct object. But that is not enough, as can be seen from the following examples:

[18] (a) *The bomb disposal unit put last night

    (b) *The bomb disposal unit put the package last night

    (c) The bomb disposal unit put the package on a truck last night

Sentence [18a] shows that *to put* is a transitive verb; sentences with *to put* are ungrammatical without a direct object. But [18b] shows a further restriction. *To put* requires not only a direct object, but also an adverbial complement, and without an adverbial complement sentences whose main verb is *to put* are ungrammatical. Only sentence [18c], which has both these elements, is fully grammatical.

The prepositional phrase "on a truck" in [18c], then, is an adverbial complement. Unlike a postcore adverbial, an adverbial complement does not state a circumstance that frames the action of the sentence as a whole, but specifically adds something to, or *extends,* the meaning of the *verb* or the *predicate.* To go back to our example of Chapter 5,

[19] That maniac next door rode his motorcycle through my shrubbery last night

"through my shrubbery" is an adverbial complement because riding something normally involves a trajectory (that is, motion in a particular direction), and therefore the trajectory completes the report of riding.

An important difference between the adverbial complement and the postcore adverbial is that *an adverbial complement is part of the predicate.* In other words, an adverbial complement is attached to the node PredPhr. You will remember that noncore phrases are not part of the predicate, but are attached instead to the high S node. Thus, [18c] is diagrammed as follows:

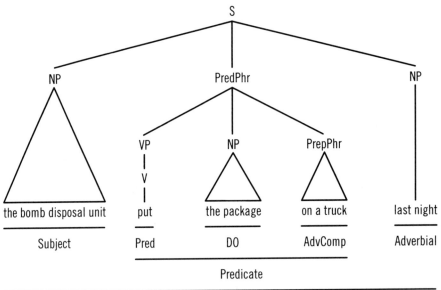

Diagram 7D.   Diagramming adverbial complements.

Adverbial complements often denote the direction of an action; in fact, any prepositional phrase that points an action in a certain direction is almost certainly an adverbial complement:

[20] Friar Tuck shot five arrows *at the hot air balloon*

[21] Then you have to pour the mixture *over the sautéed potatoes*

[22] Cautiously, the Adventurous Four crept *into the cave*

[23] I sent the fake diaries *to a well-known Harvard historian*

The compound prepositions *into* and *onto* are especially frequent in adverbial complements.

The movability test that we mentioned in Chapter 5 in discussing pre- and postcore phrases works reasonably well in reverse for adverbial complements. We saw that a prepositional phrase that can be moved to the front of the sentence without sounding stilted or artificial is usually identifiable as a noncore phrase. Conversely, a prepositional phrase that cannot be moved to the front is at least a likely candidate for being an adverbial complement:

[24] Muffy reminded him *of their wedding anniversary*

[25] I copied the memo *onto a piece of scratch paper*

[26] Our agent lived *in Paris*

[27] The general talked *about his early career*

Adv comp

The italicized phrases are all adverbial complements. Examples [24] and [25] differ from [26] and [27] in transitivity: the first two have direct objects (*him* in [24], *the memo* in [25]); the second two have no direct object.

Notice, again, that the adverbial complement is always in some sense a *typical accompaniment* of the verb: "to remind" requires necessarily that you be reminded *of something*; "to live" means necessarily to live *in a place*; "to copy" in the sense of "write a copy" means necessarily to copy something *onto something*; "to talk" means necessarily to talk *about something*. On the other hand, postcore phrases are extras—they do not have this quality of necessity that is characteristic of adverbial complements:

[28] Muffy reminded him of their wedding anniversary *during the concert*

[29] I copied the memo onto a piece of scratch paper *for John's benefit*

[30] Our agent lived in Paris *between the two wars*

[31] The general talked about his early career *for several hours*

adverbial

In all these examples, there are two prepositional phrases, the first being an adverbial complement and the second (italicized) a postcore adverbial.

7.3 Prepositions in Phrasal Verbs

In Chapter 2, we encountered the phenomenon of the marooned preposition, which we can think of as a prepositional phrase that lacks a noun phrase complement. Thus in

[32] Buster handed the money over

"over" is a preposition whose complement is absent.

It is characteristic of English that combinations of verbs and marooned prepositions form **phrasal verbs,** pairs of words which act in some respects like a single verb, and in other respects like two separate entities, one a verb, the other an adverb. This ambiguity in phrasal verbs—the fact that they are simultaneously like single verbs and combinations of verb plus adverb—causes a few difficulties in their analysis. While no analysis is completely satisfactory, the one chosen here works reasonably well for our present purposes.

Meanings of Phrasal Verbs

The meanings of phrasal verbs are sometimes predictable from the combination of verb and preposition:

[33] Vito *took* the pizza *out*

[34] They have *cut down* all those big oak trees in the plaza

Sometimes, however, the combination of verb and preposition is idiomatic; that is, the meaning cannot be deduced from the sum of its parts:

[35] Her disguise *took* the nightclub owner completely *in* (to take in = to deceive)

[36] She *told* her assistant *off* in front of all the other employees (to tell off = to reprimand)

As in the above examples, phrasal verbs with idiomatic meanings often have a single-word Latinate counterpart (take in = deceive, tell off = reprimand). In the past, student writers were encouraged to use the longer single-word verbs in preference to the shorter two-word phrasal verbs, the assumption being that the longer single words were more appropriate to the more formal registers found in writing. The recent tendency has been to alternate them so as to produce a more varied style.

By the Way:

The Basic English movement earlier in this century recommended replacing long, complex words with shorter, simple ones. This movement did not take root, however, and you can see why when you consider that it is no easier to learn idiosyncratic combinations like *take in* and *tell off* than longer words like *deceive* and *reprimand.*

Transitive and Intransitive Phrasal Verbs

In illustrating phrasal verbs, we have so far used exclusively transitive ones—that is, verbs that are followed by a direct object. In this type, we have seen, the preposition may appear either before or after the direct object:

[37] (a) We filled up our gas tank

      (b) We filled our gas tank up

If the direct object is a pronoun, only one possibility is available:

[38] (a) We filled it up

(b) *We filled up it

Here the [b] sentence is ungrammatical. The choice between [37a] and [37b] is a stylistic one, having to do with the balance between the verb and the noun.

Notice that phrasal verbs may not take an indirect object as we have previously defined it. Indirect objects are unmarked; that is, they do not have a preposition. For example:

[39] (a) She passed the surgeon a new scalpel

(b) She passed a new scalpel to the surgeon

In [39a], *surgeon* is an indirect object; in [39b] *to the surgeon* is not an indirect object but the adverbial complement of *passed*. When a phrasal verb such as *hand over* or *pass along* is used, an indirect object is not possible:

[40] (a) I handed my keys over to the valet

(b) *I handed the valet over my keys

(You may find such sentences acceptable as long as the indirect object is a pronoun, for example, *?I handed him over my keys*.)

Phrasal verbs can also be intransitive, as in

[41] The Martians peered inside

[42] Burton passed out

[43] A squadron was just taking off

The prepositional status of the second element in such verbs is often uncertain. There is enough similarity between [41] and [41]′

[41]′ The Martians peered inside the farmhouse

to show that "inside" is a straightforward preposition. Often, however, there is no obvious ellipsis of a noun phrase. In [42], "passed out," and [43], "taking off," we cannot supply a possible NP that would confirm the prepositional status of "out" and "off." In such cases, the difference between a preposition and an adverb is rather slight. Perhaps the best way of conceiving of the difference is through a diagram in which a group of words like *up, down,* and *along* share with adverbs the property of appearing without a NP, and with prepositions the ability to form prepositional phrases with a NP, somewhat as follows:[1]

---

[1]There are slight variations; for instance, (£?)*bring him to* for "bring him to consciousness, bring him around"; *stand to* in a military context = "take up a position of alertness"; *come with* in some dialects/registers for "accompany" (*Would you like to come with?*). In £, for careful users, *round* is a preposition, *around* an adverb, so: £*He ran round the park/The children were playing around*. In written $, *round* is not permitted as a preposition in the formal register, and if used has the apostrophe '*round*.

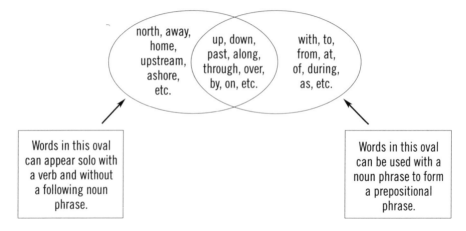

Diagram 7E. Prepositions and adverbs.

In any case, we must be very careful to separate the marooned prepositional phrase from the direct object noun phrase. Thus in

[44] The unkind workman has chopped down my tree

"down" must be analysed as a *prepositional phrase,* and "my tree" as a direct object NP, part of the predicate phrase *but not part of the prepositional phrase:*

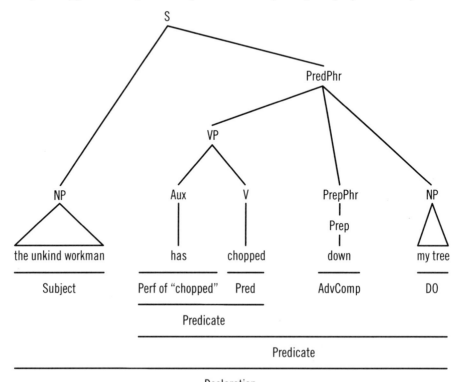

Diagram 7F. Diagramming direct object NPs and marooned prepositions.

Because phrasal verbs are analyzed as including an adverbial complement, they ought technically to be assigned to new sentence patterns—(6) S-V-AC (intransitive) and (7) S-V-O-AC (transitive). (The first five patterns were discussed in 5.6. Here AC refers to "Adverbial Complement.") It is, however, more reasonable to restrict these two patterns to adverbial complements that are not simply marooned prepositions but full prepositional phrases. In the absence of a true adverbial complement, then, phrasal verbs will be classified as simple verbs for the purpose of identifying them with one of the seven basic sentence patterns.

It also follows that a sentence may have more than one adverbial complement, as in

[45] Gideon gave up on the state lottery

to be diagrammed as follows:

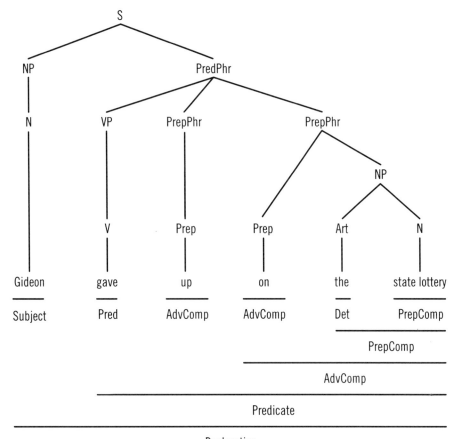

Diagram 7G.   Diagramming multiple adverbial complements.

But there is in principle no limit to the number of adverbial complements a sentence may contain; sentences like *we drove from Nashville to St. Louis,* for example, contain two adverbial complements, and *we drove northwards from Carbondale to Chicago* has three.

7.4 Prepositional Verbs

We have noted that adverbial complements have a close relationship to the verb. In

[46] Michael referred to the strange incident several times

"referred" suggests something that is referred to. The preposition "to" is not replaceable by any other preposition; "refer" can only be followed by "to." When, as in [46] above, a verb has an adverbial complement such that the preposition of the adverbial complement is fixed for that particular verb, we speak of a **prepositional verb.**

Characteristics of Prepositional Verbs

In the following examples, notice that the prepositions are fixed—different prepositions cannot be substituted without altering the sense of the verb:

[47] Her husband *looks after* the children

[48] Our victory *calls for* a celebration

[49] For the next year, John *concentrated on* his studies

[50] The executive board *approved of* the subcommittee's decision

The difference between a prepositional verb and any other verb that is followed by an adverbial complement is that the preposition following a prepositional verb is invariable. With the meaning *tend, supervise,* the verb *look* must be followed by *after.* Moreover, this meaning can usually be paraphrased by a transitive verb (*look after = tend, call for = demand, concentrate on = pursue, approve of = endorse*). Contrast this with an ordinary verb taking an adverbial complement, such as *to jump:*

[51] He jumped onto the roof

[52] He jumped off the roof

[53] He jumped into the pond

[54] He jumped through the window

and so on. Here the preposition is not fixed, but varies according to the direction of jumping. Nor are there readily available transitive verb paraphrases of "jump onto," etc.

With regard to their meanings, prepositional verbs have much in common with phrasal verbs. However, the preposition is not structurally separate from the NP, as it is in the case of a phrasal verb, but rather the preposition and the NP form a prepositional phrase. This means, among other things, that the preposition cannot be moved across its complement (*looked the childen after* is ungrammatical).

Transitive Prepositional Verbs

Verbs like *look after, call for, concentrate on,* and *approve of* in these examples are intransitive, even though they have a semantic goal very much like transitive verbs, because what follows the verb in each case (that is, *look, call, concentrate, approve*) is a prepositional phrase functioning as an adverbial complement (*after the children, for a celebration, on his studies, of the subcommittee's decision*).

However, it is also possible to have a transitive prepositional verb, in which the verb is followed by a direct object and *then* by the prepositional phrase:

[55] They attributed their victory to the geese

[56] She congratulated the team on their success

[57] Farmers are blaming the poor crop on the wet summer

[58] Farmers are blaming the wet summer for the poor crop

[59] You must forgive my young friend for his hasty temper

Notice that as with other prepositional verbs, the relationship between the verb and the preposition is a fixed one; it is not possible to substitute a different preposition. Combinations like *make fun of, take part in, keep tabs on, give way to,* and *catch sight of* also belong here. In these combinations, the direct objects ("fun," "part," "tabs," "way," "sight") and the specific verbs they occur with ("make," "take," "keep," "give," "catch") make up fixed sequences that are commonly used together; they are often referred to as idiomatic expressions. A wrong combination, for example writing *place importance on,* rather than the more correct *place emphasis on* or *attach importance to,* can make a writing style seem awkward.

Phrasal-Prepositional Verbs

Phrasal verbs can also simultaneously be prepositional verbs, yielding the characteristically English combinations of prepositions. They can be intransitive:

[60] I have been putting up with his late hours

[61] They look down on their neighbors

[62] A SWAT team burst in on the faculty meeting

[63] We could not keep up with the rest of the team

or transitive:

[64] John took his anger out on the employees

[65] The manager has been letting his staff in on the secret

Diagramming Phrasal-Prepositional Verb Sentences

The last sentence would be diagrammed as follows. Notice that there are two adverbial complements (each abbreviated AdvComp in the diagram), one of which is the marooned preposition of the phrasal verb.

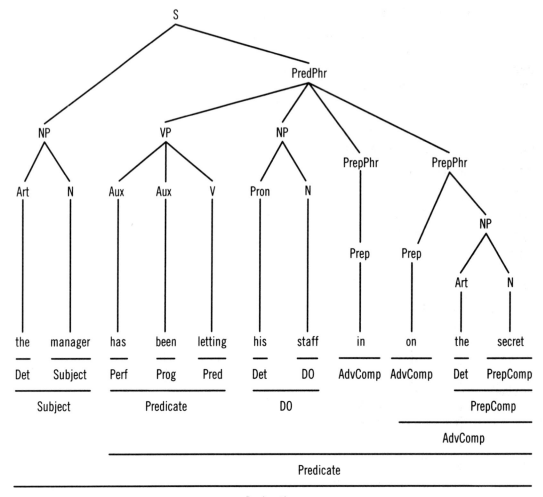

Diagram 7H.   Diagramming phrasal-prepositional verbs.

7.5 Adverbials inside the Core Sentence

Up to now we have encountered adverbials only as noncore phrases, either as pre-core or as postcore constituents of the sentence. Adverbials can, however, also occur inside the core sentence. Consider, for example, the following sentence:

[66] We gazed for several minutes at the setting sun

Here "at the setting sun" is of course an adverbial complement; it completes the sense of "gazed." But "for several minutes" does not complete the sense of "gazed" and so is not an adverbial complement. Yet because it occurs between the verb phrase and the adverbial complement, it cannot be a postcore phrase. Adverbials that are not a postcore phrase are simply part of the predicate phrase.

Diagramming Adverbials

A typical tree involving a prepositional phrase functioning as an adverbial would look as follows:

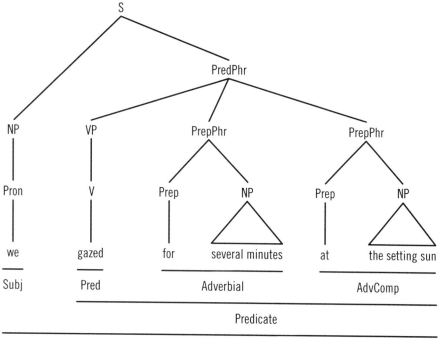

Diagram 71.   Diagramming adverbials.

Adverbials within the Verb Phrase

Adverbials can also be placed in the verb phrase. This is particularly the case with a class of adverbs of time that includes *always, often, still, yet, sometimes, then, frequently, occasionally,* and others. Adverbs that relate the sentence to other sentences and to the context often appear within the verb phrase, too.

Examples are *however, never, also, perhaps, nonetheless.* (The general negator *not* also belongs here, as will be discussed more fully in Chapter 10.)

Here are examples of such adverbs:

[67] We have *also often* visited the Tate Gallery in London

[68] You must *always* remove your outdoor shoes in the hallway

[69] He is *often* in his office

[70] He *often* works in his office

[71] They may *still* be working for the telephone company

The usual place for these adverbs is *after the operator,* or immediately before the verb if there is no operator. The verb *to be* is an exception in that it normally requires the adverb to follow rather than precede it, even when it is the main verb; see example [69]. More than one such adverb can appear in the same verb phrase.

> **REMINDER!**
>
> **The operator (see Chapter 6) is the first auxiliary. It is the one that shows tense (present or past) for the whole verb phrase.**

The diagram of [71] (a sentence with an adverbial within the verb phrase) looks as follows:

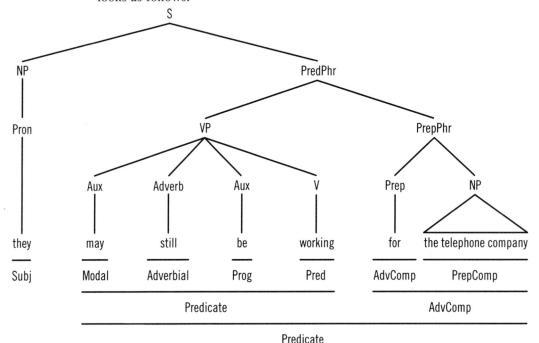

Diagram 7J.   Diagramming adverbials within VPs.

7.6 A Survey of Basic Sentence Patterns

The two kinds of sentences with an adverbial complement that we have encountered in this chapter constitute the sixth and seventh sentence patterns, which can be summed up as S-V-AC and S-V-DO-AC, depending on whether the verb is transitive or intransitive. (Here AC stands for "Adverbial Complement.") We now have

(1) S-V

(2) S-V-SC

(3) S-V-DO

(4) S-V-IO-DO

(5) S-V-DO-OC

(6) S-V-AC

(7) S-V-DO-AC

This completes our inventory of basic sentence patterns. Every English sentence that is a declarative statement can be fitted into one of these types. It is therefore well worth the investment of time and memory to study these patterns carefully and to make sure you can supply examples of them.

EXERCISES

Exercise 7.1

Draw form-function diagrams of the following noun phrases. Assume that the NP is within a sentence and that it is the direct object.

1. the woman with the small dog

2. the danger to the public from the fumes

3. the color of the cover of the book on the table

4. the opposition of the members of the union to the election of a new president

5. the painting of a dragon with large teeth in a gloomy cave on the wall of the living room

6. the capital of the state with the smallest population in the country

7. the capital of the state with its impressive skyscrapers

8. a history of a regiment of cavalry by an amateur scholar from Iowa

Exercise 7.2

Describe, on the basis of the following sentences, the principle for deciding whether to write *on+to*, *up+on*, and *in+to* as unit words or as two separate words. Use the grammatical concepts that have been taught in this book, including diagramming.

1. We sent the letter on to my parents.
2. They poured concrete onto the tiles.
3. Someone turned Lefty in to the FBI.
4. Mario turned Princess Jacinta into a frog.
5. The roof rested upon stately columns.
6. The construction workers were resting up on the patio.

Exercise 7.3

Identify sentences that have adverbial complements and sentences that have postcore phrases.

1. She was lecturing to a hundred students.
2. He exchanged his Volvo for a Ford.
3. Rollo has had nothing to eat since Saturday.
4. Hans directed his question to the pompous officials.
5. Ms. Jackson was a stubborn woman, in my opinion.
6. They played "Rudolf the Red-Nosed Reindeer" to the delighted children.
7. The fiesta lasted until midnight.
8. The group played country and western music until midnight.
9. Al drove a truck for many years.
10. They built a neat little treehouse in their backyard.

Exercise 7.4

(For class discussion) What changes would you want to make in the following sentences, and why?

1. We complimented the twins about their pretty dresses.
2. At page ninety-six John opened the book.
3. Two teenaged boys were watching the younger members of the family over.
4. You will be borrowing always money from them.
5. Someone had filled up it.
6. They sold rich financiers off their estate.
7. We moved the dynamite farther away the fire.

8. With hamburgers and french fries they plied those little brats.

9. We are looking greatly forward to your party next week.

10. The judge confined to the matter of the trust fund.

Exercise 7.5

Sentences to diagram.

1. John lost touch with the friends of his roommate.

2. You should look in on Ms. Bills on your way to the school.

3. I would put his success down to hard work by the Red Team in the design phase of the project.

Exercise 7.6

Choosing from the list of words provided, create two grammatical sentences of each of the seven basic sentence patterns; vary the words as much as possible. The sentence patterns are repeated here for your convenience.

1. S-V

2. S-V-SC

3. S-V-DO

4. S-V-IO-DO

5. S-V-DO-OC

6. S-V-AdvComp

7. S-V-DO-AdvComp

Determiners: the, a, this, that, some
Nouns: prince, dragon, wizard, cave, ring, dungeon
Verbs: carried, escaped, gave, turned, seemed, made, fainted, handed, considered, ran
Adjectives: frightened, fierce, angry, scary, clever
Prepositions: with, into, from

Exercise 7.7

Which of the following sentences contain phrasal verbs?

1. Our new Volkswagen could turn on a dime.

2. Partisans had blown up all the bridges.

3. We touched down at exactly 7:23 a.m.

4. Patti insisted on the champagne.

5. The new provost has already turned in his resignation.

6. A cold wind was blowing up the narrow canyon.

7. A member of the audience was reading off every name on the program in a loud whisper.

8. His recklessness with facts would have made his old professor turn in his grave.

9. None of the adults knew how to turn on the VCR.

10. One of the gang showed up next day with a bouquet of flowers.

Exercise 7.8

Find, in the following sentences, examples of prepositional phrases with an NP; prepositional phrases without an NP; prepositional phrases modifying a noun; prepositional phrases functioning as adverbials; adverbial complements other than phrasal verbs; phrasal verbs; prepositional verbs. (Of course there may be more than one of these in the same sentence.)

1. Over the years Harvey has simply lost touch with all his old college friends.

2. He could not keep up with his correspondence.

3. Dr. Strange was absentmindedly tapping his pipe on the radiator.

4. At the end of the driveway to the house we could just see Blakeslee's station wagon.

5. He trod down hard on the gas pedal at the first corner.

6. Fred looked "hypocrite" up in *Webster's Third*.

7. Despite our fears, Julius pulled through.

8. The schooner was slowly making headway against a fierce northeasterly gale.

9. The other members of the team looked up to Janice.

10. I referred them to Eisenblut's classic study of gerbils.

8

THE NOUN PHRASE I: PRONOUNS, NOUNS, AND DETERMINERS

8.0 Noun Phrases

A noun phrase (NP) is a phrase whose head is a noun or a pronoun. NPs can range in length from a simple pronoun or name to a phrase containing one or more subordinate clauses. In this chapter we deal only with simple NPs. Constructions in which nouns are modified, for example by adjectives, are treated in Chapter 9.

8.1 Pronouns

Pronouns, as the name suggests, are usually seen as substitutes for noun phrases. This is true of what are called personal pronouns and certain others, but the class of pronouns as a whole extends into indefinite forms like *anyone* that are not obviously a replacement for another form. Pronouns are single-word noun phrases that can substitute for longer noun phrases under certain grammatical conditions.

The core of the pronoun system is the set of what are called **personal pronouns**, those that vary according to person.

Person, Gender, and Number

The personal pronouns have first-, second-, and third-person forms. The first and third persons also have a distinction of singular and plural. The third-person singular has a three-way gender distinction of masculine, feminine, and neuter forms. The personal pronouns also show a distinction of **cases**—forms that differ according to the word's function in its sentence; one of these cases, called the **nominative**, is the case of the subject of the sentence.

In the nominative case, used for the subject of the sentence, the forms are as follows:

	SINGULAR	PLURAL
First Person	I	we
Second Person	you	you
Third Person	he, she, it	they

The second person (*you*) has identical forms for the singular and plural in the written standard; but a singular/plural distinction is still needed in order to motivate the choice of a singular or a plural reflexive pronoun in cases like the following (see also the discussion of the reflexive pronoun, below), since speakers of English always understand the *you* in [1] to be addressed to a singular person, and the *you* in [2] to be addressed to more than one person:

[1] You have obviously enjoyed yourself

[2] You have obviously enjoyed yourselves

Agreement

A verb or operator in the present tense should **agree** with the head noun of the NP that is the subject of the sentence.

> **REMINDER!**
>
> The *operator* is the first auxiliary in a series of auxiliaries, or the only auxiliary if there is only one.

If this head noun is singular, the verb/operator is in the *-s* form, and if the head noun is plural, the verb/operator is in the general present:

[3] (a) The leader of the birdwatchers resides in a separate house

   (b) The members of the sect reside in a large farmhouse

[4] (a) The shopkeepers in the downtown area have raised their prices again

   (b) The owner of the two flower shops has raised her prices again

Notice that the heads of the subject NPs are "leader" and "members" in [3], and "shopkeepers" and "owner" in [4]; it is with these nouns that the verbs and operators should agree (although usage may be slowly changing in this respect). The prepositional phrases "of the birdwatchers" (plural) and "of the sect" (singular) in [3] are modifiers of the head nouns, and are irrelevant to the choice of verb form; similarly in [4].

> **REMINDER!**
>
> In the past tense, the verb *to be* also has agreement with a singular (*was*) or a plural (*were*) subject.

Since subject NPs can be quite complex, it is important to identify the head noun in determining whether to use the *-s* form (singular head) or the general present of the verb (plural head). Diagramming the sentence (perhaps mentally) can be a useful technique for determining the head noun.

Uses of Gender-Marked Pronouns

The gender-marked pronouns *he, she,* and *it* normally suggest a three-way distinction among male humans, female humans, and nonhumans.

There is a long tradition, which is now breaking down, of viewing the masculine human pronoun as the default pronoun for general reference to singular humans. When terms like *the owner, the scientist, the writer,* and so on must be referred to with a pronoun, the accepted rule was once quite simple: use *he,* as in

[5] The recipient should sign for the package as soon as he has verified its contents

If it was necessary to justify this usage, it was usually argued that *he* was ambiguous between a specifically male reference and a gender-neutral reference (this being allegedly a fact about the English language), and that when *he* was used of *the owner* or *the writer,* it was the gender-neutral meaning, not the masculine one, that was intended.

It is easy these days to defeat this argument. For example, the *he* tended to switch to *she* if the antecedent—that is, the noun being referred to—was *nurse* or *secretary* rather than *doctor* or *attorney!* Moreover, research has shown that the supposedly neutral *he* still induces in readers a sense that the referent is male, and indeed that most significant members of the society are male.

Some authors alternate *he* and *she,* sometimes—bewilderingly—in the same sentence. Others alternate in different sections (chapters, for instance) of the work. Some stubbornly use *he* only, still others, equally stubbornly, only *she.* The use of the expression *he or she* is a solution often found in official documents. It is not only stylistically awkward, but raises the same problem of precedence (why not *she or he?*).

Of the few alternatives available, perhaps the least jarring is to swallow our prejudice about *they* being a plural pronoun and think of *they* as the third-person gender- and number-neutral pronoun. *They* would then be exactly analogous to *you* in making no reference to either gender or number. If this occasionally means that we will be using *they* to refer to a singular entity, this will be a small price to pay for equity in gender. In time it would no more be considered inappropriate than the present-day use of *you* (which was once a plural pronoun) to refer to a single addressee. Consider

> [6] If the attending physician decides that follow-up care is needed, they will refer the patient to a specialist

This solution is in fact commonly used in the spoken language, and has even made its way into the style sheets of a few journals.

The Objective Case

The personal pronouns have different forms for three grammatical cases. The forms that have already been given are called **nominative** case forms. They are the ones used when the pronoun is the subject of the verb. But some pronouns, including the personal pronouns, have forms for the **objective** case (the case of the nonsubject pronoun) and the **possessive** case (the case of possession).

The forms of the objective case in personal pronouns are as follows:

	SINGULAR	PLURAL
First Person	me	us
Second Person	you	you
Third Person	him, her, it	them

The objective case is used whenever the pronoun has some function other than the subject or the possessive. This includes:

- object of the verb, whether direct or indirect:

  [7] The FBI arrested *her* on a conspiracy charge

  [8] Georgina cooked *us* one of her meat pies

- complement of preposition:

  [9] The elephants looked at *him* curiously

Pronouns serving as subject complements are usually also in the objective case. The automatic translation of Latin rules into English has resulted in some uncertainty, since Latin requires the nominative (*ego sum* = "It is I"), and this rule is sometimes stated for English also. In certain set phrases where grammatical correctness is scarcely an issue at all for the written language, usage is fairly uniform:

[10] (a) (In answer to a telephone call) "This is she"

(b) (In answer to "Who's there?") "It's me" "It's him (her, us . . .)"

In written English, pronouns rarely appear as subject complements, probably because people are uncertain about the rules for choosing the right case. When they do appear as subject complements, they are often followed by *who*. In this context, the nominative is needed:

[11] It was he who first glimpsed the waters of the Pacific Ocean

Otherwise, the objective case is standard:

[12] The only person to hear the news was me

I in this context would sound stilted and old-fashioned. There is still some resistance to using *me*, however, and some writers prefer to use the *-self* pronouns here (*myself*), which avoids the problem but at the cost of using a more emphatic form than is needed. Probably the most usual alternative is to avoid the dilemma altogether by finding a different way to write the sentence, such as:

[12]′ I was the only person to hear the news

The case—nominative or objective—of a pronoun that is joined by *and* to a noun or another pronoun is always the same as if the pronoun were alone. There are two contexts to watch out for. One is when the joined pronoun is the subject:

[13] (a) Ronald Martinez and I are going to the Legion Ball

　　 (b) *Ronald Martinez and me are going to the Legion Ball

Here, of course, "me am going . . . " is impossible. But writers must be careful not to overcorrect and extend the "and I" to the objective case:

[14] (a) Colonel Canter has invited Ronald Martinez and me to the Legion Ball

　　 (b) *Colonel Canter has invited Ronald Martinez and I to the Legion Ball

The [14b] sentence here results from leaning over backwards to avoid the mistake of [13b]. Some version of this error is surprisingly common in speaking, and it occurs often enough in writing to suggest that sentences like [14b] are gaining in acceptance.

Possessive Pronouns

The personal pronouns have a third case form, the possessive, used to indicate possession:

	SINGULAR	**PLURAL**
First Person	my	our
Second Person	your	your
Third Person	his, her, its	their

Notice that the neuter form is always spelled without an apostrophe. (*It's* is used only as a contracted form of *it is*.) In function, these forms can be regarded either as modifiers of the noun or as determiners, since they replace the class of determiners that includes *a, the, this, that,* and others. The analysis chosen in this book is the determiner one, and these possessive pronouns will be called **possessive determiners**. NPs like *my new car* are therefore diagrammed:

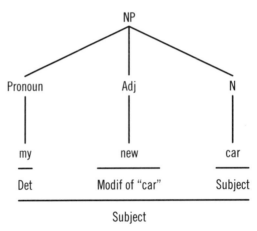

Diagram 8A.   Diagramming possessive determiners.

In addition to the set of possessive determiners, there is a similar-looking set of pronouns that function as the heads of NPs in their own right. We will refer to these as **independent possessive pronouns**. The forms are as follows:

	SINGULAR	PLURAL
First Person	mine	ours
Second Person	yours	yours
Third Person	his, hers	theirs

They are found in such sentences as

[15] *Mine* is the one with the funny round thing on the lid

[16] Someone has stolen *hers* from her locker

[17] The waiter took *yours* away, I'm afraid

Strangely, the third-person singular of this set lacks a neuter, the expected *its* not being used in the standard written language:

[18] We inspected the abandoned car. ?The hubcap we had found earlier was obviously its.

Notice that the -*s*, in the forms that have it, is not spelled with an apostrophe. Illogical as it is, the personal pronouns differ in this respect from full nouns.

Unlike the possessive determiners, the independent possessive pronouns can have any of the major sentence functions that are available to an NP, such as subject, object, and so on. Examples:

[19] I haven't had my lunch yet, but the dog has eaten hers already (direct object)

[20] The next boat along is ours (subject complement)

8.2 Special Pronouns

Special pronouns are those whose function is always linked closely to a noun in the same sentence. These pronouns include the pronouns ending in -*self* or -*selves*, whose forms are as follows:

	SINGULAR	PLURAL
First Person	myself	ourselves
Second Person	yourself	yourselves
Third Person	himself, herself, itself	themselves

Notice that some of the forms are based on the possessive (*my-*, *your-*, *our-*), others on the objective (*him-*, *it-*), while *her-* is ambiguous, being either objective or possessive. The plural forms have the plural of *self*, which is *selves*, including the second person, which thus distinguishes between singular and plural here (*yourself*, *yourselves*), though not elsewhere.

The other set of pronouns that belong under the heading of special pronouns are the reciprocals *each other* and *one another*.

Emphatic Pronouns

One function of the special pronouns is to emphasize a noun:

[21] The Chief Justice herself authorized the search

[22] The Chief Justice authorized the search herself

Notice the different word order possibilities in [21] and [22]. In [22], the emphatic pronoun has floated to the other side of the direct object "the search."

The forms *own* and *very own* are the possessive case of the -*self* forms. Instead of **himself's*, for example, we have *his own* or *his very own*:

[23] The undertaker's assistant wiped off the lipstick with his own handkerchief

[24] Professor Koldhardt gave his very own daughter a C–

[25] I myself saw it with my very own eyes

Reflexive Pronouns

The special pronouns are also used as object pronouns whenever the object has the same identity as the subject:

[26] I reimbursed myself out of the company's pension fund

[27] You may treat yourselves to some more ice cream

When they occur in this context—that is, when the object has the same reference as the subject—the special pronouns are called **reflexive pronouns**, or **reflexives**. Reflexives may also occur after prepositions:

[28] Amanda was angry at herself

In some cases of this sort, the personal pronoun is also a possibility, and it is not entirely clear whether "herself" should be viewed as a reflexive or an emphatic:

[29] (a) He closed the door behind himself

     (b) He closed the door behind him

[30] (a) Jill showed us a picture of herself when she was eight years old

     (b) Jill showed us a picture of her when she was eight years old

A perceptible difference of meaning between the personal pronoun in the objective case and the reflexive is involved in such cases as [28], "Amanda was angry at herself," versus "Amanda was angry at her." Here the two sentences make reference to two different people, one the same as the subject, the other someone else. However, since "him" in [29b] and "her" in [30b] do not preclude reference to the subjects "he" and "Jill" respectively, the meaning difference between the (a) and (b) sentences in [29] and [30] is rather obscure.

Reciprocal Pronouns

The **reciprocal** relationship, in which the subject and the object are interacting, is expressed by using *one another* or *each other* in place of the *-self* pronouns:

[31] Lefty and his attorney congratulated one another

[32] Lefty and his attorney congratulated each other

There seems to be no difference in meaning between *each other* and *one another*.

8.3 Demonstrative Pronouns

The demonstratives *this/these, that/those* can be used as pronouns as well as determiners:

[33] These are my cousins from Macedonia

[34] Chiang Kai-Shek himself gave me that

Especially frequent is a discourse in which *this* and *that* refer to things that have just been written or said:

[35] The firm had sold supercomputer technology to countries on the proscribed list. *This* was in conflict with recently passed laws.

The previous words to which the demonstrative refers are known as the **antecedent** to the pronoun. In example [35] the antecedent of *this* is fairly clear; but writers should be careful to avoid the "sloppy" antecedent in which the referent of *this* is ambiguous:

[36] The mayor spoke out in support of the stadium initiative, significant new sources of funding became available, and eventually the voters approved the measure by a wide margin. There were many reasons for *this*.

In general, the more specific the antecedent of *this*, the better. In [36], there is more than one competing antecedent, including the entire first sentence.

8.4 The Impersonal Pronoun *one*

The pronoun *one* has two forms, *one*, which is both the nominative and the objective form, and *one's*, which is possessive. (This time, the apostrophe is required!) It also has a reflexive form, *oneself*. The pronoun *one* is third-person singular. The possessive pronoun based on *one* is *one's own*—unlike the other pronouns, the possessive form of *one* (that is, *one's*) is used only as a determiner, never alone as a pronoun.

In Standard Written English, as in spoken English at all registers, there is a strong tendency to be sparing in the use of *one*. It generally sounds old-fashioned and conservative, and overusing it draws too much attention to your style. Its replacement is *you*, as illustrated in the following sentences:

[37] One should have one's car thoroughly overhauled, and one should take care to replenish one's supply of fresh water, before one drives across the Mojave Desert

[38] You should have your car thoroughly overhauled, and you should take care to replenish your supply of fresh water, before you drive across the Mojave Desert

Most present-day writers would feel more comfortable with the version represented by [38], although some style manuals still insist on the use of *one*.

8.5 Nouns

The noun is the most prominent category of all, both in quantity and in usefulness to discourse. It is customary to distinguish among **concrete, abstract,** and **proper** nouns. Concrete nouns can furthermore be either **mass nouns** or **count nouns.**

Kinds of Nouns

Of the many types and subtypes of nouns, we will here deal only with those that have a noticeable effect on grammar.

Proper nouns. Proper nouns are what are usually called names. They are distinct from other kinds of nouns in that they are used to refer to a specific individual rather than to a member of a class and do not ordinarily take determiners (there are one or two exceptions). Proper nouns may be accompanied by titles. Examples:

[39] John; Jane Doe; Charlene; the Adirondacks; the Ohio River; Senator Specter; Mrs. Smith; Pennsylvania; Andrew Carnegie; Schenley Park; Carnegie Mellon University; Fido; The Strand; Tigger; Dobbin; Argentina; Ulan Bator; Lord Vader; the Grand Tetons

Typical bearers of proper names include humans, domestic animals, countries, and cities. The general rule that names do not have determiners can be overridden in the case of geographical names, or if there is competition for reference or some reason to emphasize identification:

[40] The Abe Lincoln that lives in the apartment above us is a medical supplies salesman

[41] My Marvin would never say such a thing

[42] Who is this "Reverend Jimmy Joe Whitelock" that keeps sending us mail?

The mass/count distinction. The mass/count distinction separates nouns that refer to countable objects from those that refer to masses of material. Here are some examples of count [43] and mass [44] nouns:

[43] dream; letter; inauguration; arm

[44] water; sugar; soccer; applesauce; steel

The features that distinguish count from mass nouns are the following:

- Count nouns can take the indefinite article *a* or *an*. Count nouns have both a singular and a plural (except for a few that are idiosyncratically plural, such as *trousers*, *scissors*, and a few others).
- Mass nouns are only singular. They can take the definite article *the* or the indefinite quantifier *some*.

The word *some* can be used with singular mass nouns or plural count nouns: *some popcorn* (mass), *some students* (count). When *some* is used with singular count nouns, it takes on a special meaning of "some or other," as in these examples:

[45] Some student phoned while you were out

[46] Some student or other phoned while you were out

[47] Some students are waiting to see you (indefinite quantifier with plural count noun)

[48] There is some popcorn on the kitchen table (indefinite quantifier with mass noun)

You may be able to hear a slight difference in how the word "some" is said between sentences like [45] and [46] on the one hand and sentences like [47] and [48] on the other. In [45] and [46] "some" (= "some or other") is stressed a little more. *Some* can also be used to express surprise (exclamatory use), as in:

[49] That Raphael Gork is some student!

> ### By the Way:
> **You may remember that Wilbur the Pig, in E. B. White's *Charlotte's Web*, was "Some Pig!"**

A number of nouns can be used as count or as mass nouns, and again the test using *some* or the indefinite article *a/an* will tell us which is meant:

[50] After they had renovated the house, some carpet was left over ("Carpet" is a mass noun)

[51] We bought a carpet for the living room ("Carpet" is a count noun)

Finally, note that it is often possible to treat a mass noun as a brand or variety or as a serving or portion, and thus convert it into a count noun:

[52] The tobaccos of the Balkan Peninsula have a strong, rich aroma

[53] We ordered three coffees to go

Concrete nouns. The entire category of nouns is divided not only into the two groups mass and count, but also into the groups abstract and concrete. Concrete nouns refer to things that are tangible or perceptible, such as:

> wolf, machine, fork, sugar, ditchdigger, bishop, shoestring, dollar

In the singular, concrete nouns readily take the article *the*.

Abstract nouns, on the other hand, refer to ideas such as qualities and activities rather than to tangible things. They overlap to some extent with mass nouns. Many abstract nouns, for example, cannot be plural: *beauty, baseball, generosity, appreciation.* Others, however, can be plural: *injustices, events, confessions.* Singular abstract nouns also resemble mass nouns in being used quite often without an article:

[54] Honesty is the best policy

[55] Beauty is in the eye of the beholder

[56] Basketball is fun to watch

Moreover, like mass nouns, they do not readily take an indefinite article, but they may occur with *some:*

[57] You could have shown some appreciation for his kindness

[58] Joyce and David played some chess, but they soon got bored

---

By the Way:

We think of the nouns *cherry* and *pea* as count nouns with the plurals *cherries* and *peas*. But in earlier times these were mass nouns, *cherys* (French *cérise*) and *pease* (French *pois*). They were generally eaten mashed up in porridge like the *pease porridge hot* of the nursery rhyme. Later the *-s* came to be understood as the plural ending, and a "wrong" singular was constructed without the *-s*: cherry, pea.

Possessive Forms

The possessive form of a noun has a **morphological** form, making use of the suffix *-s* spelled with an apostrophe ("John's hat"), and a **periphrastic** form, using the preposition *of* ("the height of the building").

In the morphological form, the apostrophe precedes *s* if the possessive noun is singular. If the noun is plural and forms its plural in *-s*, the apostrophe follows the plural *s*. The following examples illustrate singular and plural forms of the possessive:

the surveyor's chart, the surveyors' chart

the deliveryman's van, the deliverymen's van

the child's story, the children's story

The apostrophe is the bane of the English spelling system. We would be better off without it. It is almost never a necessity. It has, of course, no spoken counterpart, and speakers of English invariably turn to the *of* (periphrastic) possessive if there is a real ambiguity:

the judges'/judge's decision:

- the decision of the judges, or
- the decision of the judge

As a suffix, the possessive *'s* has the peculiarity that it is attached to the end of the entire noun phrase, rather than just the head noun. Thus instead of:

*the mountaineer's holding the rope glove

it is necessary to say or write

the mountaineer holding the rope's glove

More commonly, however, writers will avoid this construction, which to some seems a little too colloquial (lower register) for formal writing. Again, the periphrastic "of" construction offers another option:

the glove of the mountaineer holding the rope

The choice between using the periphrastic *of* and the morphological possessive form (with *'s)* is often a stylistic one. But the morphological form has a preference for human and animate nouns, especially proper nouns. Thus

(a)   ? this theory's advantages

the advantages of this theory

(b)   Rory MacGregor's factory

? the factory of Rory MacGregor

(the question mark indicates a less-preferred option). When a name ends in *-s,* which is quite frequent, written usage varies a bit, and you should consult a trusted (or mandated!) style manual:

Charles Dickens' novels

Charles Dickens's novels

Roy Harris' symphony

Roy Harris's symphony

Whether or not spelled with an extra *s,* these possessive forms are pronounced as if the extra *s* were there: [Charles Dickenses novels], [Roy Harrises symphony].

Confusion between possessive and plural is common when households are referred to by the family name. The Henderson family can be referred to in the plural as *the Hendersons* in such contexts as

[59] The Hendersons have invited us over to dinner

The apostrophe is required in

[60] We are going to dinner at the Hendersons'

which is elliptical for *at the Hendersons' house,* "Hendersons'" being, of course, possessive plural and therefore having the apostrophe *after* the *s*—singular *the Henderson's* would be wrong. As a house sign, *The Hendersons'* is also correct, since this too is understood as elliptical for *The Hendersons' house.*

Gender

Gender divisions in nouns are less prominent these days, as older automatic occupation assignments like *doctor/nurse, manager/secretary,* and so on disappear. Explicit marking of gender, such as the suffixes *-ess* and *-man,* is usually avoided. For example, *chairman* is changed to *chair,* and *poetess, actress, waitress* are replaced by the gender-neutral terms *poet, actor, waiter,* though one occasionally hears *waitperson* for *waitress. Hero* may have too many male associations to be a gender-neutral replacement of *heroine.*

Plurals

The default plural sign is *-s:*

> dreams; letters; inaugurations; arms

A few words have special plurals:

> child: children
>
> woman: women
>
> man: men

Words for common animals also often have special plurals. This is true of certain farm and other domestic animals, for example:

> cow/bull: cattle
>
> sheep: sheep
>
> goose: geese
>
> mouse: mice

Some game animals (animals that are hunted) also have no distinct plural forms:

> deer: deer
>
> fish: fish
>
> elk: elk
>
> moose: moose

Latin and Greek Plurals

Words that come from Latin and Greek may form their plurals according to the rules of Latin and Greek. Since in these languages there was not one but several systems of plural marking in nouns, there is some variety in English loan words. There is a strong tendency to simplify these systems and even to replace them with the English *-s* plural. This tendency is stronger in less technical writing; for example, *index* has the plural *indexes* in everyday writing, but *indices* in certain specialized fields. The following examples are representative of the more conservative system that retains the Latin and Greek plurals.

- Words whose singular form ends in -*us* usually make their plurals in -*i:*

  fungus: fungi

  nucleus: nuclei

  focus: foci

  hippopotamus: hippopotami (also hippopotamuses)

  alumnus: alumni

- Several words of Latin origin ending in -*a*, such as *formula,* have a plural in -*ae (formulae).* Since this was a feminine suffix in Latin, a few words have both male and female forms:

  alumna: alumnae (compare alumnus: alumni)

  emerita: emeritae (compare emeritus: emeriti)

- Words with a singular in -*um* (Latin) or -*on* (Greek) form their plural in -*a*:

  desideratum: desiderata

  erratum: errata

  criterion: criteria

  phenomenon: phenomena

  corrigendum: corrigenda

Often, writers identify the -*a* plural of this type with the singular of the -*a* type (*alumna*), and hence make *phenomena* and *criteria* into singular nouns:

  this criteria, this phenomena . . . is

Although this usage is gaining ground, it leaves us without a well-established plural of the new singulars *criteria* and *phenomena.* At the present time it seems best to keep to the more standard usage:

  these criteria, these phenomena . . . are

  this criterion, this phenomenon . . . is

But with a few words the new singular has won out. *Agenda* is now always singular; *data* is still variable (*the data is/the data are*). The plural form *media* (singular *medium*) is also now sometimes interpreted as a singular (*this media*).

Words that form their singular in -*is* have a plural in -*es*. The -*is* singular sounds like "hiss" without the [h], and the plural suffix sounds like "ease":

  crisis: crises

  analysis: analyses

  basis: bases

In the last form, "bases" is spelled the same way as the regular plural of *base*, though the pronunciations are different.

8.6 Determiners

We have already encountered determiners in the form of articles such as *a* and *the*, demonstratives such as *this* and *that*, and possessive pronouns such as *his* and *my*. Determiners form part of an expression that is potentially quite complex and can be analyzed as a determiner phrase. The determiner phrase comes at the start of the noun phrase, before the head noun and any modifiers that may precede the head noun.

The determiner is a ragbag of different forms, which break down into several categories each with a small number of members. The term "determiner" is actually a *function* name rather than a formal category; it is the only one of the parts of speech whose name refers to a function rather than a lexical class.[1] It follows from this that there will be no above-the-line label that is simply Determiner, as there is for preposition, adjective, and so on. There is, however, a determiner phrase.

Types of Determiners

The determiner phrase may include different kinds of determiners, which are named, according to their position, central determiners, pre-determiners, and post-determiners.

(1) **Central Determiners.** These are the definite and indefinite articles, the demonstratives, and the possessives. Because the central determiner is the head of the determiner phrase, it will be designated simply *determiner* in the function part of a form-function diagram.

The indefinite and definite articles go with both count and mass nouns, with two gaps: indefinite mass nouns and indefinite plural nouns are not preceded by an article. Consider the following table:

	DEFINITE	INDEFINITE
Count, Singular	the paintbrush	a paintbrush
Count, Plural	the paintbrushes	paintbrushes
Mass	the rice	rice

The absence of the article in two of the right-hand column items is a fact of English, but from the point of view of the analyst it is an inconvenient fact.

---

[1] The reason for this inconsistency is that the members of the determiner class are actually several distinct categories, including articles and pronouns. Combining them into the single functional class of determiner is a decision of convenience rather than of linguistic justification.

There are times when it is useful to assume the existence of an article in this position. We can meet this requirement by positing an empty item (**zero indefinite article**), to be represented with the symbol Ø when needed, that occupies the position of the missing article before indefinite mass and plural count nouns. The above table is thus redrawn as follows:

	DEFINITE	**INDEFINITE**
Count, Singular	the paintbrush	a paintbrush
Count, Plural	the paintbrushes	Ø paintbrushes
Mass	the rice	Ø rice

The zero indefinite article will be useful when the determiner phrase is analyzed in more detail.

(2) **Pre-determiners.** These are the **quantifiers**, words that denote a quantity, such as *all, none, few, many, some* and *both*. **Multipliers** like *twice, double, three times* and **fractions** such as *half* and *one-third* also belong here. For convenience we can include quantifiers, multipliers, and fractions all under the general category of quantifier, so the above-the-line name for all of these will be "Quantifier." The below-the-line function name for these elements will be "Pre-determiner" because they are capable of preceding the central determiners like *the*—for instance, *none of the ballbearings, many of his sheep, three times our annual GNP.*

As in these examples, it is characteristic of some pre-determiners that they are linked to the central determiner by the preposition *of,* as in *none of my three children were at the wedding.* The preposition *of* is here not the head of a prepositional phrase, as it normally is, but rather it functions as a **link** between the pre-determiner and the central determiner; if this point is not clear, see the diagram at the end of the chapter.

Quantifiers notoriously cause problems in verb agreement. *Each of* and *none of* are examples of quantifiers that display variation between agreement as singulars and as plurals:

[61] (a) Each of my three children *was* in a different row

(b) None of my three children *was* at the wedding

[62] (a) Each of my three children *were* in a different row

(b) None of my three children *were* at the wedding

Conservative usage is represented by [61a] and [61b], but increasingly the plurals [62a] and [62b] are used.

It should be pointed out that the choice of singular or plural here reflects a choice between two quite different analyses. The plurals in [62] are compatible with analyzing "each of" and "none of" as pre-determiners, with "children" as the head noun. The singular verbs in [61], on the other hand, are compatible with the analysis of "each" and "none" as singular head nouns modified by the prepositional phrase "of my three children."

With names of groups, too, there is some variation between singular and plural interpretation:

[63] A flock of geese *was/were* flying overhead

[64] A gang of children *was/were* playing in the street

The factors that determine the form of the verb here are rather complex. One is a difference between British and American usage, British English being perhaps more inclined to use the plural *were*. Another is how *conventional* the combination has become; for example, *a lot of* is never interpreted as singular:

[65] (a) A lot of sports enthusiasts *are* subscribing to our channel

     (b) *A lot of sports enthusiasts *is* subscribing to our channel

Another factor is a conceptualization of the head noun as a single entity or as a more diffuse set of individuals:

[66] (a) In the painting, a bunch of red grapes *lies* on a green-and-yellow cloth

     (b) A bunch of teenagers *were* playing basketball in the backyard

(3) **Post-determiners.** These are numbers, including the **cardinal** numbers like *one, two, three*, and the **ordinal** numbers such as *first, second, third*. The words *few* and *many* can also be used as post-determiners:

[67] Several of these *eleven* candidates have failed to qualify

[68] All of my *first* attempts were unsuccessful

[69] These *few* pitiful sheets will have to tell our story

The Determiner Phrase

A noun phrase, then, can consist of a determiner and a noun. There may in addition be adjectives preceding the noun (which will be dealt with in Chapter 9) and a modifying prepositional phrase following the noun. The determiner in its fullest form may have a pre-determiner, possibly joined to the central determiner by a link, and a post-determiner. The central determiner is the head of the determiner phrase:

[70] All *these* three boxes are to go upstairs

[71] Both *my* two daughters were willing to attend

If the central determiner is Ø (because the head noun is a mass noun or a plural count noun), there may still be a pre-determiner and a post-determiner. In the next examples, the zero central determiner is written with the symbol Ø in order to make the structure clear:

[72] All Ø three boxes are to go upstairs

[73] Both Ø daughters were willing to attend

In [72] there is a pre-determiner "all," a central determiner Ø, and a post-determiner "three."

It is important to distinguish the determiner phrase from adjective modifiers that may precede the head noun of the entire noun phrase. In

[74] None of these three incompetent judges remained in office

notice that the words "none of these three" constitute the determiner phrase (with pre-, central, and post-determiners) and "incompetent" is an adjective that is not part of the determiner phrase. Example [74] is diagrammed as follows:

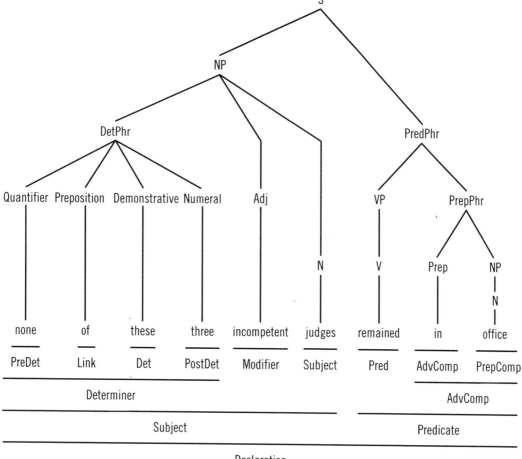

Diagram 8B.   Diagramming determiners.

EXERCISES

Exercise 8.1

Change the following sentences by converting the italicized forms into pronouns with the person indicated.

1. *I* have always imagined *myself* to be easygoing. (third-person singular feminine)
2. The assistant principal took *hers* away from *her*. (first-person singular)
3. The only person in the room at that time was *you*. (third-person singular masculine)
4. *I myself* made this soup from *my own* recipe. (second-person singular)
5. The judges will grant *you* an extension. (third-person singular feminine)
6. *You yourself* stated this in *your own* report. (first-person plural)
7. *She* surprised *herself* with *her own* boldness. (first-person singular)
8. *You* could go off on *your* vacation by *yourself*. (indefinite pronoun "one")
9. The scientist must consider the data *the scientist* has gathered before *the scientist* commits *the scientist* to an explicit hypothesis. (third person)
10. A poet must plunge *a poet* deeply into personal experience before *a poet* can make that experience part of *a poet*. (third person)

Exercise 8.2

Substitute a single pronoun for the italicized word or phrase. If there is more than one possibility, so state; assume, however, that identical names refer to the same person.

1. Lefty and Marvin slapped *Marvin and Lefty* on the back.
2. Jenny Roth indulged *Jenny Roth* in some more peanut brittle.
3. Mitch Funai had already eaten *Mitch Funai's*.
4. Skippy invited *Skippy's* Mom and Dad into *Skippy's* treehouse.
5. *A person* must always pay careful attention to *a person's* grammar when writing *a person's* résumé.
6. Nancy had lost *Nancy's* on the subway.
7. Mike and Susan, *Mike and Susan* must behave *Mike and Susan* while I am away.
8. Bill and Emma sold *Bill and Emma's* car, and Grenville and I sold *mine and Grenville's* too.
9. You and your husband can earn *you and your husband* some extra money.
10. The lieutenant showed Lucy and Verona an old photograph of *me, Verona, and Lucy*.

Exercise 8.3

Analyze the italicized NPs in terms of the determiner phrase that determines the head noun. Specifically: Identify the head of the determiner phrase. Identify any pre- and post-determiners and any links (*of*). Be sure to distinguish between the elements of the determiner phrase and any adjectives that might precede the head noun.

1. Bill was going to collect *his new eyeglasses*.
2. *All of the first thirty eager competitors* received Pittsburgh Marathon T-shirts.
3. They had an expanded retirement package for *all those fifty-nine former employees*.
4. *A lot of those twenty-three million undecided voters* will be interested in a third party.
5. *Some of my many friends* sent me birthday cards.
6. *His entire collection of ancient coins* was put up for sale.
7. This compromise will alienate *all of their few supporters*.
8. The mayor gave a red rose to *each of the proud veterans*.
9. *Several of the attorneys* left on the next train.
10. *None of these twelve upright citizens* will vote for acquittal.

Exercise 8.4

Fill in the blank with the appropriate form (-*s* present or general present) of the verb.

1. The new criteria for defining a controlled substance _call_ for a change in our enforcement policy. (call)
2. A coven of witches _take_ to the air on Halloween. (take)
3. The strange phenomena in the sky _have_ attracted the attention of a bright young astronomer. (have)
4. The agenda _includes_ Mr. Hlubik's promotion. (include)
5. Gymnastics _is_ the only sport at which she excels. (be)
6. The newly invented automata _attaches_ the chips to the exact place on the motherboard. (attach)
7. The wealthy alumna _has_ donated money for the equipment. (have)
8. The corrigenda _are_ to be added to the end of the proofs. (be)
9. A large number of voters _is_ troubled by the rising unemployment rate. (be)
10. Every one of Bill's children _has_ graduated from college. (have)

Exercise 8.5

Identify the underlined nouns as mass or count, and as abstract or concrete.

1. Marsha felt a sharp *pain* in her upper arm as the medic inserted the needle.
2. Someone threw the *basketball* directly at the dean of arts and sciences.
3. The old law resulted in numerous *injustices*.
4. The barbell was made of *steel*.
5. In the courtyard some boys were playing a raucous game of *basketball*.
6. The children got mugs of steaming hot *chocolate*.
7. One of the police used a vulgar *expression*.
8. Mr. Krepke found the head waiter's *arrogance* disturbing.
9. The full *exploration* of the Antarctic took place in the twentieth century.
10. Lefty handed the *money* to the precinct captain.

Exercise 8.6

(For class discussion) What changes would you want to make in the following sentences, and why?

1. We would like you to meet next week with several members of the administration and I. me
2. A number of species on the island has already become extinct.
3. By this criteria, all club members with children would qualify for a dues reduction.
4. That orchard of apple and peach trees as far as the stone wall is all our's.
5. An efficient receptionist will always keep her address file up to date.
6. The Anderson's are putting new siding on their house.
7. A basket of lovely spring flowers were lying on the table.
8. Mr. Hodges was in charge of the childrens' literature section.
9. We were looking forward to the speech of Mr. Breitman.
10. The police line was blocking the people's in the front row view of the stage.

Exercise 8.7

Indicate for each of the sentences which *some* is intended: the one for the indefinite mass or plural noun, or the one for the singular count noun.

1. Some idiot with diplomatic license plates has parked their car in our driveway.
2. Some water had leaked into the gas line.
3. That was some whale we saw out in the channel.

4. Oliver asked for some more of the delicious soup.

5. Some paint was on the car and some on the driveway.

6. Mattie had to go to the hardware store and get some nails.

7. Somehow some arsenic had found its way into the fondue.

8. Jim had gone to Acapulco with some woman he had met in Los Angeles.

9. Some quick-thinking bystanders grabbed the child.

10. That idiot Podgieter has deleted all my messages—some "facilitator" he has turned out to be!

THE NOUN PHRASE II: MODIFIERS OF THE HEAD NOUN

9.0 Elaborations of the Noun Phrase

Within the core noun phrase, along with its determiners, there may be other words that elaborate and amplify the noun in various ways. Nouns can also be elaborated through subject and object complements that are outside the noun phrase.

9.1 Compound Nouns

Nouns can act as modifiers of other nouns, as in *apple pie, laser printer*. A noun that is modified by another noun will be called a **compound noun,** or **compound.** In the extreme case, the two nouns are so close that they are written as a single word:

> motorboat, fingernail, cornfield, schoolhouse, expressway, locksmith, thunder-storm

In such cases, we do not have to be concerned with analyzing the word into its components; these compounds can be treated as single words and diagrammed just like other nouns:

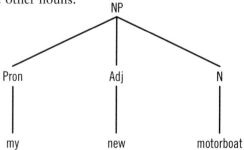

Diagram 9A.   Diagramming compound nouns.

But there are other cases in which a noun modifying another noun is a distinct phrase and is written as a separate word—for example, *brick house, toy soldier, highway robbery.*

By the Way:

The distinction between single word nouns composed of two nouns, like *headway, stepson, bedroom, footnote,* and compounds written as two words, like *office chair, coffee cup, sports jacket,* is not always a sharp one. To the degree that there is uniformity in usage, this comes largely from dictionaries and spellcheckers! The hyphen is used sparingly unless a combination of nouns itself modifies another noun: *right wing,* but *right-wing terrorists.*

Quite often in English several nouns are put together in a single noun phrase, as in *an East Coast radio station.* In longer compounds of this kind, we must be careful to group the various nouns together in a way which shows their relationship to one another; *an East Coast radio station,* for example, is not a Coast radio station which is in the East, nor a station which broadcasts East Coast radio, but a radio station which is on the East Coast, and this must be revealed in the diagram of the noun phrase:

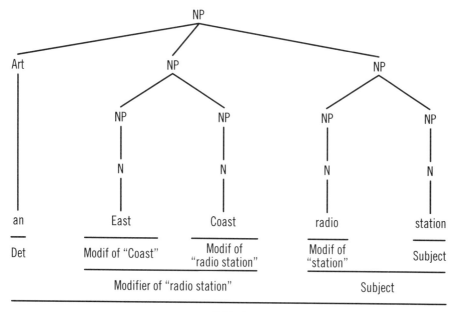

Diagram 9B.   Diagramming NPs with multiple nouns.

When one of the modifying NPs itself contains an adjective, there may be a real ambiguity about the scope of the adjective—does it modify the head noun or one of the modifying nouns? Consider the NP *a large automobile factory,* which could be a large factory making automobiles, or a factory making large automobiles. Compare the two trees 9C and 9D.

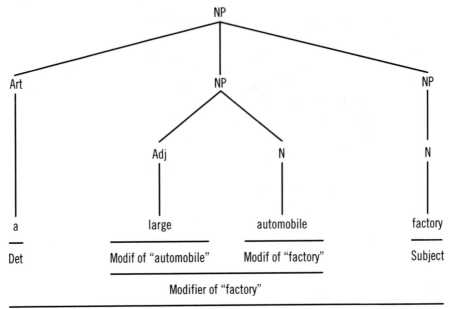

Diagram 9C.   "A factory making large automobiles."

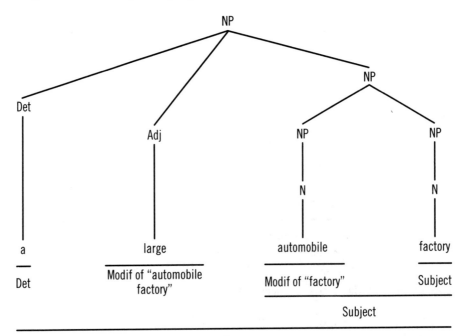

Diagram 9D.   "An automobile factory that is large."

It should again be emphasized that diagramming does not remove ambiguities of this kind, but only shows which analyses both interpretations entail. Yet an ability to analyze sentences sharpens the writer's awareness of potential ambiguities.

9.2 Possessive Nouns

The analysis is exactly the same in cases where the modifying noun has the possessive form—for example, *those large men's shoes, some amazing magicians' tricks*. Diagrams of two interpretations of *those large men's shoes* follow. In Diagram 9E the meaning is "those large shoes for men":

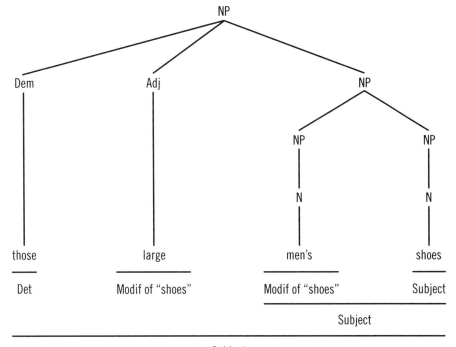

Diagram 9E. *"Those large shoes for men."*

In 9F, on the other hand (following page), the meaning is "(the) shoes of those large men."

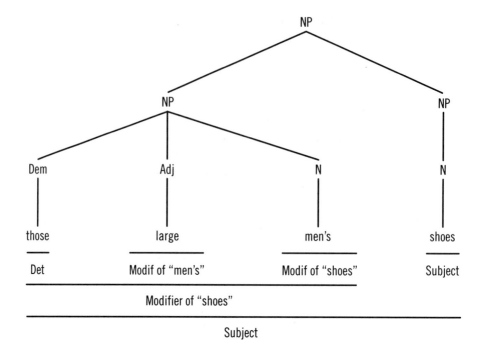

Diagram 9F.   "Shoes of those large men."

Other interpretations of this noun phrase are also possible, but they are not diagrammed here.

9.3 Adjectival Phrases

Let us first refresh our memories about the notion of a *phrase*. A phrase, you may remember, is a set of words that is exhaustively dominated by a single node. A phrase thus defined also has a *function* assigned to it. Furthermore, every phrase has a *head,* the word around which the other words in the phrase, so to speak, revolve as *dependents*.

An adjectival phrase is a set of words having an adjective as its head. The most important kinds of adjectival phrases are known as **predicative** and **attributive** ones.

Attributive Adjectival Phrases

The attributive adjectival phrase is placed before the noun, as in *a tasty stew.* The predicative adjective normally occurs after a linking verb, as in

[1] John's beard had turned white

[2] Mandy's cheeks looked pale

A small number of adjectives can only be used predicatively:

[3] The secretary is ill/*the ill secretary

[4] The patient is now well again/*the well patient

[5] The inhabitants are afraid/*the afraid inhabitants

Well has recently assumed an attributive use in health-care contexts (*the well child, the well body*).

Certain adjectives take on a different sense when they are used attributively. Sometimes this sense is an archaic one: *ill* is used in its original sense of evil in the proverb *It's an ill wind that blows nobody good. Late* when used attributively means *deceased,* and *old* means *aged* when predicative, but can also mean *of long standing* or *experienced* when attributive:

[6] The prime minister is *late* (= tardy)

[7] The *late* prime minister (= deceased)

[8] Mr. Higgins was too *old* to be promoted

[9] She is an *old* hand at office politics

[10] He is an *old* friend of the dean's

Adjectives can be formed from the *participles* (that is, the *-ing* and *-en* forms of the verb):

an ongoing project

a spent bullet

Some of these participles are clearly full adjectives, such as *interesting*, while others are more similar in meaning to verbs, such as *flowing*. Occasionally the spelling reveals a form to be verblike (*passed, burned*) as opposed to an adjective (*past, burnt*), and hidden away in the English vocabulary are some ancient participles that are no longer recognized as such (*unkempt* originally meant uncombed; *wrought* is from the same word as *worked*). Sometimes it is possible to diagnose a form as being more adjectivelike by putting *very* in front; but this test cannot be relied on.

Adjectival Complements

An adjective can have a complement, usually a prepositional phrase:

[11] Marcie is very fond *of her children*

[12] The manager was angry *at the team*

The first of these is diagrammed as follows:

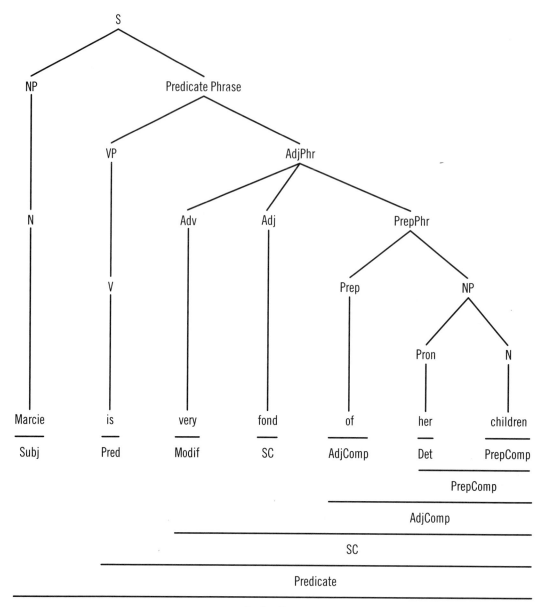

Diagram 9G.   Diagramming adjectival complements.

Adjectival complements can be of many forms, and not all types can be dealt with here. Infinitives are an important type, as in *easy to perform, delightful to watch*.

> **R E M I N D E R !**
>
> The infinitive is the preposition *to* followed by the base form of the verb: *to write, to call.*

The Comparison of Adjectives

Adjectives can be involved in *comparison,* as in

[13] I would prefer a rounder neckline

[14] I would prefer more pronounced cuffs

A compared adjective has one of two forms: in [13], the adjective takes a suffix *-er,* and this kind of comparative is called a **morphological** comparative, because it is formed by changing the shape of a word. In [14], the adjective is preceded by "more"; it is called a **periphrastic** comparative, because it is formed by using more than one word. Short (one- or two-syllabled) adjectives generally take the *-er* suffix, while longer adjectives take the periphrastic form with *more.*

> **R E M I N D E R !**
>
> The terms "periphrastic" and "morphological" were introduced in Chapter 8 when possessives like *the size of the hat* (periphrastic) versus *the mailman's uniform* (morphological) were presented. "Periphrastic" means a construction that is spread out over more than one word (as in *of the hat*). "Morphological" means the construction is formed by a suffix on the word (as in *mailman's*).

A small number of adjectives have special forms of the comparative:

ADJECTIVE	COMPARATIVE
good	better
bad	worse
far	further/farther

The noun phrase following the *than* in the comparative construction is known as the **standard** of the comparison. A controversy exists in English grammar over whether the *than* in the comparative construction is a preposition or a conjunction. The consequences of this decision are as follows:

If *than* is a preposition, then of course it forms a prepositional phrase with the standard NP, and therefore if the NP happens to be a pronoun, it must be in the objective case just like any prepositional complement. The result of this decision would then be that sentences like

[15] My girlfriend is taller than me

are fully grammatical.

On the other hand, if *than* is a conjunction, there is a choice of nominative or objective case depending on the pronoun's function. According to this decision, then, we would have contrasts of the following kind:

[16] (a) My girlfriend is taller than I

(b) The verdict made him angrier than me

Some people would prefer to keep such a distinction between the nominative and objective cases on the grounds that sentences like [16a] are elliptical for "taller than I am (tall)," and so on, with *than* interpreted as a conjunction rather than as a preposition, while sentences like [16b] are elliptical for "than it made me." There is no doubt that in the spoken language the objective case is more frequently heard, but conservative writers will still distinguish the nominative (in sentences like [16a]) and objective cases (in sentences like [16b]) after *than*.

There are also pairs of sentences where there is a difference of meaning:

[17] (a) She makes him angrier than me

(b) ?She makes him angrier than I

However, there is some question as to the correctness of [17b]. Most writers would put *she makes him angrier than I do* in [17b], and the use of an operator is in general to be preferred if the standard (the NP in the *than*-phrase) is logically the subject of an elliptical sentence.

Different from/than/to

There is disagreement about the preposition that follows the adjective *different*. Most handbooks on style recommend *from*:

[18] The languages of the coastal regions are different *from* those of the mountainous interior

However, *different than* is widely used, probably because *different* shares many contexts with a comparative (for example, to say something is bigger than something else also means that it is *different*).

[19] The languages of the coastal regions are different *than* those of the mountainous interior

To complicate matters, the corresponding preposition in British English is *to*, and so you may also encounter £*different to* in some works.

Diagramming Comparatives

Examples of the diagramming of morphological and periphrastic comparatives will now be given. Notice that we have here chosen the prepositional analysis of *than,* and also that the entire *than*-phrase is analyzed as an adjectival complement of the comparative adjective.

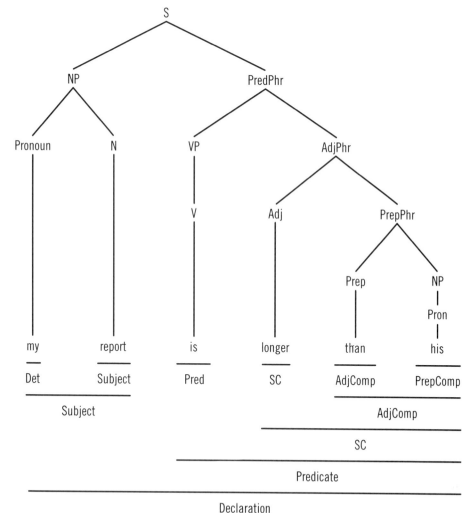

Diagram 9H.   Diagramming morphological comparatives.

In the periphrastic comparative, the *than*-phrase is still analyzed as a prepositional phrase, and the *more* is an adverb modifying the adjective:

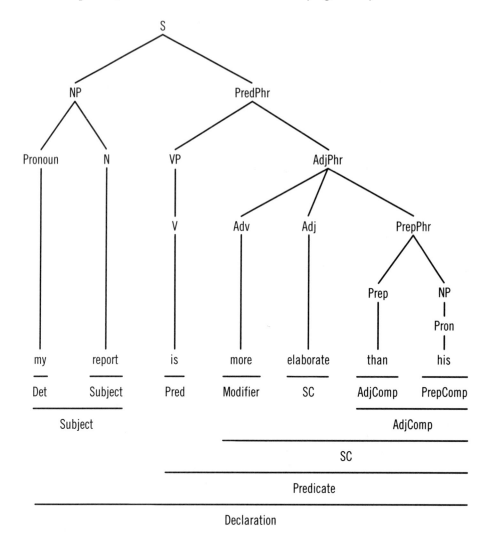

Diagram 9I.   Diagramming periphrastic comparatives.

No attempt will be made here to analyze the more complicated types in which the *than*-phrase is indisputably a conjunction, such as:

[20] This news makes me happier than I can ever tell you

The Superlative Degree of Comparison

The superlative degree of an adjective is the extreme end of the comparison, as in

[21] Jamie is the oldest child in the preschool

[22] Nuclear power is the most dangerous of all the sources of energy

These examples illustrate the morphological [21] and the periphrastic [22] forms of the superlative. Both are preceded by the definite article *the*. The morphological form has the suffix *-(e)st*, and the periphrastic form the adverb *most*. The same adjectives that have irregular comparatives also have irregular superlatives:

ADJECTIVE	COMPARATIVE	SUPERLATIVE
good	better	best
bad	worse	worst
far	further/farther	furthest/farthest

Sentence [22] also illustrates the use of a prepositional phrase with *of* as the complement of the superlative. The diagramming of superlative adjective phrases is exactly parallel to the diagramming of comparatives, as illustrated above. *Most*, in the periphrastic form, is an adverb modifying the adjective, and the *of* phrase is an adjectival complement. As in sentence [21] ("in the preschool"), other prepositions can introduce the adjectival complement in the superlative.

Conjoined Adjectives

More than one adjective can appear in an adjectival phrase: *a long, dull, rather amateurish performance*. These are diagrammed as a simple sequence of adjectives. Each adjective is its own adjective phrase. Notice that it would be inappropriate to analyze the string of adjectives together as a single adjectival phrase, since such a phrase *would not have a single identifiable head*; there would be no logical reason to think of one of the adjectives as the central one and the others as satellites. The form taken by the diagram of a sequence of adjectives is therefore nonhierarchical:

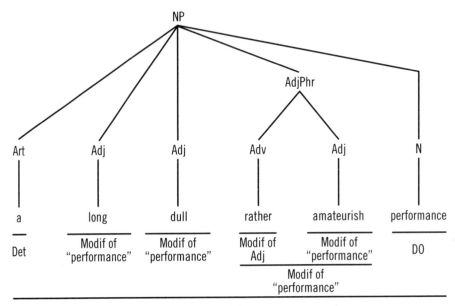

Diagram 9J.   Diagramming phrases with multiple adjectives.

9.4 Prepositional Phrases as Modifiers

The use of prepositional phrases as modifiers of the noun was mentioned in Chapter 7. The normal place for modifying prepositional phrases, as with all extended modifiers, is after the noun.

Sometimes there is a risk of confusion between a modifying prepositional phrase and one that is an adjunct or adverbial complement:

[23] The engineers have been looking for a problem in the hydraulic system

   (Is the hydraulic system the *focus* of their search for the problem, or the *place* where they were located when they conducted the search?)

[24] Mr. Oliphant became ill at a party after the concert

   (Was this a post-concert party, or merely the time at which he became ill?)

[25] Julie went to the post office with a letter for her mother

   (Did she go to the post office for her mother, or was the letter being sent to her mother?)

The writer needs to be aware of this kind of ambiguity and to avoid it where possible. Sentences like *Fred was writing the message to his assistant,* even though ambiguous in a very minor way, should ring a warning bell and possibly even be reformulated. One simple way of avoiding this error (which is both common and serious, since it can significantly change meaning and disrupt communication) is to be very parsimonious with prepositional phrases, especially at the end of a sentence. But mentally diagramming the sentence can help in diagnosing the problem.

9.5 Nominalizations (Infinitives and Gerunds)

A **nominalization** is a sentence or a predicate that has been collapsed into a noun, so that it can be used as a noun phrase in the sentence. We will here discuss infinitives and gerunds that are used to modify noun phrases. A further treatment of infinitives and gerunds is given in Chapter 15, which is devoted to noun clauses.

The Infinitive as Modifier

The infinitive, recall, is the base form of the verb preceded by the preposition *to*. It can modify noun phrases, and when it does so, it is placed after the noun phrase:

[26] Fish is the easiest food *to cook*

[27] Sylvia would be the best person *to play Lady Macbeth*

These two examples point to a remarkable fact about infinitive modifiers: the noun they modify can be either the subject or the object of the infinitive. In [26], we are talking of cooking food, and so *food* is the object of *to cook*. In [27], we are discussing the possibility of Sylvia playing Lady Macbeth, and so *Sylvia* is the subject of *to play*.

Infinitives are especially compatible with superlative adjectives and with other modifiers suggesting uniqueness, such as *the only*. However, an adjective is not necessary, as the following examples show:

[28] Midsummer is the time *to visit* St. Petersburg

[29] They attended a ceremony *to mark* the anniversary of the coup

Infinitive modifiers follow the noun phrase, and also usually follow any modifier after the head noun, such as "of the epidemic" in

[30] The first cases of the epidemic *to be reported* were in Africa

However, a very heavy post-noun modifier can be dislocated past the infinitive:

[31] The first cases to be reported *of an apparent epidemic of a virulent strain of the disease* were in Africa

The Gerund as Modifier

The gerund, which was introduced in Chapter 6, is formed by adding the suffix *-ing* to the base form of the verb. When it modifies a noun, it does so by forming a compound with the gerund as first element:

[32] The green ones in the back are not eating apples

[33] Leslie went to driving school this summer

Since the gerund is formed with the *-ing* suffix and is identical to the progressive, we must be careful to distinguish the gerund, as in *a sleeping pill,* from the progressive used as an adjective, as in *a sleeping baby.* A good rule of thumb is to mentally place "which *or* who is/are" in front of the *-ing* form. If the result has the same sense, the *-ing* form is a progressive and should be analyzed as an adjective; if the result doesn't make sense, or has a different sense, from the original, the *-ing* form should be analyzed as a gerund:

> a sleeping baby = a baby which is sleeping

> a sleeping pill ≠ a pill which is sleeping

Moreover, the adjective can be modified by an adverb, while the gerund (being a noun) cannot:

> a soundly sleeping baby

> *a soundly sleeping pill

In speech, you will hear a distinct difference in the stress pattern between [a sleeping **baby**] and [a **sleeping** pill], [a **driving** school] and [a driving **rain**]. Usually, too, common sense will distinguish which is meant; for example, [32] could, but is unlikely to, be an observation on the behavior of Martians sitting in a car.

By the Way:

Here are two more ways you can tell the difference between the progressive *-ing* form and the gerundal *-ing* form:

(1) Put the *-ing* form after the head noun and add the preposition *for* in front of the *-ing* form. If the noun phrase makes sense, it is a gerund: **a baby for sleeping, a pill for sleeping.*

(2) Put the *-ing* form after the head noun and put the words *in the process of* before the *-ing* form. If the noun phrase makes sense (more or less), it is a progressive: **a pill in the process of sleeping, a baby in the process of sleeping.*

Apposition

The relationship known as **apposition** means that a word or phrase supports the head word, reinforcing it by repeating it by using different words. In English the head word precedes the apposition, for example:

[34] (a) John, my best friend, is visiting us

(b) My best friend, John, is visiting us

In [34a], the head word is "John," and the NP "my best friend" is in apposition to "John." In [34b], it is the reverse: in [34b], "friend" is the head word, and "John" is in apposition to "friend." So in [34a], the subject of the sentence is "John," and in [34b], the subject is "friend." Notice the punctuation: the appositional NP has commas on *both* sides.

EXERCISES

Exercise 9.1

Diagram the following NPs as subjects. Assume the most natural interpretation of the NP. If you nonetheless feel the phrase could with about equal likelihood be understood two ways, diagram it both ways.

1. the complex motor vehicle regulations
2. some quietly reading library users
3. a loud unpleasant metallic screech
4. a very badly frightened babysitter
5. a fairly acceptable examination answer

Exercise 9.2

Identify any adjective phrases that contain adjectival complements.

1. They made the essay subject to strict length limits.
2. Their attempt to open the door was successful on the third try. *no Adcomp*
3. The children were afraid of the strange creature in the closet.
4. Alphonse appeared unwilling to write the letter.
5. They gave a new essay subject to the students. *None*
6. Gregory is good at chess.
7. The spooky story made the children glad for their warm, secure beds.
8. The rest of the class went green with envy over Marsha's score.
9. We quickly became exasperated at the staff's incompetence.
10. They found that Schreiber was quick to anger and slow to forgive.

Exercise 9.3

(For class discussion or group work) Fill out the table by checking adjectives that are

(A) only attributive

(B) only predicative

(C) used either attributively or predicatively but with somewhat different meanings

(D) able to take a complement

(E) used only with a complement

		A	B	C	D	E
(1)	main					
(2)	erroneous					
(3)	utter					
(4)	comfortable					
(5)	fond					
(6)	tantamount					
(7)	latest					
(8)	very					
(9)	glad					
(10)	chief					
(11)	enough					
(12)	ready					
(13)	absolute					
(14)	amazing					
(15)	able					
(16)	suicidal					
(17)	ancient					
(18)	aware					
(19)	red					
(20)	jealous					

Exercise 9.4

Diagram each of the following three sentences (discussed in 9.4 of the text) two ways to reflect the structural ambiguity

1. The engineers have been looking for a problem in the hydraulic system.

2. Mr. Oliphant became ill at a party after the concert.

3. Julie went to the post office with a letter for her mother.

Exercise 9.5

Expand the adjective(s) in these sentences to a comparative, using the NP in parentheses as the standard for the comparison.

1. Ulan Bator is far away. (St. Petersburg)
2. A pound of feathers is heavy. (a pound of nails)
3. The wines of the Asti region are bubbly. (champagne)
4. The Newburg *Gazette* is an old, good, and highly regarded journal. (the Oldville *Dispatch*)
5. A freelance mechanic will often give an honest and straightforward appraisal. (the average employee of a large chain of garages)
6. Dotheboys College is a large, prestigious, and expensive institution. (St. Jasper's)
7. The Nashville Nukes are bad losers. (the Knoxville Niners)
8. Octopus Industries Limited have pursued the merger for a long time and obstinately. (Coordinated Widgets Incorporated)
9. A pasta and salad diet is healthy, low in cholesterol, and nutritious. (some of the faddish new health foods)
10. The bond market has performed badly and given holders little return on their investment. (the mutual funds)

Exercise 9.6

(For class discussion) What changes would you want to make in the following sentences, and why?

1. We were aware for the finance committee's objections.
2. Barbieri's ice cream is more tasty, more costly, and refreshinger than Mozzarelli's.
3. With Hrdlicka's theory, several scientists have independently noted a serious problem.
4. The first to cross the finish line runner was June Novak.
5. With his bonus he bought a quietly and efficiently washing machine.
6. David did real well in his examinations.
7. Attorneys and financial planners will work together for their client to make the largest possible profit.
8. We wanted a conference that would be different in significant ways than that of the previous year.
9. We examined most of the files on the top shelf in my office.
10. Because of his tact and good manners, Peter would be the best person to telephone.

10

NEGATION

10.0 Negative Sentences

Declarative statements can be **affirmative** or **negative.** A negative sentence can be formed from an affirmative one by adding *not* or some other negative word in the verb phrase, as in [1], or by placing a negative word in one of the NPs, as in [2] and [3]:

[1] They *will not hold* a meeting tonight

[2] *None of the players* left the field

[3] The Goodshoes permitted *no alcoholic drinks* to be served at the party

10.1 Negation in the Verb Phrase

The usual way of negating a sentence in English is through an adverb in the verb phrase, typically *not.* The adverbs that accomplish negation in this way are called **negators.**

Not

The usual place for the negator is the same as for other adverbs within the VP, namely after the first auxiliary (the operator). Thus the negative of the affirmative sentence "That motorist will see the sign" is

[4] That motorist will not see the sign

It is diagrammed as follows:

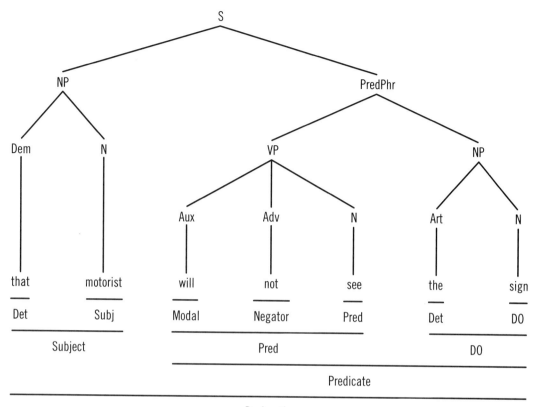

Diagram 10A. Diagramming negators.

If there is no operator in the affirmative sentence, the "dummy" operator *do* is inserted when making the negative. *Do* in this context is referred to as a dummy because it carries no meaning, but serves as a purely structural carrier of tense.

> **REMINDER!**
>
> The verb *to do*, which is used as the dummy operator, has the following tensed forms:
>
> | general present | *do* |
> | -s present | *does* |
> | past | *did* |
>
> Since the operator's job is to indicate tense, only a tensed form of *to do* can be used as a dummy operator.

Thus, the negation of the past-tense sentence "That motorist saw the sign" is "That motorist did not see the sign," diagrammed as follows:

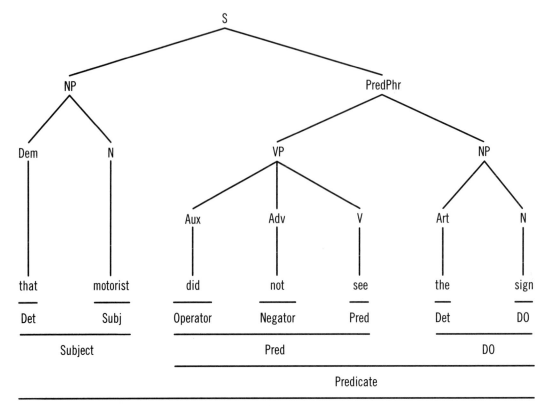

Diagram 10B.   Diagramming dummy operators.

Notice that "saw" in the affirmative sentence has become "did not see" in the negative. The tense of "saw" is past, and so in the negation the tense of the dummy operator "do" must also be past ("did"). Like the modals, the dummy operator "do" is always followed by the base form of the verb, in this case *see.* If there is already an operator in the affirmative, there will be no *do,* and the auxiliary will have its own function in the diagram, such as "Perfect," "Modal," or "Progressive," as in the first diagram above.

The combination *can not* is preferably written as a single word, *cannot,* although both ways are acceptable.

In less formal registers, *not* can be replaced by the contracted form *n't.* There is some tendency for the shorter (contracted) form to move into the written registers also, especially if a chatty style is the goal, but in formal writing this trend should not be followed. A few combinations of modal plus *n't* must be specially learned, for example *won't, can't.* The verb *to be* is regular except for the first-person singular *I am,* whose original contracted form *I ain't* has become taboo.

Have and *Be* as Main Verbs

As auxiliaries, *to have* and *to be* behave as predicted when negated:

[5] The art cinema has not made a profit for many years

[6] We are not enjoying this hot, humid weather

As a main verb, *to be* has the peculiarity that it forms its negative without *do*:

[7] The engineers are not sure of the bridge's safety

To have allows *to do* in the negative in U.S. English, but in British English may appear without the dummy auxiliary:

[8] (a) $We don't have enough fuel to reach the border

    (b) £We haven't enough fuel to reach the border

Other Negators in the Verb Phrase

Although *not* is the only negator that requires an operator, other adverbs that negate the sentence can appear in the VP. These are *never, barely, hardly, scarcely, rarely,* and *seldom*. All can be reinforced with *ever*. Because these adverbs are already negative, they cannot occur with *not* in the written registers:

[9] Jill can scarcely qualify for any of these jobs

[10] Dudley hardly ever exercises

[11] Dr. Teidtfist seldom sends his mother any money

[12] *Dudley doesn't hardly ever exercise

Notice that when there is no operator, these adverbs do not employ the dummy operator *do*.

10.2 Negation Elsewhere in the Sentence

A number of words that occur elsewhere than in the VP are also intrinsically negative and cause the sentence to become negative.

Negative Words

Negation through one of the NPs in the sentence can be accomplished with the pronouns *no one, nobody, nothing,* and the determiners *few, no, neither*. In all higher registers, the presence of one of these words in the sentence, especially *no, nothing, no one,* and *nobody,* makes the presence of a negator anywhere in the predicate either ungrammatical or subject to a special interpretation, such as a special register or dialect:

[13] "Nobody doesn't like Sara Lee" (advertising slogan)

[14] Few people don't like Sara Lee

[15] *No one didn't say nothing about no lawsuit

[16] ?Neither of the twins didn't kiss their grandmother

One interpretation of a "double negative" sentence (such as [13] or [16]) follows the principle that two negatives make an affirmative. According to this principle, [13] is intended to mean "Everyone likes Sara Lee," and [16], if used at all, means "both of the twins kissed their grandmother."

> ### By the Way:
>
> Multiple negatives such as the ones in [15] are commonly heard in the spoken registers in almost all dialects of English and are historically justified (multiple negation was perfectly grammatical in Old English). For many, perhaps most, speakers of English the starred sentence [15] is the natural way to say this. There is perhaps no other aspect in which spoken English and the formal written standard diverge so radically.

A negative in the VP or the subject may force a change of the indefinite determiner *some* elsewhere in the predicate to *any*:

[17] (a) The guests brought some wine to the party

      (b) The guests did not bring any wine to the party

[18] (a) The children saw some ducks on the lake

      (b) None of the children saw any ducks on the lake

However, sentences like [17b] and [18b] with *some* in place of *any* are possible:

[19] (a) The guests did not bring some wine to the party

      (b) None of the children saw some ducks on the lake

They have a somewhat different sense from the same sentences with *any*. Thus, [19a] suggests that the writer of the sentence knows about some specific wine that the guests didn't bring; and [19b] similarly suggests that the writer of the sentence saw the ducks even though the children didn't. Technically, *some* presupposes that the object is already known to the writer, whereas *any* leaves this presupposition open.

Negative Verbs

Some verbs are intrinsically negative and behave in certain respects as if there is a negator in the VP, as in *deny, dissuade*. For example, they allow *any* rather than *some* later in the sentence:

[20] Harvey has denied making any untrue statements to any of the jurors

[21] We dissuaded them from bringing any expensive wine to the party

In such sentences, it is possible to use *some* in place of *any*. For example, in [21], with the use of *some*

[22] We dissuaded them from bringing some expensive wine to the party

there is a sense that the proposal to bring expensive wine to the party had already been made, and even perhaps that the wine had already been bought. Here again, the use of *some* presupposes the writer's prior knowledge of the object.

Scope of Negation

Negation is said to have **scope**, the range of words that is affected by the negative. For example, in

[23] They did not hire Sanford because of his police record

it is probable that Sanford was not hired, and that the reason for his not being hired was his police record. But in

[24] They did not hire Sanford because of his handsome face

it seems more likely that Sanford was hired, but for some reason other than his handsome face. In [23], "hire Sanford" is **in the scope of** *not*. In [24], "because of his handsome face" is in the scope of *not*. Another example:

[25] The ambulance did not come to the house quickly enough

In [25] it is declared that the ambulance did come to the house, just not quickly enough. So "quickly enough" (an adverb phrase functioning as an adverbial) is in the scope of *not*. But in

[26] The ambulance did not come to the house, strangely enough

it is denied that the ambulance came to the house at all. (Here "strangely enough" is a post-adjunct.) In [26], therefore, "come to the house" is in the scope of *not*. Similarly in

[27] The boys didn't break the window deliberately

[28] The boys didn't break the window, fortunately

In [27], "deliberately" is in the scope of *not*, and the boys did break the window. In [28], "break the window" is in the scope of *not*, and the boys did not break the window.

A third, less common kind of example consists of cases where the negator appears in the VP but the element in its scope comes *earlier* in the sentence:

[29] Surely all those clowns can't get into that one little Volkswagen

[30] The employees were not responsible for the deficit

In [29] and [30] the subjects are in the scope of the negation, and these are equivalent to "Surely not all those clowns can get into that one little Volkswagen," and the ungrammatical "*Not the employees were responsible for the deficit."

The scope of the negation can often be in a different clause from the negation itself. The negative of verbs like *believe* and *think* is usually transferred to the next clause, as for example in

[31] He doesn't believe that he passed the examination

Here the meaning is more like "He believes that he did not pass the examination." Note, however, that the position of the negator is often determined by rule of grammar rather than of logic, and it is therefore somewhat dangerous to appeal to what the sentence "really" says before deciding on the word order.

Until is often in the scope of a negative in a preceding clause:

[32] Clarence did not fire the starting pistol until the competitors had stopped talking

Notice that it is not stated that Clarence did not fire the starting pistol, only that he did so after waiting for the talking to stop.

Adverb-Operator Inversion

Certain negative adverbs at the beginning of the sentence have the unusual property that they must be followed immediately by an operator:

[33] Hardly had we entered the room when the fire alarm began buzzing

[34] Rarely do the board members lavish such praise on one of the employees

Such cases of adverb-operator inversion may also involve longer phrases with a negative meaning, and even entire clauses:

[35] *Not until the early hours of the morning* did the sounds of revelry finally fade

[36] *Only when the judge himself intervened* did the prosecuting attorney drop her insulting manner

Some other adverbs that typically cause this inversion are *never, neither, nor,* and *scarcely*.

Negative Idioms

A few special words and expressions appear only in the negative: *one little bit, a drop, lift a finger, spend a penny, say a word.*

[37] Buster did not leave a smidgeon on his plate for the dog

[38] Not a word did any of us say about the affair afterwards

Such expressions reinforce the negator, often in a highly idiomatic fashion. They characteristically make use of exaggeration. Especially colorful are such phrases as *a rat's ass* and many others that are used by all speakers in the informal registers.

By the Way:
Public restrooms in England used to require a one-penny fee, from which is derived the British expression £*spend a penny* = $*go to the bathroom.* Foreign visitors in London may sometimes encounter an amused reaction (especially from older inhabitants) to statements like *We stayed in the museum all day and didn't spend a penny.*

EXERCISES

Exercise 10.1

(For class discussion) What changes would you want to make in the following if you were writing formal sentences, and why? (Which of the sentences are possible in spoken dialects or older usage, or in less usual contexts?)

1. We knew not the reason for his anger.
2. The babysitter does not will come over tonight.
3. Few of the guests ate some of the stuffed olives.
4. All of the board members received any e-mail messages.
5. The children didn't be good all day.
6. No one has bought no cheese today.
7. The new highway has not hardly had any effect on the congestion at rush hour.
8. Scarcely the echoes of the explosion had died away when a squad of agents burst in through the front entrance.
9. John slept a wink the night before the trial.
10. Motorists are forbidden to bring some inflammable items through the tunnel.

Exercise 10.2

Determine the possible scope of the negation in each sentence. Note any places where more than one scope interpretation is possible.

1. Dr. Skimpitt had not read the report carefully.
2. One of the committee members did not approve of the idea.
3. Not one of the committee members approved of the idea.
4. The CEO didn't donate a single penny to the Widows' Fund.

5. I don't believe that the IRS cares a fig about your convenience.

6. He did not speak very clearly.

7. They had not read all of *War and Peace*.

8. I am not going because she asked me.

9. Sometimes she does not eat a thing all day.

10. Johnny Mack Brown did not meet Pancho until the very end of the movie.

Exercise 10.3

Diagram the following sentences from Exercise 10.2.

1. Dr. Skimpitt had not read the report carefully.

2. One of the committee members did not approve of the idea.

3. He did not speak very clearly.

4. They had not read all of *War and Peace*.

5. Sometimes she does not eat a thing all day.

THE PASSIVE

11.0 A Review of the Auxiliaries

We have considered the following basic members of the verb phrase:

(1)   the modal auxiliaries, which express "modalities"—ways of modifying the meaning of the verb by suggesting an obligation or degree of probability

(2)   the perfect aspect, which suggests a past event that has a continuing effect in the present

(3)   the progressive aspect, which backgrounds a process to a real or implied foregrounded event

(4)   the lexical verb itself

   To these can be added the various adverbial elements that have been discussed, such as *already*, and the negators such as *not*. The formula for the verb phrase (VP) that sums up items (1)–(4) can be stated as follows:

   VP: (Modal)(*have+en*)(*be+ing*) Verb

In this formula, the suffixes *-en* and *-ing* are bundled together with *have* and *be* respectively because they are always associated with these elements; *-en* is always used on the word following the perfect aspect *have*, and *-ing* is always found on the word following the progressive aspect *be:*

[1]   Someone *has* stol-*en* my wallet

[2]   Your Public Morality Campaign *is* ruin-*ing* the tourist industry

11.1 The Forms of the Passive

We now add to this formula one further element: the passive, whose form is *be+en*. The passive is, in other words, characterized by the auxiliary verb *to be* followed by a verb in the *-en* form. The passive is always the last auxiliary in a string of auxiliaries.

The Structure of the Passive Sentence

The passive is, however, far more than simply an extra auxiliary. It also involves a wholesale transformation in the order of words in the sentence, as in the following example:

[3] These lines were written by one of Ruritania's most famous poets

Notice that the auxiliary is *be* in its past plural form, "were"; it is in the plural, of course, because the subject ("these lines") is plural. The verb "written" is the *-en* form of the verb *to write;* the verb in the passive construction is always in the *-en* form.

A little reflection will point up an unusual fact about the relationship between the subject and the verb in sentences like this. This is that the subject of the verb is not *undertaking* the action of the verb, but *receives* the action of the verb. The person who undertakes the action of the verb is not the subject, but is tucked away in the complement of a prepositional phrase headed by *by:* "one of Ruritania's most famous poets." We will be referring to this prepositional phrase as the **by-phrase**.

A passive sentence like [3] has an obvious similarity in meaning to what is called an **active** sentence in which the NP in the *by*-phrase is a subject:

[4] One of Ruritania's most famous poets wrote these lines

It is customary, in fact unavoidable, to think of any passive sentence as related to a corresponding active sentence in the same way that [3] is related to [4]. The recipe for making a passive sentence out of an active one is:

(1)   The object of the verb becomes the subject.

(2)   The auxiliary *be+en* is added immediately before the verb in the VP.

(3)   The subject is placed in the predicate phrase as the complement of a prepositional phrase whose head is the preposition *by*.

It is a peculiarity of English that the object that is to be the subject of the passive (or, as we say, "passivized") may be direct or indirect. The active sentence [5] has two possible passives, [6] and [7]:

[5] Their uncle told the children this story

[6] This story was told [to] the children by their uncle

[7] The children were told this story by their uncle

In [5], the verb *to tell* has two objects: an indirect object, "the children," and a direct object, "this story." In [6], the passivized object is the direct object ("this story"), and in [7] it is the indirect object ("the children").

The Agent

The NP of the *by*-phrase is the **agent** of the passive. It is a normal prepositional phrase in form and could perhaps be considered an adverbial complement or adverbial; its function as an agent, however, seems to suggest that we should distinguish it from adverbials and adverbial complements that also happen to have the preposition *by* (such as *by the side of the road, by* [=*near*] *the war memorial*). We will acknowledge its special status by designating its function as **agentive**. Here is a diagrammatic analysis of [3]:

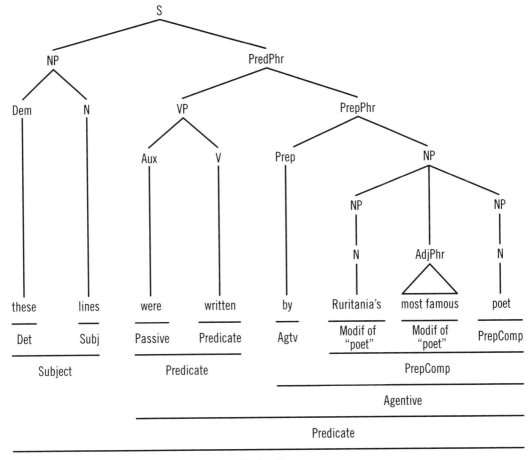

Diagram 11A. Diagramming agentives.

The Passive with Other Tenses and Aspects

The passive auxiliary *be* is, as we have seen, always the last auxiliary in the VP. It can be preceded by modal and aspect auxiliaries, as in the following examples:

[8] John will be promoted by his department

[9] All the wine has been drunk by June's guests

[10] Farquhar is being questioned by the FBI

[11] The silverware must have been stolen by one of the guests

> **REMINDER!**
>
> It might be useful to review the various forms of the verb that were discussed in Chapter 6. Recall that for many verbs, the *-en* form will have the same form as the past tense; this is usually *-ed*, as in "promoted" in sentence [8] and "questioned" in sentence [10]. Be careful not to confuse this *-ed* with the past tense *-ed*, however. For many other verbs these two are quite distinct—for instance *to drink* in sentence [9] and *to steal* in sentence [11]. Notice that the *-en* form of the verb has two functions: (i) it is used with the auxiliary *have* to make the perfect aspect, and (ii) it is used with the auxiliary *be* to make the passive.

Theoretically, both aspect auxiliaries, perfect and progressive, are possible before the passive, but in practice passive sentences that contain both aspects are considered awkward, because there are two untensed forms of *to be*, namely *been* and *being*. The same holds for combinations of modal with the progressive:

[12] (a) ?This site has been being excavated for the past three years by a team from Yale

(b) ?Ms. Winsocky will be being entertained by the Dean tomorrow evening

It is often preferable to reformulate such sentences as actives:

[13] (a) A team from Yale has been excavating this site for the past three years

(b) The dean will be entertaining Ms. Winsocky tomorrow evening

But if the active form is not possible for some reason, the progressive *be+ing*—that is, the *be* that precedes the *-ing* form and the *-ing* form itself—should be omitted; it doesn't contribute much to the sentence in the passive anyway:

[14] (a) This site has been excavated for the past three years by a team from Yale

(b) Ms. Winsocky will be entertained by the dean tomorrow evening

The formula for the order of auxiliaries in the verb phrase given in 11.0 can now be extended with the addition of the passive to

VP: (Modal) (*have+en*)(*be+ing*)(*be+en*) Verb

The last (*be+en*) is, of course, the passive. Like the other auxiliaries, the form taken by the *be* of the passive will depend on its place in the string of auxiliaries. If it is the operator (the first auxiliary) *be* will be tensed, and its form will depend on the tense—present or past—of the sentence:

[15] The interviews *are* conducted by a Spanish-speaking reporter

[16] The interviews *were* conducted by a Spanish-speaking reporter

Here *be* has the form "are" in the present tense, as in [15], and "were" in the past tense, as in [16]. If some other auxiliary comes first, the passive *be* will appear in a non-tensed form such as "being" or "been."

R E M I N D E R !

Non-tensed forms of the verb are ones that do not show tense independently. These are the *-ing* form, the *-en* form, and the base form. The non-tensed forms of the verb *to be* are therefore

-*ing* form: being

-*en* form: been

base form: be

If you had forgotten about non-tensed forms of the verb, reread Chapter 6!

Here are some further examples of passive sentences with auxiliaries. Remember that the passive auxiliary is the form of *be* that occurs immediately before the main verb:

[17] The interviews are/were being conducted by a Spanish-speaking reporter (progressive aspect)

[18] The interviews have/had been conducted by a Spanish-speaking reporter (perfect aspect)

[19] The interviews will be conducted by a Spanish-speaking reporter (modal auxiliary)

[20] The interviews will have been conducted by a Spanish-speaking reporter (modal auxiliary with perfect aspect)

It is worth recapitulating the forms of the passive by constructing the active voice counterparts of [15]–[20]. Except for [16]′, they are given in the present tense:

[15]′ A Spanish-speaking reporter conducts the interviews

[16]′ A Spanish-speaking reporter conducted the interviews

[17]′ A Spanish-speaking reporter is conducting the interviews

[18]′ A Spanish-speaking reporter has conducted the interviews

[19]′ A Spanish-speaking reporter will conduct the interviews

[20]′ A Spanish-speaking reporter will have conducted the interviews

11.2 The Agentless Passive

Up to now, we have been assuming that the passive invariably comes with an expressed agent. This is in fact not so, as the following sentences illustrate:

[21] John will be promoted

[22] Steinmetz was arrested

Sentences [21] and [22] are said to be **agentless passives**. The corresponding active sentences lack a subject:

[23] ( ) will promote John

[24] ( ) arrested Steinmetz

The reason for leaving out the agent is that it is unimportant or unknown. The agent may be unimportant because it can be filled in from general knowledge of how verbs like *to arrest* are used. In actual usage, agentless passives account for a large proportion (something like 80 percent) of all passives.

When the *by*-phrase is absent, there can be a question as to whether we are dealing with an agentless passive or a linking verb with an adjective:

[25] Their electrical power was disconnected

[26] Jill's favorite dress was torn

[27] Our CD player was damaged

The meaning difference can often be ascertained from the context. Is the focus on the activity (suggesting the passive) or on the present state (suggesting the adjective)? Does it make sense to supply an imaginary agent? If so, the sentence should be analyzed as a passive; if not, as an adjective. Take, for example, sentence [27] above, with the following two possible contexts:

[28] The den in our basement was flooded during the storm. Our paintings and rugs were ruined and *our CD player was damaged*.

[29] Last night we wanted to play one of our new disks. But when we tried to turn on our CD player, we found that *it was damaged*.

Here the damage to the CD player in [28] was one of a series of events, and the clause is therefore in the passive. But in [29], the damage is a *state* the CD player is in as a result of something unspecified that had previously happened. In [29], "damaged" is an adjective.

A few other criteria can be used to identify adjectives. Is it possible to modify the form with an intensifying adverb such as *very* or *rather?* If so, the form is an adjective. (Unfortunately, however, the reverse criterion is not so helpful; an inability to be modified does not always mean that the form is a verb.) Some adjectives that look like verbs simply cannot be used as verbs: in *The fields were unplowed*, there is no verb **to unplow*, and no corresponding active sentence **They unplowed the fields*.

Once the obvious cases are taken care of, however, there remain many cases where, without a wider context to indicate to us whether a writer is describing a state (adjective) or reporting an event (verb), the distinction between an adjective and a passive verb in its *-en* form is undecidable.

11.3 The Passive of the Prepositional Verb

Prepositional verbs, and indeed other kinds of adverbial complements, can participate in passivization:

[30] (a) Many travelers have written about this bizarre ritual

(b) This bizarre ritual has been written about by many travelers

[31] (a) Rival clans had fought over the valley for centuries

(b) The valley had been fought over by rival clans for centuries

[32] (a) Ornithologists often refer to Imogene's book on migrant finches

(b) Imogene's book on migrant finches is often referred to by ornithologists

[33] (a) Daniel Pinkwater slept in this bed

(b) This bed was slept in by Daniel Pinkwater

Adverbial complements differ in this respect from postcore phrases. The prepositional complement in an adverbial complement can be made into a passive subject, whereas this is not the case with postcore adverbials:

[34] (a) The council decided on a new course of action

(b) A new course of action was decided on by the council

[35] (a) The council retired at six o'clock

(b) *Six o'clock was retired at by the council

> **REMINDER!**
>
> Postcore phrases are phrases that occur after the predicate phrase.
> They may be post-adjuncts, like *in my opinion*, or adverbials of place,
> time, or manner, such as *in Denver*, *after Labor Day*, *with vigor*.
> Postcore phrases were discussed in Chapter 5.

In [34a], "decide" has the adverbial complement "on a new course of action."
Because it is in an adverbial complement, the NP "a new course of action" can
be thematized and made into the subject of a passive, just as if the verb were
"decided on" with "a new course of action" as its direct object.

In [35a], on the other hand, the prepositional phrase "at six o'clock" is not
an adverbial complement but a postcore adverbial. Here there is no quasi-tran-
sitive verb *retire at* comparable to the "decide on" of sentence [34a].

Note that if the verb also has a direct object, the prepositional complement
in an adverbial complement cannot become a passive subject. This means that,
for example,

[36] The bandits robbed them of their new camera

(where "of their new camera" is an adverbial complement of the transitive
verb "robbed") cannot be converted into

[37] *Their new camera was robbed them of by the bandits

One way of looking at this constraint is to say that the complement of a preposition can only become the subject of the passive if there is not already a direct
object in competition for this role. For this reason,

[38] They were robbed of their new camera by the bandits

(where "they" corresponds to the direct object "them" of the active verb in
[37]) is perfectly acceptable.

11.4 Functions of the Passive in Discourse

The passive has a bad reputation. Some stylists recommend avoiding it altogether. It is said to be awkward in comparison to the simpler active. More
darkly, there is the suggestion of a sinister intent in omitting the agent:

[39] Senator Eustace has been accused of having Marxist sympathies

The senator's accusers are not identified, but a politically unpopular stance is
attributed to her nonetheless. Disparagers of the passive note that if sentences
of this kind are formulated in the active, there is no possibility of sneakily
avoiding identifying the accusers and pinning an attitude on the subject without saying what the source of the information is.

But the unethical use of language will not be made to disappear by reducing the number of available grammatical constructions. (It would be no less evasive to formulate [39] as an active: "People have accused Senator Eustace of having Marxist sympathies"; "They have accused Senator Eustace of having Marxist sympathies.") As to the charge of stylistic awkwardness, in fact the reverse is true. There are discourse circumstances in which the passive is the more graceful alternative to the active.

In order to understand why the passive is sometimes more natural, we must first understand the notion of **theme**.

The theme of a section of a discourse is the person or thing that is the central concern of the passage. To use an analogy from film or television, the theme of a scene is the person or object whom the camera is following during the scene. The relationship between theme and grammar is the following: *There is a strong association between the theme of a passage in a discourse and the subject of a given clause or sentence in the passage.*

Whether a given NP is the theme of a passage is often to be decided quite liberally. NPs can become themes by association with another NP that is more obviously the theme. Consider:

[40] The Ogilvys have had nothing but bad luck with their new house. First the foundations leaked, then the plaster came away from the ceiling in the living room, and just last week *a falling tree damaged the roof.*

In [40], "the roof" is thematic by reason of a natural association with the word "house" (houses normally have roofs) and by its association with other parts of the house that were affected. The passive could therefore be used, perhaps with an improved stylistic effect:

[40]′ The Ogilvys have had nothing but bad luck with their new house. First the foundations leaked, then the plaster came away from the ceiling in the living room, and just last week *the roof was damaged by a falling tree.*

In the following passage, taken from a history of the Balkans, the theme is set up in the first sentence as "the present bloody struggle":

Consider, for instance, the present bloody struggle between Croats and the Serbian minority in southern parts of the Croatian republic. No doubt the conflict *is being systematically promoted* by the government of Serbia, but there can be no doubt about a certain degree of local involvement. (*The Black Book of Bosnia: The Consequences of Appeasement*, ed. Nader Mousavizadeh [New York: Basic Books, 1996] 11. Italics added.)

Now in the second sentence "the conflict," which continues the idea of struggle in the first sentence, is thematic, and becomes the subject of the verb "promote" even though it is logically the object; hence the passive verb phrase "is being systematically promoted." The government of Serbia, however, the logical subject of "promote," which has not been mentioned before in this paragraph, is placed into a *by*-phrase.

We are talking here of a question of style rather than one of grammar. The point is that the passive, far from being a construction to be avoided, is actually preferable to the active in some circumstances.

One important function of the passive, then, is to thematize the object of the verb by making a thematic direct or indirect object into a subject. The passive is in fact a grammatical manifestation of a more general tendency in English style to place the less novel (older) parts of a sentence earlier and the more interesting, newer parts later. We will return in Chapter 17 to some other manifestations of this tendency. But one by-product of it is that there is a tendency to balance sentences by placing short and uninformative material before the verb and longer and more interesting material after it. The passive is therefore typically found if the shorter material is the direct object and the longer material the subject. Compare [41], where the active sentence (long subject, short object) is unbalanced, with [42], where the passive (short item before the verb, long item after the verb) restores the balance:

[41] A strange figure in a chequered costume carrying a monkey on his shoulder preceded the band

[42] The band was preceded by a strange figure in a chequered costume carrying a monkey on his shoulder

The various grammatical constructions of a language can be seen as a repertoire available to writers, permitting them to vary their sentences and add vitality and flexibility to the way information is delivered. In English, the basic sentence structure (subject-predicate) cannot be altered, but constructions like the passive enable us to move NPs around the sentence in interesting ways without violating this basic structure.

EXERCISES

Exercise 11.1

Convert the following sentences into the passive.

1. The War Office has canceled Franklin's leave.

2. The negotiators for the IRS insisted on this guarantee.

3. The attorneys and the board of governors drew up a new agreement.

4. FBI agents were secretly taping the proceedings.

5. One of the work-study students must have stapled the copies back to front.

6. A snowplow has been clearing our street.

7. A team from *National Geographic* will be photographing the eruption.

8. Only James Bond can identify the second agent.

9. The mayor offered the protesters a chance to leave quietly.

10. The government attorneys went closely into the question of Rookhurst's dealings with the union leaders.

Exercise 11.2

Rewrite, changing the parts in italics from active to passive or vice versa in order to place thematic NPs in the subject position. Delete any of the NPs if this would improve the sentence.

1. Mr. Holthausen was suffering from chest pains, and *medics took him to the hospital.*

2. Fran got up wearily from her armchair and *the front door was closed by her.*

3. Our street was blocked by snow, but *a municipal plow cleared it before I had to leave for work.*

4. The students cannot do the exercise, but *one of the TAs is helping them.*

5. Michelle sautéed the shrimp, stir-fried some fresh vegetables, and put the garlic bread in the oven, while *a bottle of 1991 Mouton Cadet was opened by her boyfriend.*

6. Prince Gundolf founded a new university, and *schools and hospitals were built by his brother.*

7. There was a storm last night, and *their neighbor's toolshed was blown away by one especially strong gust of wind.*

8. One of the boxers was badly cut, and so *they stopped the bout in the third round.*

9. We tried to reach the hospital, but *a fallen tree blocked our way.*

10. *Plenty of money was paid by me for these tickets* and I intend to see the performance no matter what.

Exercise 11.3

Use the ability to passivize to decide whether the prepositional phrases are adverbial complements or postcore adverbials. (There may be more than one prepositional phrase in the sentence!)

1. Stanley and Livingstone met in the middle of Africa.

2. The faculty did not approve of the appointment.

3. They read from the Book of Job at the funeral service.

4. Every citizen was talking about the affair.

5. The economic crisis will call for some creative new approaches.

6. Connie was weeping during the funeral service.

7. The children have been sleeping since yesterday evening.

8. Astonished passersby were staring at the notice board.

9. The other motorists were cursing at the slow old Cadillac.

10. Several different families have lived in this house.

Exercise 11.4

Decide whether the *-en* forms in the following sentences are adjectives or verbs.

1. A number of trees were blown down in the storm.

2. The union members were unperturbed by the actions of the management.

3. The younger undergraduates were rather confused.

4. The site of Troy was discovered in the nineteenth century by German archeologists.

5. Economists were surprised at the price increases.

6. Dr. Gladhand was quite interested in the progress of the project.

7. The gardens of strongly aromatic flowers and herbs are appreciated by the blind residents.

8. All this time the planet Earth was being closely watched by the distant Martians.

9. Professor Skatter's desk was cluttered.

10. Some of these garments are manufactured by companies with headquarters in Asia and Mexico.

12

COORDINATION

12.0 Introduction

Up to now we have been studying the grammar of phrases and sentences that are **simple**—that is, they are not joined to another sentence or phrase by a conjunction like *and* or *because*. We now move on to more complex constructions.

Sentences can be **coordinated** with one another, as in

[1] Milhouse played "Sweet Georgia Brown" on his teeth, and Bart did his imitation of the principal

in which there is one longer sentence consisting of two shorter ones joined by *and*. The shorter sentences that make up a longer sentence are known as **clauses**. In order to qualify as a clause, a phrase must contain a verb phrase or a recognizable form of a verb phrase, such as an infinitive or gerund. We will say that example [1] consists of two clauses coordinated with one another. One clause can also be **subordinated** to another, as in

[2] We cannot watch the game tonight because the transmitter has been knocked out by lightning

In [2], one of the clauses, "because the transmitter has been knocked out by lightning," is given as the reason for the other clause, "we cannot watch the game tonight." In [2], the clause introduced by "because" is said to be **subordinated** to the first; the clause to which it is subordinated is known as the

main clause. In subordination, one clause is *part of* a phrase of another sentence. Subordination forms the subject matter of Chapters 13 through 16, and detailed discussion is found there; but examples of subordination (in italics) are:

[3] We explained to Farquhar *that he would need a ticket*

[4] The young man *she brought to the party* had a pocket protector with four pens

[5] There was an embarrassed silence *when June mentioned the new jail*

12.1 The Coordination of Full Sentences

The simplest way in which two clauses can be combined is through **coordination**. Coordination calls for a conjunction such as *and* to serve as a **coordinator**, as in

[6] A heavy snow had fallen the night before, *and* the fields were clothed in a dazzling white

The other most frequently used coordinator is *but,* which suggests a contrast with the first clause:

[7] Mr. Guzzlit ordered a red Bordeaux, *but* the waiter brought them a white Zinfandel

Sentences [6] and [7] are examples of **compound sentences**. A compound sentence is one that consists of two or more coordinated clauses. Compound sentences are different from **complex sentences**, sentences that consist of a main clause and a subordinate clause.

Diagramming Compound Sentences

Assuming that each clause in a compound sentence has a full subject and predicate, as is the case with [6] and [7], the diagram will involve at least two S nodes that are dominated by the highest S of the sentence. In other words, S itself appears at some point lower down in the diagram. Sentence [7] above is diagrammed as follows:

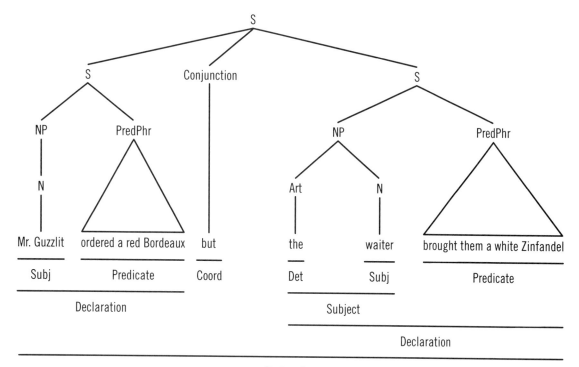

Diagram 12A.   Diagramming compound sentences.

12.2 The Coordination of Other Phrases

Not only full clauses, but all types of phrases can be coordinated; for example:

[8] The response to my memo was *rapid* and *effective* (adjective phrases)

[9] The next candidate *discussed Slovakian folk dancing* and *named all the geological eras* (predicate phrases)

[10] Imogene selected *a dirndl blouse* and *a shell necklace* for the senior prom (noun phrases)

We will look at some of these different sorts of coordination.

Coordination of predicate phrases. Predicate phrases can be coordinated, sharing a common subject. Consider, for example,

[11] Ms. DiCamillo *picked up the phone and called the police*

Here "picked up the phone and called the police" together form the predicate of the sentence whose subject is "Ms. DiCamillo." But, since both "picked up the phone" and "called the police" function equally as predicates of "Ms. DiCamillo" (both report something that she did), each coordinated phrase is also a predicate. The entire predicate therefore consists of two coordinated predicates dominated by the node Predicate Phrase. The diagram makes this clear:

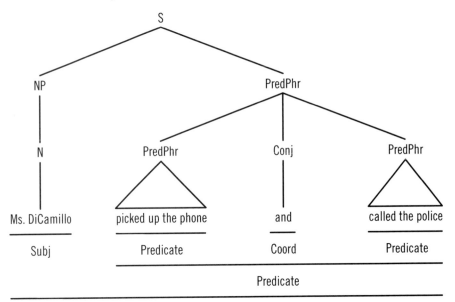

Declaration

Diagram 12B.   Diagramming compound predicate phrases.

The two conjoined predicates, then, are taken up under a single node, itself a predicate phrase. Coordination always results in a situation in which a node with a certain label dominates two or more nodes, each with the same label. This reflects an important fact about coordination: *only two phrases of the same type can be coordinated.* Consider the following nonsentence:

[12] *Sebastian had fallen into a ditch and muddy shoes

Assuming that the fully expanded sentence here is "Sebastian had fallen into a ditch and Sebastian had muddy shoes," the explanation of why the second "had" cannot be omitted is that the two instances of "had" are of quite different kinds. The first is the perfect auxiliary, the second a lexical verb. "Fallen" is of course the *-en* form of the verb *to fall* and "muddy shoes" is an NP that is the direct object of "had." Therefore the roles of the words "fallen" and "muddy shoes" are also quite different from one another. This means that "fallen into a ditch" and "muddy shoes" are not phrases of the same type and therefore they cannot be coordinated.

Verb and verb phrase coordination. Verb phrases can also be coordinated, as in

[13] Jane *peeled and boiled* the potatoes

This is a fairly simple problem of analysis; it is diagrammed as follows:

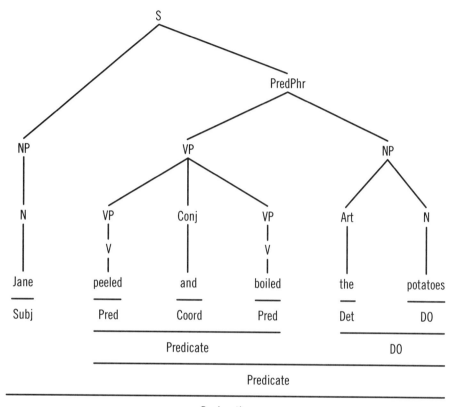

Diagram 12C. Diagramming compound verb phrases.

Note, however, that coordination of verb phrases results in the two verb phrases being clustered together. On the face of it, we might expect ellipsis of the direct object to produce sentences like *Jane peeled the potatoes and boiled,* with the second occurrence of *potatoes* being dropped. But coordinated phrases, as we have seen, normally form together a third larger phrase of the same kind as the two coordinated phrases, and this can only happen if they are adjacent.

Some further complexity is introduced when auxiliaries occur in one or both of the verb phrases. Of the many theoretically possible combinations, only a few occur with any frequency. By far the most important, and the only one we will consider here, is that in which two *verbs* share a common auxiliary:

[14] We will *encourage and finance* your crazy scheme

[15] Michael has *written and directed* several plays

The last of these is diagrammed as follows:

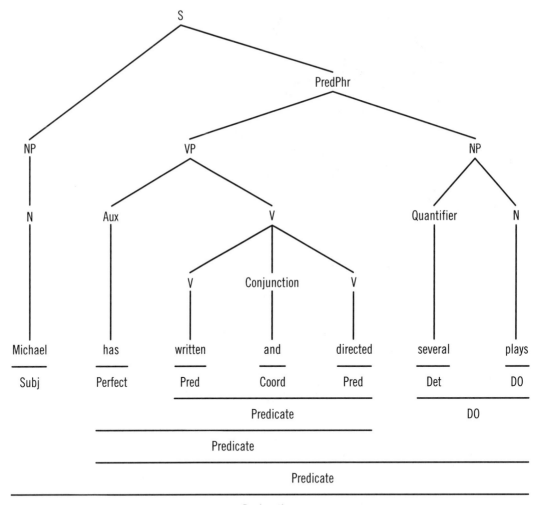

Diagram 12D.   Diagramming verbs with shared auxiliaries.

Rarely, both subjects can be present, as in

[16] ?Jane peeled and Michael boiled the potatoes

Although much loved by grammatical theorists (you are invited to consider the difficulties of diagramming this one), such sentences are likely to be avoided by careful stylists.

Coordination of noun phrases. NPs in all the possible functions for NPs can be coordinated. If the coordinated NPs are the subject of the verb, they form a plural NP and the verb will agree accordingly:

[17] Marvin and his sister are going to medical school

The conjoined subject is plural, as is shown by the auxiliary "are." An alternative to [17] is available for all conjoined NPs, making use of the word "both":

[18] Both Marvin and his sister are going to medical school

We will analyze the word *both* as a (discontinuous) conjunction in parallel with *and*; this is made clear by the following diagram:

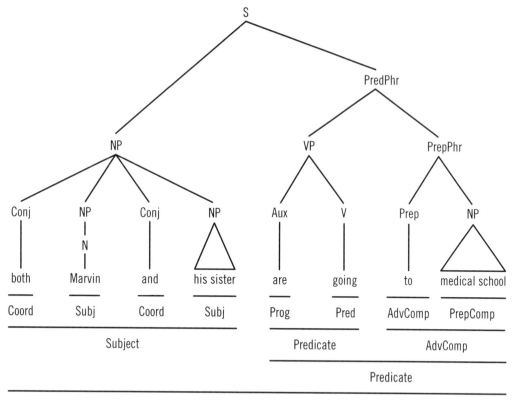

Diagram 12E.   Diagramming compound subjects.

It is clear that [18] means the same as "Marvin is going to medical school and his sister is going to medical school," and that the common predicate is "are going to medical school." But often, coordinated subjects are *joint,* as in the following:

[19] Marcie and Herbie shook hands

[20] Linda and Antonio were dancing the tango

The natural interpretation of a sentence like [20] is that Linda and Antonio are partners, and so we would not normally think of this statement as being elliptical for "Linda is dancing the tango and Antonio is dancing the tango." Joint NPs like "Linda and Antonio" are not usually coordinated with *both . . . and.*

Respectively and *on the one hand*

The more elaborate possibilities of coordination in the written language sometimes bring about ambiguities in the phrase structure. For example:

[21] Dr. Jane Michaels and Dr. Michael Michaels teach Renaissance poetry and postmodern criticism

More than one interpretation is possible: the two subjects could both teach both courses, they could co-teach both courses, Jane could teach postmodern criticism and Michael Renaissance poetry, or the other way around, and so on *ad nauseam.* By adding *respectively,*

[21]′ Dr. Jane Michaels and Dr. Michael Michaels teach Renaissance poetry and postmodern criticism respectively

we can sort out their teaching assignments unambiguously. *Respectively* matches equivalent parts of two coordinated clauses.

The next example of ambiguity resulting from coordination involves a similar problem of phrasing. Consider:

[22] It is difficult to compare the political rivalry between Republicans and Democrats and Conservatives and Socialists in Britain

The problem is that *compare* always involves two objects joined by *and;* consequently there are at least as many interpretations of the sentence as there are instances of *and* (in this example, three*). On the one hand, . . . on the other* makes clear the terms of the comparison:

[22]′ It is difficult to compare the political rivalry between Republicans and Democrats on the one hand, and Conservatives and Socialists in Britain on the other

Coordination of adjectives. An unlimited number of adjectives can be placed before a noun, coordinated with commas and *and.* British practice (and that of a minority of American style manuals) is to omit the comma before the last *and:*

[23] $your crazy, juvenile, irresponsible, completely unworkable, and brilliant idea

[23]′ £your crazy, juvenile, irresponsible, completely unworkable and brilliant idea

Since commas serve to keep apart the different adjectival phrases, without the comma there is an obvious danger of reading £"completely unworkable and brilliant" as a single phrase.

Strings of coordinated adjectives are simply placed before the noun with equal status, as shown in the next diagram. Such a "marquee tent" analysis is preferable to one in which adjectives are all made part of a larger adjectival phrase, however tempting this may be. As was noted earlier, a string of attributive adjectives is not normally a phrase, because there is no natural way to determine which one is the head. As in this example, the label AdjPhr should be reserved for groups headed by a single adjective and containing a modifier or complement of the adjective (such as *completely unworkable*). Inspect the tree diagram carefully:

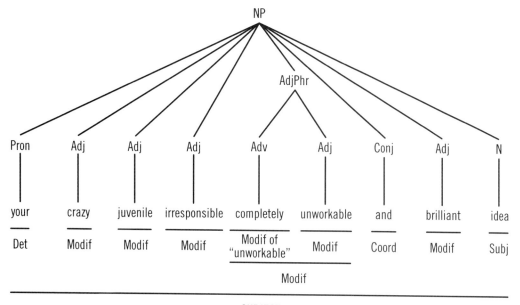

Diagram 12F. Diagramming coordinated adjectives.

Coordination of a Series of Phrases

The use of the comma in showing coordination of a series is not restricted to adjectives. In fact, any sequence of phrases can be coordinated with commas and a final conjunction, including NPs:

[24] The floor was littered with books, newspapers, old magazines, and typewritten sheets

and verbs:

[25] Rachel had planned, financed, and launched the project all on her own

In constructing a coordinated series of this kind, it is important to make certain that the phrases are of the same type. There is a danger of inadvertantly slipping a different kind of phrase into the last slot, as in

[26] ?The missing man was thirty-five years old, dark-haired, of average height, and spoke with a stammer

Notice what has happened here: "was thirty-five years old" and "spoke with a stammer" are both complete predicate phrases, whereas "dark-haired" and "of average height" are only subject complements whose linking verb *was* has undergone ellipsis. The sentence can be repaired in either of the following ways:

[27] The missing man was thirty-five years old, was dark-haired, was of average height, and spoke with a stammer

[28] The missing man was thirty-five years old, dark-haired, and of average height, and spoke with a stammer

The second of these is preferable, in that the verb *was* is not repeated. In [28], three subject complements following "was" are made to form a coordinated set ("thirty-five years old," "dark-haired," "and of average height") and a new conjunct is made out of the last phrase ("spoke with a stammer").

Other kinds of conjunction are also sensitive to phrase structure. Consider the following example:

[29] ?As a youth Jason rebelled both against his parents and his teachers

Better: As a youth Jason rebelled against both his parents and his teachers

In [29], the position of "both" shows that two unlike phrases, one a prepositional phrase ("against his parents") and the other a noun phrase ("his teachers"), have been coordinated.

12.3 Disjunction

One variety of coordinated sentence is what is called **disjunction**, in which two clauses or phrases state alternatives. The alternatives may be positive or negative.

Positive Disjunction

The coordinator in such clauses is *or*, and the first clause may be preceded by *either*, as in

[30] Either the foundations are leaking or the main pipe has burst

This sentence would be diagrammed as follows, with *either . . . or* represented as what it is—a discontinuous coordinator:

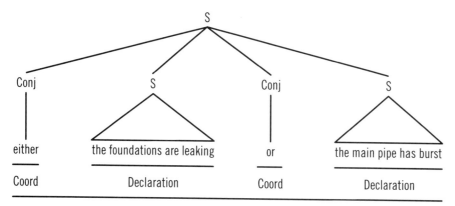

Diagram 12G. Diagramming disjunctions.

The presence of *either* may be used to suggest that the alternatives are exclusive of one another.

Negative Disjunction

Negative disjunction involves the conjunctions *nor* and *neither . . . nor. Or* is replaced by *nor* if the first term of the disjunction is also negative:

[31] Neither Billie nor Millie would go on the new rides

[32] Billie would neither ride The Monster nor go through the Haunted House

If the disjunction between two clauses is complete (that is, there is no ellipsis) adverb-operator inversion takes place.

> **REMINDER!**
>
> Adverb-operator inversion (see Chapter 10) is the rule that requires a clause-initial negator such as *never, hardly, scarcely, not once* to be followed by an operator:
>
> - Scarcely had we left the house when it began to rain
> - Not once did they invite us to their home
>
> In this last example, the dummy operator *do* must be used because the verb phrase has no other auxiliary to serve as an operator.

In [33], "nor" in the second clause triggers inversion of the modal auxiliary "would" with the subject "Millie":

[33] Billie would not ride The Monster, nor would Millie go through the Haunted House

As usual (see the box above), if there is no other auxiliary, the dummy operator *do* must be used:

[34] Mr. Scrounger would not give any money to the orphanage, nor did he offer to host the holiday party

Agreement of Conjoined Subjects and Verb

It will be recalled that agreement refers to the question of whether the general present or the *-s* form is used in the present tense of the verb. The *-s* form is used if the subject is third-person singular, and the general present for other kinds of subjects in the present tense. The verb *to be* has the further peculiarity that it agrees with the subject in the past tense also, using *was* for singular and *were* for plural. We have also seen that a conjoined subject is plural:

[35] The horrified caterers discovered that the wedding cake and the champagne *were* missing

"The wedding cake" and "the champagne," both singular, together form a plural subject, and so the verb must be "were." But there are a few traps to be aware of.

Apparent conjunctions. There are sets of words that function to join phrases but are not considered true conjunctions, and which therefore, in the formal written language, do not create conjoined subjects. *As well as,* for example, is close in meaning to a conjunction *and,* but does not make a new NP with the subject. From the point of view of standard written English, then, the following agreement pattern should be avoided:

[36] ?The president of the union, as well as many of the rank-and-file members, *do* not support the strike

Does, rather than *do,* would be more correct here. Similarly, *together with, not to mention,* and some others:

[37] ?Philippa Jenkins, together with her husband and children, *were* present at the funeral

[38] ?The unfair exchange rate, not to mention the outrageous import duties, *contribute* to the high price of foreign-made motorcycles

Only the first NP in such sentences is the subject; therefore, in [37] "was" rather than "were" is correct, and in [38] "contributes" should be substituted for "contribute."

Disjoint subjects. A problem of **number conflict** occurs when the verb must be made to agree with disjoint subjects. Consider the following examples:

[39] Michael was playing rock music in the reading room again

[40] Michael and the twins were playing rock music in the reading room again

[41] Either the twins or Michael (was? were?) playing rock music in the reading room again

Sentences [39] and [40] present no problems of verb agreement. In [39] the subject is singular; in [40] the subject is joint and therefore plural. But [41] does present us with a problem, since the subjects are **disjoint**. Disjoint subjects with different numbers like those in [41] are awkward when it comes to verb agreement because they compete with one another for the verb agreement.

No ordinary grammatical principle accounts for the verb agreement in such cases. Instead we must fall back on an arbitrary rule that is not well motivated grammatically, but which has the support of grammarians generally. The rule is this: If there is number conflict in disjoint subjects, the verb agrees with *the most recent NP,* in other words, with the NP *closest to the verb.* This means that in [41], since the NP closest to the verb is *Michael,* the correct form is *was.* Notice the following examples, which illustrate the agreed-upon usage:

[42] Either the club manager or the members of the team *are* responsible for clearing the trash

[43] Either the members of the team or the club manager *is* responsible for clearing the trash

This rule seems to be purely artificial, but it provides a consistent solution to the problem of number conflict.

EXERCISES

Exercise 12.1

Decide whether the following sentences are *simple* (consist of only one clause), *compound* (consist of coordinated clauses), or *complex* (consist of a main clause and a subordinate clause).

1. Entwhistle can start the barbecue while Crawford mixes the fruit punch.

2. The early settlers would not eat kangaroo meat, and many of them came close to starvation within easy reach of food.

3. Cheryl was balancing a basketball on her head and doing a tap dance in the foyer.

4. After Sheriff Kunitz had delivered the eulogy, the mournful procession made its way back to the town.

5. With the advent of new submarine technology, underwater archeology at hitherto unthinkable depths has become possible.

6. Dr. Martinez together with all the members of the cheerleading team finally boarded the bus.

7. The minuet's popularity declined so much that by 1815 only a few of the older courtiers could still remember how to do it.

8. The patron insisted that the screen should be carved from mahogany.

9. This wood is tough, and the erratic nature of its grain makes it an unusually difficult medium for the carver.

10. The poor provinces could not grow enough rice for their needs, nor would the wealthier provinces give up any of their surplus.

Exercise 12.2

Coordinate the following pairs of sentences with *and, but, (either)/or*, or *(neither)/nor*, using ellipsis, passive, and pronouns where good style would require it.

1. Clouds had moved in during the afternoon. By evening a light rain was falling.

2. Our car has been stolen. The police have towed our car away.

3. Their flight was delayed because of the fog. They are stuck in traffic on the way from the airport.

4. Jake has looked my phone number up. Jake has written my phone number down.

5. Tatwina did not inform us of her plans. Tatwina did not finish the report before she left.

6. Robert was not only the youngest person to receive a doctorate. The university awarded Robert's thesis a prize.

7. The crew struggled heroically to save the *Mariposa*. By nightfall the *Mariposa* had foundered in the heavy seas.

8. They must have shredded the incriminating documents. They must have burned the incriminating documents.

9. The security officers did not notice the break-in. The secretaries did not report the missing documents.

10. Kanaka's fantastic story is a pure fabrication. Something very strange happened at the deserted farmhouse last night.

Exercise 12.3

Diagram these sentences *without* using the triangle convention.

1. Peter will be invited to the party but will not be introduced to Janine.

2. The attorneys did not appear, and the judge was very offended.

3. The project got Milford interested, but funding was denied by the agency.

Exercise 12.4

(For class discussion) What changes would you want to make in the following sentences, and why?

1. Our neighbor, not to mention her two children and their dog, are coming over for supper.

2. By replacing the chief of police, the mayor hopes to strengthen and make the force more efficient.

3. The Roman Catholic archbishop, as well as clergy of other faiths, have spoken out against the proposed law.

4. They replaced the fenders, the badly dented hood, the cracked windshield, and repainted the entire car.

5. Because of the incessant rain, Vanessa could not play tennis nor the children could go on their picnic.

6. Sergei was dissatisfied both with his job and his family life.

7. Cheryl left this cigarette butt under the sofa, or Gregory.

8. Sam trimmed the artichoke hearts and marinated.

9. Either the wheel axles or the chain are slipping.

10. Davie was nervous about the dispatch slips and questioned by the harbor police.

13

SUBORDINATION: RELATIVE CLAUSES

13.0 An Introduction to Complex Sentences

We have seen that sentences with more than one clause are of two kinds: compound and complex.

When clauses or phrases are coordinated to give a compound sentence, as described in Chapter 12, we have a symmetrical pattern such as *S and S*; the coordinated clauses or phrases are adjacent and parallel. When the coordinated elements are full clauses, each clause makes a separate declaration and the two clauses are combined together into a joint declaration.

Subordination is different from coordination in that in subordination the two clauses are arranged with one clause *inside* another. One clause, the **main clause** or **matrix clause**, is more important and more independent, and the other, the **subordinate clause**, is backgrounded to it. The combined main clause and subordinate clause make only one declaration. The subordinate clause is *part of* the matrix or main clause.

Subordinate clauses have functions in the sentence that are similar to those of categories such as "noun," "adjective," and "adverb." For example, in

[1] Michael shouted an insult

"an insult" is a NP headed by the noun "insult" and is the direct object of "shouted." In

[2] Michael shouted *that he was ready*

"that he was ready" is also the direct object of "shouted," but it happens to be a clause, rather than a NP with a noun as its head.

> **REMINDER!**
>
> **Recall that to qualify as a clause a phrase must have a verb phrase or a recognizable form of a verb phrase, such as an infinitive or a gerund.**

In the next example

[3] The stony soil was unsuitable for farming

"stony" is an adjective acting as a modifier of "soil." Clauses can also function as modifiers, as in

[4] They sold the land *which lay to the north of the gully*

Here "which lay to the north of the gully" modifies "land." Clauses can also function the same way as pre- and postcore adverbials, as in

[5] *While Merlin was entertaining the inspector in the living room,* Janice made coffee in the kitchen

The different kinds of subordinate clauses have standard names in grammar. The type exemplified by [2], which functions like a NP, is called a **noun clause**. The type of [4], functioning as the modifier of a noun, is a **relative clause**. And the type found in [5], introduced by "while," functioning as an adverbial, is known as an **adverbial clause**.

As was noted above, the clause that frames the subordinate clause is known as the "main clause" or "matrix clause."

13.1 Relative Clauses as Modifiers

A sentence like

[6] We photographed the balcony *that ran along the back of the house*

contains a NP ("the balcony that ran along the back of the house") that includes a relative clause. As can be seen from the following diagram, the head of the NP here is "balcony," and "balcony" has a determiner, "the," and a modifier, "that ran along the back of the house." Notice that, being a modifier, the relative clause is *within* the NP. It is said to be **embedded in** the noun phrase:

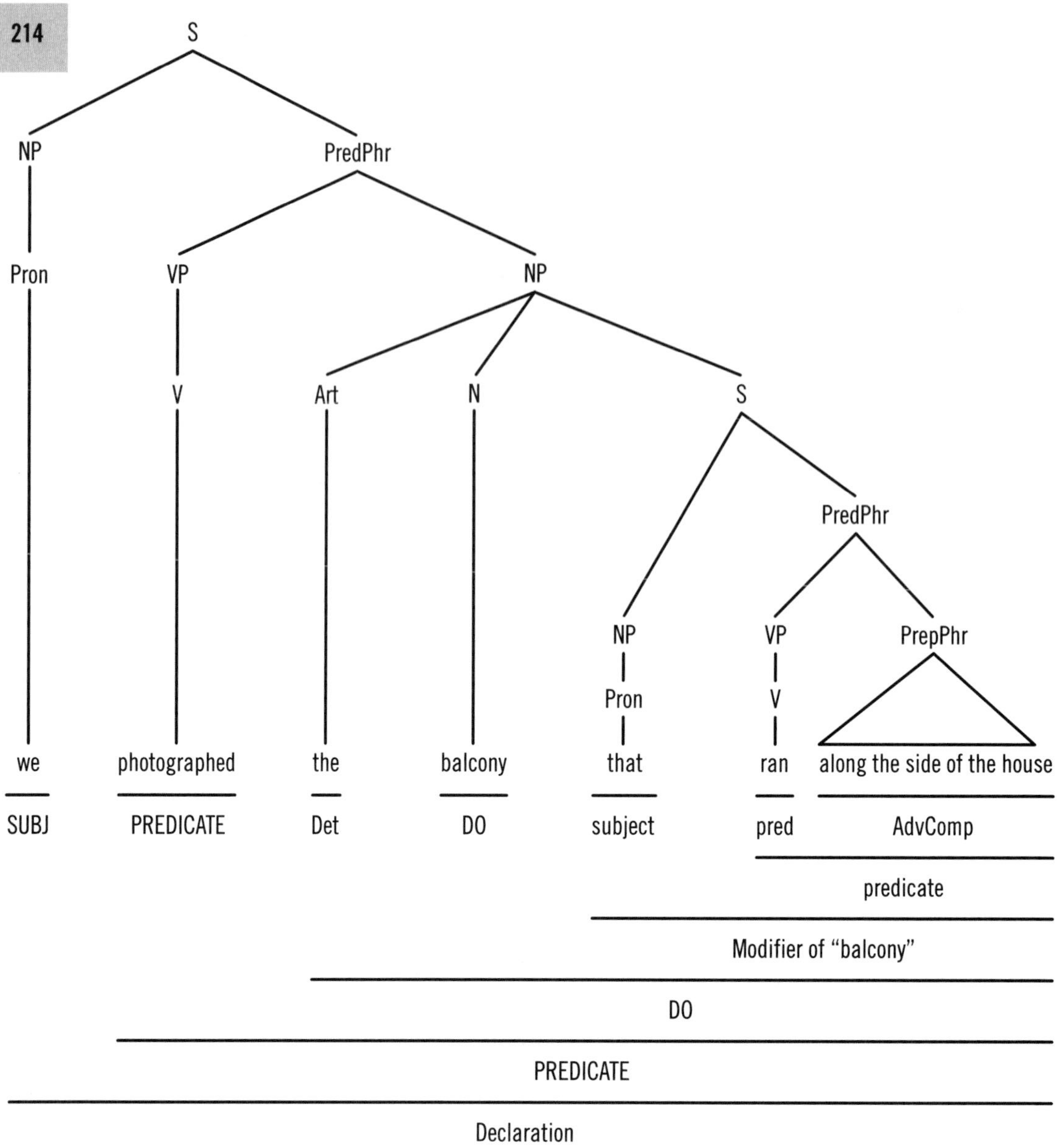

Declaration

Diagram 13A. Diagramming relative clauses as modifiers.

In [6], the relative clause is linked to the noun by the word "that." *That* has a number of different functions in English grammar, and we will encounter it again. Here, however, "that" is a **relative pronoun**. The relative pronoun has two functions:

(1) It resumes a mention of the head noun in the NP. In the example sentence, "that" refers to the head noun, "balcony."

(2) It serves some such function as "Subject," "Direct Object," or "Prepositional Complement" *inside the relative clause*. In the example sentence, "that" is the subject of the verb, "ran."

> **By the Way:**
>
> If there is any risk of confusion in the diagram between the functions of the embedded S and those of the matrix sentence, fuller function labels can be used such as "Predicate of Relative Clause," etc. One graphic device adopted here is to put the words SUBJECT and PREDICATE of the matrix clause in upper-case letters, and the terms "subject" and "predicate" of the embedded clause in lower case. It should be stressed that this a purely visual tactic—it has no grammatical significance.

13.2 The *wh*-Word Relative Pronouns

An alternative to [6] would be

[7] We photographed the balcony *which* ran along the back of the house

Which is also a relative pronoun, and in some contexts it is interchangeable with *that*. *Which* is chosen when the head noun of the NP, the noun the relative clause modifies, is not human. If the head noun is human, *who* must be used in place of *which*, as in

[8] The passerby *who* had identified the pickpocket went to the precinct station with the officers

Here "who" refers to the head noun "passerby." It is also the subject of the clause whose predicate is "had identified the pickpocket."

  Who and *which* belong to a group of relative pronouns that all begin with the letters *wh*. We will therefore call these pronouns the *wh*-relative pronouns; they are identical with the interrogative *wh*-words discussed in Chapter 4, as in

[9] *Which* hotel did you choose?

[10] *Who* told Amy about the surprise party?

13.3 Case in the Relative Clause

The relative pronoun *who* has different forms according to its **case**.

> **R E M I N D E R !**
>
> To review case, see Chapter 8. Case refers to the function a NP serves in its clause. The case of the subject of the sentence is the *nominative* case. The case of the direct and indirect objects and of the prepositional complement is the *objective* case. The case of a noun phrase that possesses another noun, such as "*his* desk," "*the attorney's* desk," is the *possessive* case.

Who is the nominative form. *Who* is therefore used in such environments as

[11] The passersby *who* have helped the police with the arrest will be rewarded

[12] The sailor *who* brought us our breakfast was unbelievably polite

In each of the two relative clauses here, "who have helped the police with the arrest" and "who brought us our breakfast," "who" is the *subject* of its clause. If we were to replace "who" with personal pronouns, making the relative clauses into full sentences, these pronouns would have the forms "they" (in [11]) and "he" (in [12]), both nominative because they are subjects of the verbs "have helped" and "brought" respectively.

Relative pronouns occur in other case functions also. There is, however, one important restriction: *Regardless of their case, relative pronouns always occupy a position at or near the beginning of the relative clause, within the first phrase of the clause.* So even when a relative pronoun is the direct object of the verb, it will still appear in the initial position in its clause:

[13] The courier *whom they sent with the message* was stopped at the border

Here the relative clause "whom they sent with the message" is a transitive clause with a direct object, "whom." *Whom* is the **objective** form of the relative pronoun *who*. The diagram of [13] shows that "whom" functions as the direct object of "sent" even though it is at the beginning of the clause:

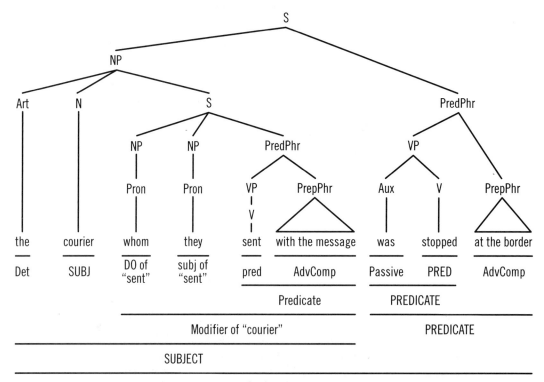

Diagram 13B. Diagramming relative clauses.

Note that if we were to convert the relative clause into a main clause, the personal pronoun that would appear in place of "the courier" would have the objective form "him" or "her," for example:

[13]′ They sent *him* with the message

There is also a **possessive** case form *whose*, which is common to both *who* and *which*. It is illustrated by [14], with the human head noun "tenants," and [15], with the nonhuman head noun "mountains":

[14] The tenants whose apartments had been condemned were demonstrating

[15] The mountains whose peaks you can see from the house are the Cascades

In [15], "whose peaks" is the direct object of the verb "see"; "whose" is a pronoun functioning as a determiner of the noun "peaks."

We have now encountered all of the forms of the *wh*-relative pronouns. They can be summed up as follows:

	HUMAN HEAD NOUN	**NONHUMAN HEAD NOUN**
Nominative	*who*	*which*
Objective	*whom*	*which*
Possessive	*whose*	*whose*

Remember that the choice between the *which* column and the *who* column depends on whether the head noun is human or nonhuman. The choice of the *case* (nominative, objective, or possessive) depends on what function the relative pronoun has *in its own clause*.

13.4 Relative Clauses Based on Prepositional Complements

The relative pronoun may be the complement of a preposition inside the relative clause, as in

[16] The buildings and monuments *past which* the procession moved were strung with ribbons and lights

[17] The audience *to whom* these words were addressed was unusually receptive

The second of these two sentences is diagrammed as follows:

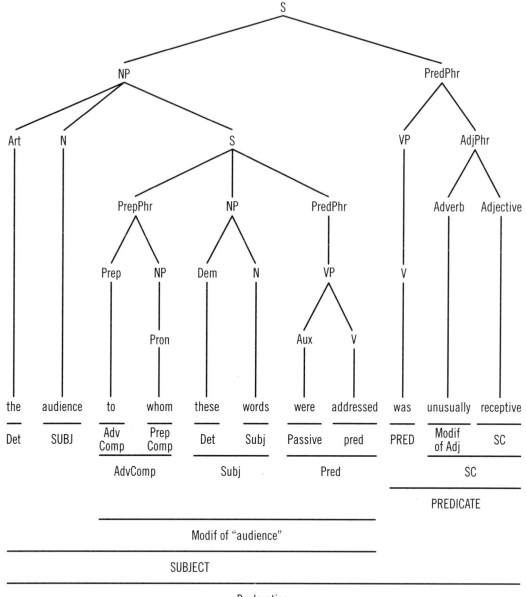

Diagram 13C.   Diagramming relative clauses as PrepComps.

Notice that when the relative pronoun (*whom* or *which*) is the complement of a preposition, the formal written style allows the preposition to accompany it. Marooning the preposition is possible, as in the following, but would result, in the view of some stylists, in a slightly less formal style:

[16]′ The buildings and monuments which the procession moved *past* were strung with ribbons and lights

[17]′ The audience whom these words were addressed *to* was unusually receptive

The last sentence is diagrammed as follows:

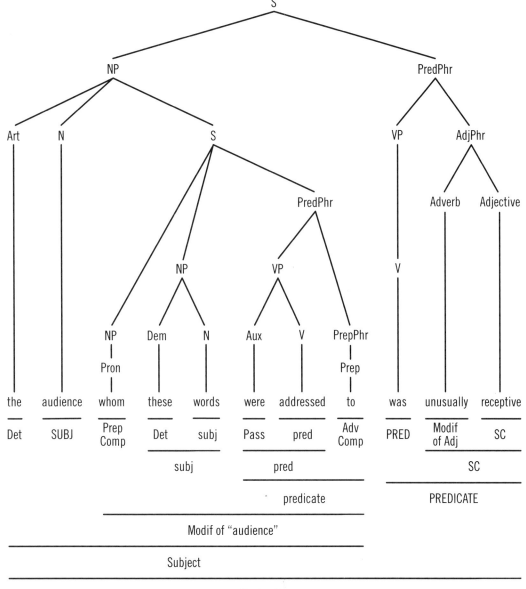

Diagram 13D. Diagramming marooned prepositions in relative clauses.

Notice that, being the complement of the preposition "to," the relative pronoun has the form "whom." The objective form "whom," however, conflicts in the minds of many writers with the subjectlike position of *who(m)* at the beginning of the clause, and nowadays *who* is acceptable here instead of *whom*.

> ### By the Way:
>
> In general, *whom* is vanishing in English. *Whom* is already effectively dead in the spoken language, where it is replaced by *who* or *that*. In the written language it is still found, especially after prepositions (*with whom*, and so on). In spoken English, the combination preposition + relative pronoun is usually avoided ("the people that I went with" rather than "the people with whom I went"). The uncertainty most speakers of English feel about when to use *whom* is a sure sign of its imminent demise. It will have few mourners.

If the prepositional phrase that includes the relative pronoun is itself part of a larger NP, the relative pronoun inside the lower prepositional phrase may remain in place without moving to the front of the relative clause. For example, suppose the relative pronoun is the complement of a preposition that itself modifies a noun, as in

[18] He gave a persuasive speech on electoral reform to the club, many of the older members of which were lifelong Republicans

We could think of this sentence as consisting of two clauses whose full form would be

[18]′ He gave a persuasive speech on electoral reform to the club. Many of the older members of the club were lifelong Republicans.

The word "club" in the second clause of [18]′ becomes a relative pronoun "which" in [18], but this relative pronoun retains its place when the clause is embedded into the NP of the matrix clause. Here is another example:

[19] They sent us a set of china as a wedding gift, some of the larger pieces of which were unfortunately cracked

[19]′ They sent us a set of china as a wedding gift. Some of the larger pieces of the set of china were unfortunately cracked.

It is a cumbersome construction, and one that is restricted to very formal writing. Somewhat simpler alternatives using "of which" or "whose" are represented by

[20] He gave a persuasive speech on electoral reform to the club, of which many of the older members were lifelong Republicans

[21] He gave a persuasive speech on electoral reform to the club, many of whose older members were lifelong Republicans

Incidentally, we have not yet made any distinction between the use of the *wh*-relative and the use of *that* as a relative pronoun. This somewhat disputed area will be dealt with in a later section.

13.5 Some General Pointers on Diagramming Relative Clauses

The diagrams for sentences containing relative clauses all have a complex NP consisting of a determiner, a noun, and an embedded S that itself has the same structure as that of a declarative sentence. Some details:

- The three parts of the complex NP are exhaustively dominated by NP; there is no *phrase* consisting only of the noun and its determiner without the S.
- The chief difference between the embedded S and a matrix sentence is that in the embedded S, the relative pronoun must be *part of the phrase that begins the clause* no matter what its function. So even a direct object relative pronoun must be the first item in the relative clause (see 13.9).
- Notice that the information that there is a relative clause or a relative pronoun does not appear explicitly in the diagram. The configuration of lines and the function label "modifier" under the embedded S adequately supply this information.

13.6 Restrictive and Nonrestrictive Relative Clauses

Consider the following two sentences:

[22] The planets of the solar system whose orbits lie between Jupiter and the sun are known as the inner planets

[23] The Commonwealth of Pennsylvania, whose capital is Harrisburg, is full of historical interest for the educated tourist

There are two relative clauses, "whose orbits lie between Jupiter and the sun" and "whose capital is Harrisburg." Notice that in [23] the relative clause is set off with commas, whereas in [22] there is no punctuation of the relative clause. Relative clauses like that in [22] are known as **restrictive** relative clauses, and relative clauses like those in [23] are **nonrestrictive** relative clauses.

A restrictive relative clause, as the name suggests, restricts or limits the head noun in some way. In [22], it is not being claimed that the planets of the solar system are known as the inner planets; rather, only those with particular orbits are so called. But in [23], which contains a nonrestrictive relative clause, it is asserted that the Commonwealth of Pennsylvania is full of historical interest for the educated tourist. That its capital is Harrisburg has no effect on how the rest of the sentence is interpreted. We could answer [22] in response to a question like *Which planets are known as the inner planets?* But [23] is not understood as an answer to *Which Commonwealth of Pennsylvania is full of interest for the educated tourist?* Instead, "whose capital is Harrisburg" simply adds a bit more information to "the Commonwealth of Pennsylvania." A non-restrictive relative clause can always be replaced with a coordinated clause without any loss of meaning; compare [24a] and [24b], which mean the same, with [25a] and [25b], which do not mean the same:

[24] (a) The Commonwealth of Pennsylvania, whose capital is Harrisburg, is full of historical interest for the educated tourist

  (b) The Commonwealth of Pennsylvania is full of historical interest for the educated tourist, and its capital is Harrisburg *(means the same as [24a])*

[25] (a) The planets of the solar system whose orbits lie between Jupiter and the sun are known as the inner planets

  (b) The planets of the solar system are known as the inner planets, and their orbits lie between Jupiter and the sun *(does not mean the same as [25a])*

The distinction has other consequences in addition to the use or non-use of commas. Only in the restrictive relative clause can the *wh*-relative pronoun be replaced by *that:*

[26] The citizens of Pittsburgh who had failed to pay their taxes in 1991 were ordered to appear in court

[26]′ The citizens of Pittsburgh that had failed to pay their taxes in 1991 were ordered to appear in court

[27] The decision to continue classes after Christmas disappointed the students, who had been looking forward to the vacation

[27]′ *The decision to continue classes after Christmas disappointed the students, that had been looking forward to the vacation

Furthermore, in restrictive relative clauses the relative pronoun can under some circumstances be omitted. We will return to this point shortly.

Relative Clauses That Refer to a Whole Clause

A relative clause that refers to an entire main clause, rather than just one noun, is always nonrestrictive and must use the relative pronoun *which:*

[28] The mayor and the chief of police decided to permit the parade to take place, *which infuriated the community*

Here again, because the relative clause here does not *restrict* a noun, but is an add-on to the main clause, relative clauses of this kind have much in common with coordinated clauses; [28], for example, could be expressed with very little difference as

[28]′ The mayor and the chief of police decided to permit the parade to take place, *and this infuriated the community*

Wh-Relatives in Restrictive Clauses

Because *that* can only be used in restrictive relative clauses, the converse rule is sometimes asserted: that the *wh*-relative pronouns *who* and *which* must *not* be used in restrictive relative clauses. According to this "rule," sentences like

[29] The citizens of Pittsburgh who had failed to pay their taxes in 1991 were ordered to appear in court

would be ungrammatical with *who*.

There are a number of problems with the *who/that* "rule." It has no historical validity, but is an artificial rule made up quite recently, apparently to guide editors who are uncomfortable with the idea that the choice is a stylistic rather than a grammatical one. It is not grounded in the usage of good writers, but only in arbitrary regulation. And it has the further disadvantage that it simply does not work, since *that* lacks a possessive form; there is no

[30] *The planets of the solar system that's orbits lie between Jupiter and the sun are known as the inner planets

Here there is no choice but to use the *wh*-relative pronoun *whose*, even though the clause is restrictive. So defenders of the *who/that* rule must add the proviso "except when the relative pronoun is possessive." Furthermore, *that* cannot be used as the complement of a preposition:

[31] *The audience to that these words were addressed was unusually receptive

Therefore yet another limitation must be added: "and except when the relative pronoun is preceded by a preposition."

It seems far simpler, and consistent with actual usage in the written standard, to assume that *that* and *which/who* are both permissible in restrictive relative clauses, but that only *which/who* should be used in nonrestrictive clauses.

By the Way:

In *American Usage and Style: The Consensus*, page 378, Roy Copperud notes that "*which* is often used to introduce restrictive clauses ('We attended the reception which followed the concert'), and this cannot be considered an error."

13.7 Zero Relative Pronoun

In some circumstances, the relative pronoun is omitted altogether. These circumstances are

• the clause is restrictive, and

- the (absent) relative pronoun would be the direct object of its clause, or the complement of a marooned preposition.

In the following examples, pronounless relative clauses are in italics, and the equivalent sentences using the *that* relative are given for comparison:

[32] (a) The medication *the doctor prescribed* had serious side effects

    (b) The medication that the doctor prescribed had serious side effects

[33] (a) The bus *they were traveling in* collided with a pickup truck

    (b) The bus that they were traveling in collided with a pickup truck

13.8 Elliptical Relative Clauses

Certain kinds of modifying expressions are often regarded as relative clauses that have undergone ellipsis of the relative pronoun and the verb *to be*. Here are examples, with the elliptical relative clause in italics.

[34] Tourists *visiting the shrine* can now reach the summit in the newly built cable car

[35] Applicants *being considered for the doctoral program* must submit their GRE scores

[36] An article *published in 1905* presented the theory of relativity to the scientific world

[37] None of the paintings *damaged in the fire* were insured

[38] All items *to be shown at the exhibition* must be certified as American-made

Clauses of this kind are very close to being adjective phrases placed after the head noun. Notice that there are several possible functions for the omitted verb *to be*. However, the passive (illustrated in sentences [35] through [38]) is especially common. But what they all have in common is that *who/which + be* (a *wh*-word and the verb *to be*) can be restored without changing the sense. This rule is known, whimsically, as "*WHIZ*-deletion," because typically a *wh*-word and *is* have been dropped.

13.9 Other Relative Pronouns

In addition to *who* and *which*, certain other *wh*-words can also be used as relative pronouns. For example, a *when* clause can modify a word that means "a period of time":

[39] We called the meeting on the day when Professor Langweil was out of town

The *when* clause "when Professor Langweil was out of town" is a relative clause modifying "day." Similarly, a *where* clause can modify a noun that refers to a place of some kind. In

[40] They put up a monument in the field where the demonstrators were shot

"where the demonstrators were shot" modifies the place noun "field."

So-Called "Headless Relative Clauses"

A very similar set of sentences to [39] and [40] can be constructed in which there is no head noun for the relative clause to attach itself to:

[41] I showed them where Lenin had given his famous speech

[42] He pointed to where the soil had been freshly dug

[43] The sunspots explained why our radio transmission had been interrupted

[44] The pathologist was unable to state precisely when death had occurred

Notice that all of these have exact paraphrases with a general noun (italicized) in the position of head:

[41]′ I showed them *the place* where Lenin had given his famous speech

[42]′ He pointed to *the place* where the soil had been freshly dug

[43]′ The sunspots explained *the reason* why our radio transmission had been interrupted

[44]′ The pathologist was unable to state precisely *the time* when death had occurred

For this reason, many grammarians would include sentences like [41]–[44] in the category of relative clauses, calling them **headless relative clauses**. The idea here is that the head of the relative clause has undergone ellipsis. Yet this type of clause is better analyzed not as a relative clause, but as a type of noun clause. A fuller discussion of this kind of sentence is therefore postponed to the next chapter.

EXERCISES

Exercise 13.1

Combine the two clauses, with the first as a matrix and the second as a relative clause. Make sure that you indicate by the punctuation whether the clause is restrictive or nonrestrictive.

1. Their present house is on Cranberry Road. They bought it last year.

2. Teenagers should have their driver's licenses revoked. Some teenagers are arrested for curfew violations.

3. Someone stole the money. They were to pay the rent with the money.

4. The product is unsafe. This company manufactures the product.

5. The people have now left the neighborhood. The letter is addressed to those people.

6. Georgian is an inflected language of considerable complexity. Georgian is a member of the Kartvelian or South Caucasian language family.

7. Human infants pass through a short critical period. They learn the basic structures of language during this period.

8. I have grown tired of my old stereo. I bought my old stereo twelve years ago.

9. There were many voters. Many voters disapproved of the NAFTA treaty.

10. They awarded the person a prize. The needle pointed at a person.

Exercise 13.2

Diagram:

1. The guest whose watch was stolen left the party.

2. A light appeared from the direction in which they were looking.

3. A stranger has identified the woman the police arrested.

4. The house where Beethoven lived can be visited on weekdays.

Exercise 13.3

Identify and punctuate the nonrestrictive clauses.

1. The recession will benefit the public universities whose tuition fees are heavily subsidized by the state.

2. Many middle-class parents who had themselves attended Ivy League schools began looking closely at smaller colleges for their childen.

3. Many voters sympathized with the poor and unemployed who had gained little from the tax break.

4. Academic departments which did not pay attention to the changing needs of the students soon found their enrollments slipping.

5. The airplane and the motorized sled which had been introduced in the second decade of the century revolutionized the exploration of the Arctic environment.

6. Medical science began searching for the key to the control of cholesterol high levels of which were associated with heart disease.

7. Those newspapers which had at first cautiously endorsed the plan now raised critical voices against it.

8. The nightclub refused to admit customers who wore leather or other punk garb.

9. Their new car which had been left outside in front of the house all night was now covered with a generous layer of snow.

10. The president was now working fourteen-hour days which alarmed the White House doctors.

Exercise 13.4

Which of the following sentences contain relative pronouns in clauses modifying a head noun (see 13.9)?

1. She will inherit the business on the day when she graduates.

2. I asked the gardener why our rhododendrons had all died.

3. Have you found out where the demonstration is to take place?

4. The place where they spilled the mixture had turned yellow.

5. The Fourth of July, when we celebrate our independence, is a national holiday.

6. None of us could remember where we had read the story.

7. They did not understand why so many voters had stayed away.

8. The new software can tell us how to calculate the exchange rate.

9. The district where the assaults occurred has been placed under a curfew.

10. We learned from the answering machine when Mr. Harmsworth had left the apartment.

14

SUBORDINATION: NOUN CLAUSES I

14.0 An Introduction to Noun Clauses

The second type of complex sentence we will deal with is that containing a **noun clause**. A noun clause is one that can have the function of a noun phrase in the whole sentence. For example, a noun clause can be the direct object of the verb, as in

[1] You noticed *that they did not eat the shrimp*

"That they did not eat the shrimp" functions as the direct object of the verb "noticed." Similarly, in

[2] They showed us *where the demonstrators were shot*

"where the demonstrators were shot" acts as the direct object of "showed." Noun clauses can also function as subjects:

[3] *That the Twelfth Ward voters continue to reelect him* constantly baffles me

"That the Twelfth Ward voters continue to reelect him" is the subject of "baffles." Noun clauses are **subordinate** clauses in that they are part of a main or matrix clause, rather than coordinated clauses, which are parallel to one another. Noun clauses differ from relative clauses in that they do not **modify** a word in the main clause.

The *it*-Replacement Test for Noun Clauses

There is an almost infallible test for identifying a noun clause: replace the entire clause with the pronoun *it*. If what results is still a grammatical sentence, we have a noun clause:

[4] That the gas station would be closed was unexpected ->

It was unexpected

[5] The warnings *that were given* were ignored ->

*The warnings *it* were ignored

The starred sentence is impossible because "that were given" is not a noun clause, but a relative clause.

By the Way:

We said that the *it*-replacement test was *almost* infallible. The *it*-replacement test doesn't work with the appositional noun clauses we will discuss in 15.4:

The claim *that she was not at home* was investigated.

"That she was not at home" is a noun clause, but can't be replaced with *it*.

Not all verbs can take subjects and objects that are noun clauses. Verbs that can take noun clause objects are usually verbs of saying, knowing, reporting, asking, and showing. In addition, a few adjectives (usually suggesting psychological states such as *aware, certain, unhappy*) can be followed by a noun clause complement. And a small number of nouns can be followed by a noun clause complement, for example, *the claim (that the experiment had been successful), the expectation (that the Secretary of Labor would resign)*. Such nouns are usually related to a corresponding verb, such as *to claim, to expect*.

14.1 Noun Clauses and Subordinators

Noun clauses are introduced by a word called a **subordinator**. Subordinators are also often known as subordinating conjunctions. However, we will need to consider several different subtypes, and so we will avoid the term "conjunction" and use instead this more general label. In example [6] the subordinator is "that." In [7] the subordinator is "where."

[6] The parents expected *that* the school would soon reopen

[7] We found out *where* the auction would take place

That and *where* belong to the two major classes of noun clause subordinators. Those in the first, the *that* class, are known as **complementizers**. The second class of subordinators consists of the *wh*-subordinators. The basic difference between them is the following. The *wh*-subordinators are *inside* the noun clause; they play a grammatical role within the clause. Complementizers, on the other hand, are *outside* the noun clause and do not have a role within the noun clause. The two types will be discussed in turn.

Noun Clauses with a *wh*-Subordinator

Any of the *wh*-words can be used as a subordinator to introduce a noun clause.

> **REMINDER!**
>
> The list of *wh*-words includes *who, whom, which, why, how, when, where, what.* You have now encountered the *wh*-words in the contexts of
>
> (1) open interrogatives, such as "When will you move to Memphis?" (4.2)
>
> (2) relative clauses, such as "This is the house where he was born." (13.2)
>
> (3) noun clauses, as in "They asked him where he was born." (Chapter 14)

Here are some examples of noun clauses with the *wh*-subordinator:

[8] I learned *why he was fired*

[9] They told us *where the hearing was to be held*

[10] We figured out *how they had opened the window*

[11] Ms. Ramirez asked the assistant *what the drapes would cost*

[12] We could not tell *which twin was Irving*

These sentences illustrate the *wh*-subordinator appearing in different roles within its clause. It can be an adverb, such as an adverb of reason in [8], an adverb of place in [9], and an adverb of manner in [10]. It can also be a pronoun, as in [11], and a determiner, as in [12].

The entire noun clause also has a grammatical role in the main clause. For example, a noun clause can be the subject or the object of the verb, as in the following sentences:

[13] *Why Major Reno retreated across the river* has never been determined (subject)

[14] We discovered *where the weapon had been hidden* (direct object)

Complementizers

We have seen that in noun clauses with a *wh*-subordinator, there is a *wh*-word that has a function inside the subordinate clause. Thus in sentences like

[15] They informed us *who would be in charge* of the inquiry

the word "who" is a subordinator, but it is also the subject of "would be." And in

[16] We discovered *where the weapon had been hidden*

the word "where" is a subordinator, but it is also an adverb of place within the subordinate clause.

There are other subordinators, however, that are outside the subordinate clause. Consider:

[17] I asked them *whether they had taken shelter during the thunderstorm*

The noun clause here is "they had taken shelter during the thunderstorm," and the word "whether" does not have a function in this clause. *Whether* is a subordinator that is not part of the subordinate clause, but rather serves to introduce it. It is said to be a **complementizer**. Instead of having a function inside the noun clause, it acts as a grammatical link between one of the words in the main clause (in this case, the verb "asked") and the noun clause. The noun clause that follows a complementizer is the **complement** of the complementizer. In [17], "they had taken shelter during the thunderstorm" is the complement of "whether."

There are three complementizers that can introduce noun clauses: *that, if,* and *whether.* Here are some examples of sentences containing these complementizers:

[18] I do not know if they have reached the summit

[19] Scientists have established that comets are composed mainly of ice

[20] We are trying to find out whether our Little League team won the pennant

Other complementizers will be introduced when we consider adverbial clauses in Chapter 16.

Diagramming Sentences with Complementizers

In diagramming sentences with one of the complementizers *that, whether,* or *if,* notice that the complementizer is the head of the NP which dominates the clause. It follows that the complementizer is assigned the same function as this NP. If the clause is functioning as a subject, the complementizer will also be subject, and so on. The clause itself is the complement of the complementizer.

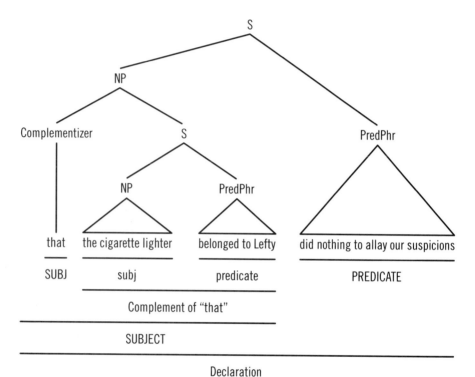

Declaration

Diagram 14A.   Diagramming complementizers.

Uses of the Complementizers *if* and *whether*

The complementizers *if* and *whether* suggest a different degree of certainty from *that*. Consider, for example,

[21] (a) They did not know *that the substance was harmless*

    (b) They did not know *if/whether the substance was harmless*

A typical use of *if/whether* is to introduce what are called **indirect questions**, in which the object noun clause stands for a question that is asked:

[22] She inquired *whether the bus service was reliable*

The noun clause in [22] can be paraphrased as the question "Is the bus service reliable?"

    The use of *if* as a complementizer must not be confused with the *if* of a conditional clause, where *if* means something like "in case" or "in the event that." The following two sentences illustrate the difference (notice that in [23], a noun clause, but not in [24], *if* can be replaced with *whether*):

[23] They asked us if we were ready (*If* introduces a noun clause after a verb of asking, and the clause is an indirect question. *If* is here a complementizer.)

[24] We will stay home if it rains (*If* introduces a condition, and the clause is not an indirect question.)

Clauses like [24] cannot be noun clauses because they fail the *it*-replacement test described earlier (*We will stay home it*). Conditionals like [24] are adverbial clauses, and they will be discussed in Chapter 16.

14.2 Grammatical Functions of the Noun Clause

By definition, a noun clause is a subordinate clause that can function like a noun phrase in a matrix sentence. Just as noun phrases can have different roles, so also noun clauses can occupy various kinds of functions in the matrix sentence.

Subject Noun Clauses

These are found chiefly in the formal written standard:

[25] *That the treaty failed to be ratified by the Congress* was a serious setback to the negotiators

[26] *That the cigarette lighter belonged to Lefty* did nothing to allay our suspicions

[27] *Why the hinge was loose* was never established by the board of inquiry

[28] *What the two leaders discussed* was not revealed in the final communiqué

The clauses in italics function as the subjects of the whole sentences. Sentences like these are usually felt to be slightly awkward in English, especially by writers who feel that the subject of the sentence should preferably be short and light rather than long and cumbersome. **Extraposition** of the subject noun clause, in which a dummy subject pronoun *it* replaces the noun clause, can be used to avoid placing the entire clause in the subject position:

[25]′ *It* was a serious setback to the negotiators *that the treaty failed to be ratified by the Congress*

Extraposition of a subject noun clause is favored when the noun clause is in some sense more complex than the predicate.

The *wh*-word noun clauses can also appear as subjects, as they do in both [27] and [28] and the following (the alternative forms with extraposition are given in parentheses):

[29] *Why their plane crashed* will always be a mystery (It will always be a mystery why their plane crashed)

[30] *That the rescue team arrived so soon* astonished the survivors (It astonished the survivors that the rescue team arrived so soon)

[31] *Who invented the calculus* is a matter of some dispute (It is a matter of some dispute who invented the calculus)

[32] *Where they had hidden the keys* was obvious (It was obvious where they had hidden the keys)

The diagrams of such sentences will differ from the type with a complementizer seen in Diagram 14A. Since the internal subordinator has a role in its own clause, the noun clause cannot also be its complement. The diagram shows the noun clause (S) to be exhaustively dominated by the matrix NP of the main clause, as is seen from [31]:

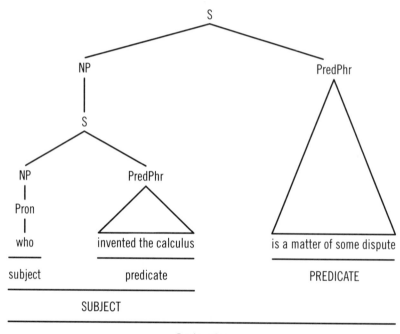

Declaration

Diagram 14B.   Diagramming noun clauses with internal subordinators.

Direct Object Noun Clauses

The direct object is probably the most frequently encountered function for noun clauses. Verbs like *notice, believe, say, report, see, hear*, and others normally take a clausal direct object:

[33] Mayberry suspects *that alien beings have colonized his espresso machine*

[34] Vicki told the children *that the teddy bear had been kidnapped*

"That" here is, as we have seen, a complementizer. However, direct object noun clauses can also have *wh*-subordinators, as in

[35] We all know *who has been getting into the petty cash drawer*

[36] They have discovered *where we hid the bag*

The following diagram of [36] is given as an example of a sentence in which a *wh*-adverb such as *where* or *when* introduces a direct object noun clause.

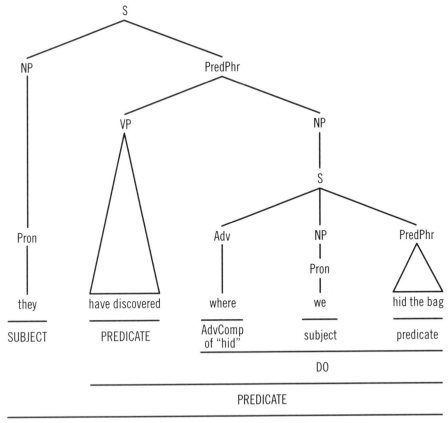

Diagram 14C. Diagramming direct object noun clauses with a *wh*-subordinator.

Note that the *wh*-word "where" is analyzed as the adverbial complement of "hid." It is as if the clause in isolation had the form "we hid the bag where" (replacing, say, "we hid the bag under the sofa"). Because *wh*-words must always go to the front of the clause, the *wh*-subordinator will usually be detached from its verb in this way. The adverbial *wh*-words (*when, where, how,* and *why*) can be analyzed as adverbials or as adverbial complements of the verb.

14.3 Noun Clauses as Complements of Prepositions

Noun clauses can be the complements of prepositions, as in

[37] Debbie was keeping a bottle of champagne in her office *for when she was offered a partnership*

[38] The negotiating team addressed the question *of whether an improved health care package was part of the deal*

[39] We questioned the author *about what the climate changes would bring the world in the coming decades*

[40] Everyone listened very carefully *to how the judge summarized the case*

Diagramming Clausal Complements of Prepositions

When a noun clause is the complement of a preposition, as in these examples, the clause, including its *wh*-word subordinator, forms the NP that is immediately dominated by the node PrepPhr, and is therefore the complement of the preposition. The diagram for [40] is therefore as follows:

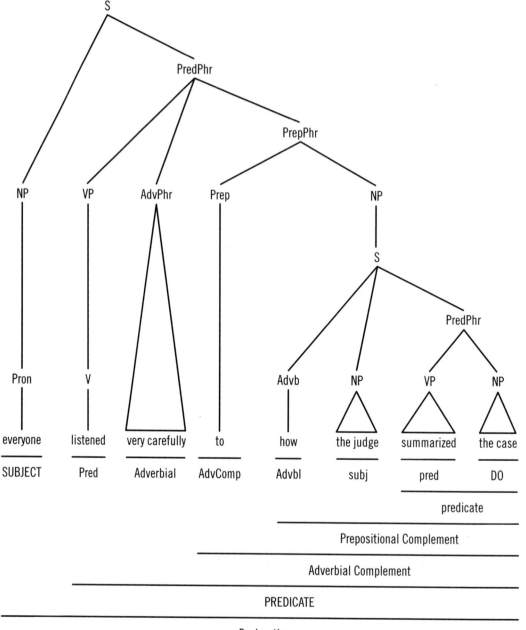

Diagram 14D. Diagramming complement-of-preposition noun clauses.

The *that*-Complementizer as Complement of a Preposition

The complementizers *if* and *that* cannot take prepositions. This restriction raises a problem for speakers of English: how we are to form a noun clause with the *that* complementizer when the clause is to be the complement of a preposition, as in a hypothetical:

[41] *Winnie was worried *about that* there was no honey in the jar

It is often possible to simply omit the preposition ("Winnie was worried that . . . "). But another commonly used way out of the problem is to expand *that* to *the fact that*:

[42] Winnie was worried *about the fact that* there was no honey left in the jar

However, writers who replace *that* with *the fact that* must take care that the noun clause complement really is a fact, or they may be taken to have made an inadvertent confession. A well-known politican is reported to have stated:

"I don't think you can find any evidence of the fact that I had changed government policy solely because of a contribution." (President Bill Clinton, *New York Times*, Dec. 31, 1997, A15)

The proper (and more harmless) construction to use here would be either a simple "that" or a gerund:

I don't think you can find any evidence that I had changed government policy solely because of a contribution.

I don't think you can find any evidence of my having changed government policy solely because of a contribution.

A few nonprepositional verbs also require *the fact that* in place of *that*: *ignore, dislike, approve, admire* are examples. Not surprisingly, these verbs have one thing in common: if their direct object is a clause, the clause must be—or be believed to be—a fact!

By the Way:

It is advisable to be cautious about using *the fact that*. But you should also be aware that language is constantly changing. Sooner or later, *the fact that* will be a standard complementizing phrase and will have lost any requirement that what follows it should be a fact. Clearly, in the spoken language it has already reached this stage, and the written language will not be far behind.

Whoever or whomever?

The suffix *-ever* can be added to several of the *wh*-words: *wherever, whichever, however, whenever*. When *whoever* occurs in a clause that is the complement of a preposition, a question of case often arises: *whoever* or *whomever*?

Note that since *whoever* and *whomever* are *wh*-subordinators, they have a role in the subordinate clause. The choice between *whoever* and *whomever* will therefore depend on its function *in the subordinate clause*, not on its function in the matrix clause:

[43] We will give the prize to whoever wins the race

[44] They will give the nomination to whomever the ward boss selects

Thus in [43] "whoever" is the subject of "wins," and in [44], "whomever" is the direct object of "selects." They owe the presence or absence of *-m-* solely to these facts, not to the prepositions "for" and "to." The diagrams of these sentences show why the *-m-* is absent from [43] but present in [44].

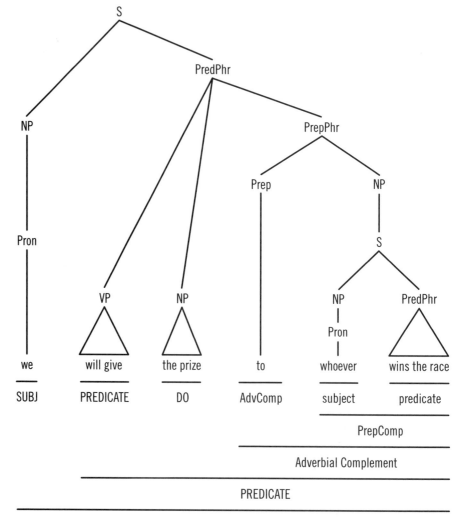

Diagram 14E.   Diagramming *whoever*.

In Diagram 14E, it can be seen that "whoever" is the subject of "wins." In the next diagram, the pronoun has the form "whomever" because it is the direct object of "selects." Notice that in both sentences, the preposition does not directly govern the pronoun; instead the prepositional complement is the entire clause, in [43] "whoever wins the race," and in [44] "whomever the ward boss selects."

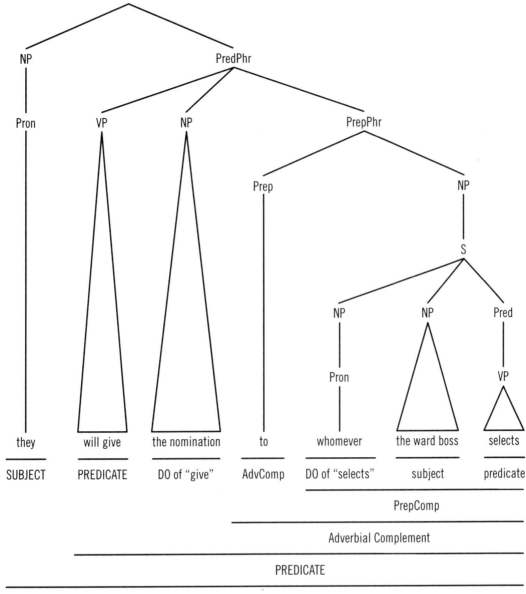

Diagram 14F. Diagramming *whomever.*

EXERCISES

Exercise 14.1

Put the correct form of *who/whom* in the blanks. The sentences include examples of both noun clauses and relative clauses.

1. The players _____ reached the semi-finals were rewarded with Orange County bonds.
2. They will promote _____ ever makes the highest sales in July.
3. They have fired the designers _____ they blamed for the failure.
4. _____ ever the court names as executor will decide on the partition of the estate.
5. Some newspaper columnists criticize _____ ever they wish to discredit.
6. _____ had drawn a pumpkin head on the principal's door was never determined.
7. No one was sure _____ the committee would nominate.
8. The chief trombonist, _____ had recently joined the orchestra, was waving to his mother in the audience.
9. _____ ever wrote this article should be thrown off the Brooklyn Bridge.
10. The police officers _____ have been taking bribes will be suspended.

Exercise 14.2

Complete the matrix sentence with a subordinate (noun or relative) clause using the subordinator indicated in parentheses. Identify the subordinator as an internal or an external subordinator.

1. I asked Jack _____. (if)
2. The reporters _____ were forced to disclose their sources. (who)
3. All the new recruits wondered_____. (which)
4. _____ was a question on many people's minds. (whether)
5. No one could possibly imagine _____. (what)
6. Many people have disputed the claim _____. (which)
7. It was hardly surprising _____. (that)
8. _____ remained a mystery. (who)
9. The suggestion _____ amazed the brothers. (that)
10. The trophy _____ had been stolen. (that)

Exercise 14.3

Draw a complete form-function diagram of the following two sentences (do not use the triangle convention).

1. Ted declared that his neighborhood had been invaded by wealthy outsiders from Philadelphia.
2. That the man who had climbed the fence was deranged was obvious.

Exercise 14.4

Rewrite these sentences using extraposition with *it* in the subject position.

1. That the aliens would invade Earth on Halloween seemed plausible to many scientists.
2. How they had gained access to the safe was not clear.
3. Why "hardly" should trigger adverb-operator inversion was a big mystery to grammarians.
4. Whether the demonstration could be stopped by force was doubtful.
5. How the mass jail break was planned was baffling to the investigators.
6. That the professors had voted themselves a big salary increase was recorded in the minutes.
7. Exactly how the Action Party had funded their campaign was revealed by one of the local newspapers.
8. How many people were taken in by the New York Sunshine scam was tragic.
9. Whether the grammar exam would include a question on extraposition was irrelevant to the students.
10. When the demonstration was scheduled was made known by posters.

15

SUBORDINATION: NOUN CLAUSES II

15.0 Noun Clauses, Part II

We have now seen noun clauses in some of their basic functions. In this chapter, we will consider some of the more complex aspects of noun clauses. We begin with indirect speech, the rules for reporting things that people say, and conclude with nonfinite clauses—that is, subordinate clauses consisting of infinitives and gerunds that do not contain a tensed verb form.

15.1 Indirect Statements and Indirect Questions

The set of constructions used to report things others have been heard to say is a central aspect of the grammar of written English. Indirect speech sentences can report statements, questions, or commands.

Indirect Statements

A noun clause is often a report or claim of some kind, and therefore implies that the author has in mind some original words that were said. A statement that is reported without quotation marks is called an **indirect statement**. If, for example, I tell someone, "The tap has been left on," my report can be expressed as follows:

[1] I told the investigator that *the tap had been left on*

Notice that the present tense of the operator *has* has been changed to a past-tense "had." The tense of the operator in an indirect statement must always agree with the tense of the main clause verb in this way.

> **REMINDER!**
>
> Remember that "tense" refers strictly to the present-past dimension. Do not confuse "tense" in this sense with "aspect" (such as the perfect *have* + -*en*) or with modals such as *will*.

Similarly, the present-tense modals *will* and *can* may appear in indirect statements as past-tense modals *would* and *could*:

[2] (a) "We can see Mount Rainier from our cabin"

(b) I told the other tourists that we *could* see Mount Rainier from our cabin

[3] (a) "Our flight will be delayed for two hours"

(b) I told the other tourists that our flight *would* be delayed for two hours

In [2] and [3], the original statement in the first person is being reported by the same person. Often, however, a first- or second-person statement has to be reported by a third person. When this happens, there is a general removal of the perspective, of which the change in tense is only one facet. Suppose, for example, I hear someone make the following statement over the telephone:

[4] "We can see Mount Rainier from here"

When I relay this report to someone else, I must say:

[5] She said that they could see Mount Rainier from there

Notice that in the subordinate clause three changes have been made in what is called **deixis**, the time-and-place orientation of the original statement:

- the **pronoun reference** has been changed from first-person "we" to third-person "they"
- the **tense reference** has been changed from present-tense "can" to past-tense "could"
- the **adverbial reference** has been changed from near the speaker ("here") to distant from the speaker ("there")

Thus the shift from first-person direct statements to third person indirect statements can be seen to involve a general **distancing** of the perspective.

The shift from first- to third-person required by grammatical rules when indirect statements are made out of direct ones can result in the presence of more third-person referents than can easily be sorted out. Consider the following:

[6] (a) "Lefty gave me the gun when he came to Philadelphia"

(b) Goodshoe told the grand jury that Lefty had given him the gun when he came to Philadelphia

In [6b], we cannot unambiguously recover the original referent of "he" in "he came": it might be Goodshoe or Lefty. There does not seem to be any elegant solution to this problem. A decidedly inelegant, but perhaps necessary, solution is to repeat the full noun phrase as an apposition:

[7] Goodshoe told the grand jury that Lefty had given him the gun when he, Lefty, came to Philadelphia

Indirect Questions

Noun clauses that are the object of a verb of asking and are introduced by a *wh*-subordinator such as *when, where, how, who,* or *what,* or by the complementizers *if* and *whether,* are known as **indirect questions**. What they report is not a statement but a question.

As with indirect statements, in Standard Written English the tense of an indirect question agrees with the main clause verb regardless of the "real" tense of the question asked. Hence:

[8] (a) Maisie asked the inspector: "When does the train leave?"

(b) Maisie asked the inspector when the train left

Here of course Maisie's question is in the present tense, but the *report* of her question is in the past tense because the main verb, "asked," is in the past tense. This is a rule of grammar rather than of logic, since we cannot now tell whether Maisie's original question was "When *does* the train leave?" or "When *did* the train leave?" It is the same problem of recovering the original referent that we encountered with third-person pronouns in the previous section. A way out of this difficulty is to use the past tense of the perfect auxiliary (the so-called "pluperfect") when reporting a sentence that was formulated in the past tense:

[9] (a) Maisie asked the inspector: "When did the train leave?"

(b) Maisie asked the inspector when the train *had* left

The same shifts of deixis (time-and-place reference) that are found in indirect statements are also found in indirect questions. For example, from an original statement

[10] "Can we buy locally made souvenirs here?"

an indirect question might be formed as follows:

[11] They asked the tour guide whether (*or* if) they could buy locally made souvenirs there

Notice again the shifts in time-and-place reference: "we" to "they"; "can" to "could"; and "here" to "there."

Like indirect statements, indirect question clauses can be embedded in prepositional phrases. For example, in

[12] Detwiler asked the officials with whom the union had been negotiating

an indirect question is embedded in a prepositional phrase. The direct question here would be: "With whom has the union been negotiating?" The diagram therefore shows the direct object of "asked" to be "with whom the union had been negotiating." (Notice, by the way, that if there is a clausal direct object, the human object of verbs like *to ask* is an indirect object.)

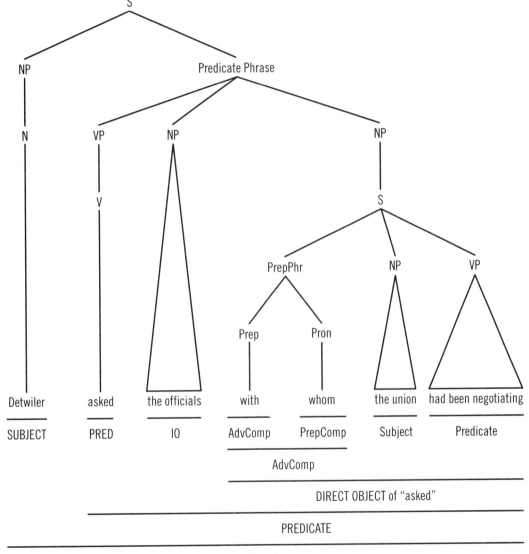

Diagram 15A.   Diagramming indirect questions.

Indirect Commands

Certain verbs in the main clause impose an expectation or obligation on the subject of the noun clause. The noun clause object of such verbs is an **indirect command**. We saw earlier (6.3) that in such sentences as

[13] The new regulations require that you be warned in writing about the risks

[14] We insist that she appear before us in person

the verb inside the noun clause is in a special form called the **subjunctive**, which is identical in form with the base form of the verb.

> **R E M I N D E R !**
>
> The subjunctive is identifiable in those forms of the verb where the base form and the present tense are distinct. These forms are (i) all forms of the verb *to be* (as in [13]) and (ii) the third-person singular of the present tense (as in [14]). If you need to refresh your memory concerning terms such as "present tense" and "base form," reread 6.1.

The subjunctive is found only in the most formal registers. It is far more usual to formulate an indirect command as an infinitive:

[15] The new regulations require you to be warned in writing about the risks

The infinitive is not always possible, however; for example, *to insist* cannot take an infinitive, and so [14] cannot be reformulated as an infinitive.

15.2 Noun Clauses as Adjectival Complements

Some adjectives that take adjectival complements permit *that* clauses as the complement.

> **R E M I N D E R !**
>
> An adjectival complement is a phrase that completes the sense of an adjective, such as *amazed at his chutzpah*, *crazy about his grand-daughter*, and so on. The ones we have encountered so far have all been prepositional phrases, but other types are possible, and here we analyze adjectival complements that consist of a noun clause. See 9.3 for a discussion of adjectival complements.

Examples are

[16] The producer was furious *that Jacques fumbled the pas de deux*

[17] We were anxious *that no one should mistake the wasabi mustard for pesto sauce*

However, not all adjectives that take a complement can be followed by a *that* clause.

15.3 Noun Clauses as Subject Complements

Noun clauses can be the subject complement of a NP joined to the noun clause by a linking verb. Overwhelmingly, this linking verb will be *to be*:

[18] My chief worry was *that the projector would short-circuit during the presentation*

[19] The question on everyone's mind was *whether the axle would bear the extra strain*

[20] The only mystery was *why no one had noticed the missing diamond*

The subject complement clause has a grammatical kinship with the next noun clause function, the apposition.

15.4 Noun Clauses as Appositions

Appositional NPs were introduced briefly in Chapter 9. Expressions like "my grandson the doctor" consist of one NP in apposition to another; the two NPs are being equated with one another. "The doctor" is an *expansion* or *supplement* to the head noun phrase, "my grandson," and so the relationship is not one of modifier to head.

Appositional clauses work the same way. Look at the next three sentences ([21]–[22]), where the italicized noun clause is placed in apposition to a head noun phrase:

[21] My concern *that the projector would short-circuit during the presentation* turned out to be unnecessary

[22] The prosecuting attorney's claim *that the defendant had hypnotized the victim over e-mail* was viewed skeptically by the jury

[23] The question on everyone's mind [*as to, of*] *whether the axle would bear the extra strain* was answered with a loud crack

(In sentences like [23], the appositional clause may be the complement of a preposition such as *as to* or *of*. But this is not necessarily the case. *As to* and *of* are not required here.)

Appositional noun clauses may bear a superficial resemblance to relative clauses, because the complementizer *that* of the noun clause happens to be identical to the pronoun *that* of the relative clause. Compare the following, where "concern" and "claim" are the heads of NPs that contain a relative clause:

[24] The concern *that many of the members had expressed* regarding freedom of speech was taken seriously by the committee

[25] The claim *that the prosecution had made* was viewed skeptically by the jury

Whereas virtually any noun can be modified by a relative clause, only a small number of nouns can take appositional noun clause complements. They are words like *claim, concern, worry, declaration, report*—that is, nouns that refer to a fact or to something said or thought. Often, these nouns are transparently related to a verb of saying, such as *to state* (statement), *to declare* (declaration), *to suggest* (suggestion). Moreover, the *that* of a relative clause, unlike the *that* of an appositional clause, may be replaced with *which*. Study the following diagrams of two similar-looking sentences, the first containing a relative, the second a noun clause:

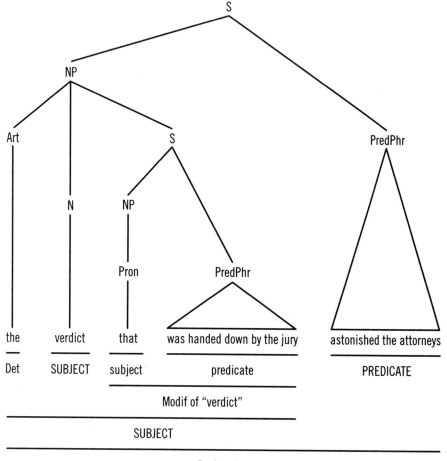

Diagram 15B.   Diagramming relative clauses.

The preceding diagram illustrates a perfectly straightforward relative clause, with a relative pronoun, "that," functioning as the subject of the predicate, "was handed down by the jury." Here "that" could be replaced by "which." Notice that in the next diagram, the clause inside the subject NP differs in two important respects from this. First, the word "that" is not a pronoun but a complementizer (that is, it has no role in the subordinate clause). And second, the clause does not modify the head noun, "verdict," but is in apposition to it. "That" cannot here be replaced by "which":

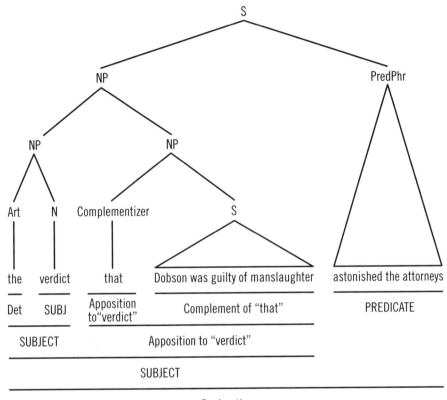

Diagram 15C. Diagramming appositional noun clauses.

15.5 Nonfinite Noun Clauses

Up to now we have been discussing noun clauses that contained a complete verb phrase. But the verb phrase can also lack a tensed verb form and appear as either a **gerund** or an **infinitive**. Both of these forms are made from the base form of the verb. The gerund adds to the base form the suffix *-ing*, and the infinitive is the base form preceded by the preposition *to*.

The diagramming of nonfinite noun clauses is a complex topic that would take us well past the scope of the present book. We will therefore bypass the problem of graphic diagrams of this aspect of sentence structure. We will discuss only a few salient details of the grammar of gerunds and infinitives.

Gerunds

The gerundal noun clause may consist of a single word (the verb with an *-ing* suffix) or a longer and more complex construction. In [26], the one word "kayaking" is itself a noun clause, the subject complement of "pastime":

[26] Maxine's favorite pastime was *kayaking*

By the Way:

Be careful not to confuse the sequence of words "was kayaking" in [26] with the verb phrase "was kayaking" in "Maxine was kayaking in Alaska when she heard the news," which is a progressive aspect form, not a gerund. For some discussion of the progressive aspect and the gerund, see Chapter 6. In example [26] above, "was kayaking" is not a verb phrase but a predicate phrase consisting of the verb "was" and the subject complement "kayaking."

But gerundal clauses can also be quite elaborate. In [27], the gerund "explaining" has a direct object and an adverbial complement:

[27] Albert liked *explaining his new theory to the undergraduates*

The aspect auxiliary *have* can also be a gerund [28], as can the passive auxiliary *be* [29]:

[28] They accused the owners of *having raided the company's pension fund*

[29] *Being addressed as "Sir"* imbued Mortimer with a glow of self-importance

However, the gerund of the progressive *to be* is avoided, probably because of the cacophonous clash of *-ing* suffixes:

[30] *Buster missed the appointment because of *being running in the Pittsburgh marathon at the time*

The modal auxiliaries do not have gerunds, but if there is a periphrastic form of the modal using *have* or *be,* this can be used in a gerundal construction:

[31] (a) *Willing dive off the top board* made Montgomery nervous

      (b) *Being about to dive off the top board* made Montgomery nervous

[32] (a) *Musting admit that he was wrong* was embarrassing for Dr. Immerwahr

      (b) *Having to admit that he was wrong* was embarrassing for Dr. Immerwahr

> **R E M I N D E R !**
>
> **"Periphrastic" means spread out over more than one word. Thus *to be about to* is often a periphrastic form of *will*; *to have to* is a periphrastic form of *must*; and *be able to* is a periphrastic form of *can*.**

Gerunds can easily take direct and indirect objects and adverbial and other kinds of complements. But the subject has a special rule: the subject of a gerund is in the possessive:

[33] *Burridge's giving the assignment to a rookie* raised some eyebrows among the executives

Note that here the noun clause is itself the subject of its main sentence. If the noun clause is not the subject of the main sentence, the possessive suffix on the subject of the gerund is often dropped even in written English, because there is a tendency to think of the *subject* of the gerund as simultaneously an *object* of the main clause (or of playing another role):

[34] The executives were surprised at *Burridge giving the assignment to a rookie*

The version with the possessive is to be preferred here for the written standard, although it is easy to see how "Burridge" can come to be interpreted as the complement of the preposition "at." Other forms of the possessive case are of course also possible, especially personal pronouns:

[35] The prosecuting attorney objected strongly to *their summoning the mayor as a witness*

In such sentences, *them* in place of "their" would be not so much incorrect as symptomatic of a somewhat lower register than the formal written one.

Infinitives

The infinitive closely parallels the gerund and is often an alternative to it:

[36] Maxine's favorite pastime was *to kayak*

[37] Albert liked *to explain his new theory to the undergraduates*

[38] *To be addressed as "Sir"* imbued Mortimer with a glow of self-importance

[39] *To have to admit that he was wrong* was embarrassing for Dr. Immerwahr

The choice of gerund versus infinitive in a noun clause that is a direct object may be conditioned by the main sentence verb and is quite idiosyncratic. While *like* can take either a gerund or an infinitive, *dislike* can (or should!) take only a gerund. *Want* and *expect* require an infinitive, *enjoy* and *begrudge* a gerund:

[40] Bill begrudges *spending* money on his children's education

[41] Brother Ambrose expects the end of the world *to be* sudden, violent, and soon

However, the choice between gerund and infinitive may involve a slight meaning difference that can be seen in the two kinds of main clause verbs. The infinitive tends to suggest something less definite than the gerund and often presents the report in the noun clause as a future possibility. The gerund often implies that the report is an established fact. (Indeed, unscrupulous lawyers and politicians will sometimes find ways to formulate statements as gerunds in order to suggest that they have already been established as facts.) This is surely why so many of the verbs that take an infinitive are future-oriented (*want, expect, like,* and so on).

The infinitive is not possible for noun clauses that are the complements of prepositions. In such cases only the gerund is used:

[42] (a) *Fiona was amused *at to have to explain compound interest to her stockbroker*

(b) Fiona was amused *at having to explain compound interest to her stockbroker*

Like gerunds, infinitive clauses can have all of the usual trappings of a sentence, such as direct and indirect objects and adverbial complements, but the subject has the special feature that it must be preceded by *for:*

[43] *For the mayor to have cheated on his income tax* was a major scandal

This is a good place to note the "split infinitive" rule that an adverb may not intrude between the "to" and the verb:

[44] ?Maggie urged the children to secretly replace the mushrooms with toadstools

In observing this rule, some flexibility is called for. Avoiding the split infinitive may cause more stylistic trouble than it is worth, since quite often the adverb that is moved could now belong to the main clause verb (in this example, with "urged" rather than with "replace"):

[45] Maggie urged the children secretly to replace the mushrooms with toadstools

In such cases (and they occur frequently), liberal stylists will want to ignore the rule, and purists should find an alternative way to express the same idea.

EXERCISES

Exercise 15.1

Replace the blank space in the first sentence with the entire second sentence, using a full clause or a partial clause (gerund or infinitive), whichever is indicated.

1. Trilby accused them of _____. They had put soy sauce in the vegetable ragout. (partial)

2. Yeoville suspects _____. The FBI has planted a tape recorder in his refrigerator. (full)

3. _____ would have made the headlines. Fenworth sailed the *Albatross* across the Pacific in ten days. (partial)

4. Mattie pretended _____. He had locked them out of the house. (partial)

5. I do not know _____. Are you serious or not? (full)

6. The workers were asking _____. What is the real annual income of the CEOs? (full)

7. They asked the farmer _____. May we put up our tents in this field? (full)

8. The graduate students objected to _____. They must pay fees for undergraduate-only events. (partial)

9. The hikers were overjoyed at _____. They could change out of their wet clothes. (partial)

10. I must ask _____. Can we afford this extravagance? (full)

Exercise 15.2

Convert the following sentences into NPs, using first the gerund, then the infinitive construction, and make each NP the subject of the predicate supplied in parentheses. Example:

John complained to the management about the staff's attitude. *(was surprising)*

(a) John's complaining to the management about the staff's attitude was surprising. (gerund)

(b) For John to complain to the management about the staff's attitude was surprising. (infinitive)

1. The patriots flew the Ruritanian flag. *(required considerable courage)*

2. All those children did well in the tests. *(is to the credit of the School Board)*

3. The government has sold the landowners the mineral rights. *(scandalized the voters)*

4. The agency has been listening to our phone conversations. *(would be a violation of our constitutional rights)*

5. You must be available at all times. *(is a requirement of the job)*

6. She will become chief financial officer. *(will calm the frantic stockholders)*

7. The power company was building a dam in the mountains. *(worried the environmentalists)*

8. Rudy contacted the foreman of the jury. *(would have resulted in a mistrial)*

9. The Dow-Jones average fell despite the low inflation rate. *(alarmed many investors)*

10. The district attorney takes the rumors seriously. *(is evidence of his stupidity)*

Exercise 15.3

Make the sentences inside quotation marks into reported speech, using the matrix clause suggested in the parentheses.

1. "The army is leaving us unprotected" (The refugees complained to the commissioner)

2. "I am innocent of this charge" (The defendant continued to insist)

3. "I had already turned on the lights when he attacked me" (The witness testified)

4. "Did you arrive here yesterday?" (Ms. Bridges asked Jenny)

5. "Our travel agent told us the museum would be open every day this week" (The tourists complained to the Visitors' Bureau)

6. "If you had bought tickets for both of us, I could have sold mine at the entrance" (Jill said to her boyfriend)

7. "I was born and grew up in this house, and by God I am going to die here!" (General Bordwehr declared)

8. "We mailed the parcel yesterday from this very post office" (Mrs. Tucker testified)

9. "I told Jack the news as soon as I returned from the hospital" (John assured Lisa)

10. "Do not return their passports until they have signed the declaration" (The chief of police ordered the customs officials)

Exercise 15.4

Identify any noun clauses or relative clauses in the following sentences. Indicate any examples of subordinate clauses that could be either.

1. The fierce determination that we could perceive on the part of the rebels made us anxious to reach a settlement of the conflict.

2. None of us believed the report that the enemy had finally submitted.

3. The monumental sculptures sprang from her deep desire that her work should not be forgotten.

4. The announcement that the concert had been canceled was greeted with boos and catcalls.

5. The warning that one out of three citizens would be audited greatly increased tax compliance.

6. Most of the inhabitants ignored the proclamation that had been issued the previous day.

7. The story that the supposedly deaf conspirators could hear made the judge angry.

8. The swim team listened to the advice that the coach was giving them.

9. The agreement that the union was about to negotiate with the management bolstered the stock market.

10. Much of the research was motivated by a deep belief that nonhuman creatures could not acquire language.

Exercise 15.5

(For class discussion) The adjective *concerned* can appear in two distinct contexts, as illustrated by

1. The social worker is concerned that he take his medication regularly.

2. The social worker is concerned that he drinks too much alcohol.

After analyzing the two sentences, what can you say about the two meanings of *concerned* and the way the meaning affects the grammar?

16

SUBORDINATION: ADVERBIAL CLAUSES

16.0 Pre- and Postcore Clauses

We saw in Chapter 5 that some kinds of phrases precede or follow the core subject-predicate sentence and state an adverbial frame within which the core sentence is valid. For example:

[1] *During the storm* a number of power lines were torn down

[2] Someone had tampered with my brake pedal *before the race*

The prepositional phrases in italics are functioning as adverbials. Clauses can also be used as pre- or postcore phrases. For example, [3] and [4] have clauses, rather than prepositional phrases or adverbs, functioning as adverbials:

[3] *When the storm passed through our town*, a number of power lines were torn down

[4] Someone had tampered with my brake pedal *before the race started*

The italicized words in [3] and [4] are **adverbial clauses**—that is, pre- and postcore phrases that consist of a clause.

> **REMINDER!**
>
> A clause differs from a phrase in having a verb or part of a verb. In [4], "before the race started" is a clause; in [2], "before the race" is not a clause but a simple prepositional phrase.

Adverbial clauses state a circumstance such as time, place, or manner that applies to the main clause or the predicate of the main clause. Because they indicate the time at which something took place, "before the race" and "when the storm passed through our town" are adverbial clauses of time.

16.1 Subordinators in Adverbial Clauses

The "when" and "before" that introduce the adverbial clauses in [3] and [4] (repeating the earlier examples) are **subordinators**:

[3] *When* the storm passed through our town, a number of power lines were torn down

[4] Someone had tampered with my brake pedal *before* the race started

In Chapter 14, we identified *wh*-subordinators and complementizers according to whether the subordinator functioned as part of the subordinate clause (*wh*-subordinator), or was a separate element that introduced the clause but did not have a function in the clause (complementizer). We saw that the clause that follows a complementizer is a complement of the subordinator.

The word that introduces an adverbial clause is a complementizer. Let us be clear about the difference by using as an example the subordinator *when*. Consider the following sentence:

[5] I told Harry when they left

This sentence has two quite distinct possible meanings. One of them is equivalent to "I informed Harry of their departure time," and the other means the same as "At the time of their departure, I told Harry."

We will say that there are two distinct sentences:

[5] (a) I told Harry when they left (i.e., "I informed Harry of their departure time")

(b) I told Harry when they left (i.e., "At the time of their departure, I told Harry")

In [5a], "when they left" is a noun clause, because it is functioning as the direct object of "told." In [5a], "when" is an **internal** subordinator. "When" refers to the time at which they left and is the focus of the information Harry is being given.

In [5b], on the other hand, the sentence states the time at which I told Harry something. "When they left" is now an adverbial clause. It is an element that follows the subject-predicate core sentence "I told Harry." Notice that moving the clause to the front of [5b] does not change the meaning or result in an ungrammatical sentence: "When they left, I told Harry." "When" does not here play a role in the subordinate clause, but merely links the main clause, "I told Harry," to the subordinate clause, "they left." In [5b] "when" is understood as a subordinator that is *external* to the main clause, or a *complementizer,* and the subordinate clause, "they left," is its complement.

In this chapter, we are concerned only with the second of these two possibilities for sentence [5], that is sentence [5b], which means the same as "When they left, I told Harry." We are not concerned with sentences like [5a], which contain a noun clause and were therefore dealt with in previous chapters.

REMINDER!

The *it*-replacement test shows that [5a] contains a noun clause: "I told Harry it."

16.2 Adverbial Clauses as Noncore Adverbials

Adverbial clauses can be placed before or after the main clause (that is, they can be pre- or postcore phrases). Usually the adverbial clause does not form a close grammatical relationship with any one word or phrase in the main clause, and can be omitted without affecting the structure or basic meaning of the main clause. It is in other words an *adverbial,* rather than an *adverbial complement.* (Indeed, we saw in Chapter 7 that adverbial complements are not pre- or postcore phrases, but part of the predicate phrase.) Thus in the following

[6] *Because they had left their passports at the hotel,* they could not cross the border

[7] They could not cross the border, *because they had left their passports at the hotel*

"they could not cross the border" is not affected grammatically by the adverbial clause "because they had left their passports at the hotel." The subordinate clause could be omitted without changing the sense or the structure of the main clause. It therefore qualifies as a noncore adverbial. Let us look at the following diagram of example [6]:

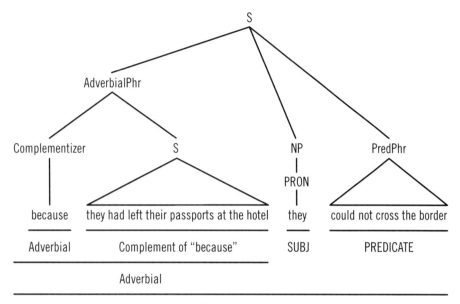

Diagram 16A. Diagramming adverbial clauses.

The diagramming of postcore adverbials is similar, except of course that the adverbial phrase is at the right. Notice that the complementizer "because" is the head of the adverbial clause "because they had left their passports at the hotel." It therefore has the same function as the entire clause. The subordinate clause "they had left their passports at the hotel" is the complement of "because." The phrase consisting of the complementizer and the S complement is labeled "Adverbial Phrase."

Complementizers that introduce adverbial clauses include the following:

- the *wh*-words *when, whenever, where, wherever, whereas, while*
- certain words that are also prepositions: *before, until, as, after, since*
- other complementizers: *because, if, as, although, unless, once*
- a number of compound complementizers made of prepositional phrases or participles, such as *in the event that, in case, given that, considering, provided [that], as soon as*

Here are some further examples of adverbial clauses functioning as adverbials:

[8] *If it rains*, they will cancel the outdoor performance of the opera

[9] *When the bell rang*, the smart dogs began to salivate

[10] *Whereas the Blue Team made fewer mistakes*, the Reds took risks and moved ahead faster

[11] *Wherever local cultural facilities are well supported,* corporate profits are significantly higher

16.3 Finite Adverbial Clauses

It is customary to classify the different kinds of adverbial clauses according to their principal meanings. We will follow this custom, discussing in turn adverbial clauses of

- time
- place
- concession
- reason/cause
- purpose
- result
- condition

Like noun clauses, adverbial clauses can be both finite (full clauses) and nonfinite (partial clauses). We will begin by discussing finite clauses, which are introduced by a complementizer.

> **REMINDER!**
>
> **The distinction between finite and nonfinite refers to the presence or absence of a tensed verb or auxiliary. Clauses that contain a tensed verb or auxiliary are finite clauses. Clauses that do not contain a tensed verb or auxiliary, but only an *-ing* form or an infinitive such as *to leave*, are nonfinite.**

Adverbial Clauses of Time

The chief complementizers that introduce adverbial clauses of time are *after, before, since, until, when, while, as,* and *whenever:*

[12] *After Constantinople fell to the Turks,* many scholars fled to Western cities

[13] Marcy had not seen George *since they graduated together from Emory in the 1980s*

[14] *As the war clouds gathered,* the embassy was besieged by anxious travelers

While has an older and more conservative form, *whilst. Until* has the peculiarity that under some conditions the main clause verb must be in the negative:

[15] (a) They did not cut down the old oak tree *until the family had left town for their summer vacation*

(b) *They cut down the old oak tree *until the family had left town for their summer vacation*

This peculiarity of *until* is connected with the scope of the negative; see 10.2. It is as if the complementizer is really *not until*, but the negative *not* has been moved to the main clause. There is, however, one condition under which *until* can be used without a negative: this is if the verb in the main clause is interpreted as an *ongoing or repeated action*. In [16], *until* in the subordinate clause does not require a negative in the main clause:

[16] (a) Sheriff O'Casey watched the Carson Kid *until the rest of the posse arrived*

(b) Franklin dialed and redialed the number *until at last the night nurse picked up the phone*

A verb like "cut down" in [15a], which reports a once-only action of brief duration, is known as a **punctual** verb. Verbs like "watched," and repeated actions like "dialed and redialed" in [16b], however, are not punctual, and this is why it is possible to have "until" in the adverbial clause. The rule for the use of *until* is, then, that if there is an adverbial clause with the complementizer *until*, a punctual verb in the main clause must be in the negative. (Notice that we could make sense of "cut down" in [15b] only if the action were understood as somehow having occurred repeatedly, as in a nightmare.)

The complementizers that introduce adverbial clauses of time have a well-known tendency to have other functions. *Since* and *as*, for example, may indicate not only time, but also reasons and causes:

[17] *Since we have not received payment for the past year*, your subscription to the *Shining Path Quarterly* has been canceled

[18] You will have to spend the night in my castle, *as the bridge was washed away in the storm*

The use of "since" in [17] obeys an old Latin principle *post hoc ergo propter hoc:* "after this, therefore because of this." The main clause is seen at first as an event that happens *after* the event in the "since" clause; but it comes to be interpreted as an event that happens *because of* the "since" clause. (Some writers prefer to restrict the use of "since" to the time meaning.)

A number of complementizers that are used for time clauses are simple nouns and adverbs that have been pressed into service: *the moment, directly, every time, once, immediately:*

[19] *The moment (every time, directly, immediately)* she saw me coming into the room, she would call out, "Pretty Polly!"

[20] *Once the curtain was lowered,* the actors put down their swords and shook hands

Adverbial Clauses of Place

Adverbial clauses of place are introduced by the complementizer *where* or its *-ever* form, *wherever*:

[21] The traffic moves at around the speed limit *wherever traffic patrols are visible to motorists*

[22] *Where local cultural facilities are well supported*, corporate profits are almost always significantly higher

Adverbial Clauses of Condition

Conditional clauses are characteristically introduced by *if*. The *if*-clause can either precede or follow the main clause:

[23] *If our velocity falls below warp one*, we will have to resort to impulse power

[24] We will have to hold classes during the summer *if the strike lasts for more than a week*

If has a negative counterpart, *unless*, which is equivalent to *if . . . not:*

[25] *Unless Catwoman testifies*, the jury is certain to convict Bruce

In sentences like [25], "unless Catwoman testifies" is interchangeable with "if Catwoman does not testify."

In simple conditions involving present-tense states of affairs, no special tense or modality is needed in the verb phrases of the two clauses:

[26] If the vehicle is over two tons, a special permit is needed

In sentences like [26], no question of the likelihood is raised of a particular vehicle's being over two tons. It is simply a general statement of two mutually exclusive categories: vehicles that are and vehicles that are not over two tons. However, the speaker may present the same state of affairs as a contingency or possibility:

[27] If the vehicle were over two tons, a special permit would be needed

Here the modalities of the verbs reflect the less definite, less assertive nature of the two clauses in [27]. The first clause, "if the vehicle were over two tons," has the verb in what is often called the **second subjunctive**, or **past subjunctive**.

The second subjunctive is used in conditional clauses like [27]. It has the form of the past plural and is therefore distinct only in the verb *to be*. With other verbs, the second subjunctive is the same as the past tense:

[28] If the vehicle *weighed* over two tons, a special permit would be needed

REMINDER!

We have already encountered the subjunctive (see 6.3, 15.1). It consists of the *base form* of the verb and is used in a subordinate clause when the main clause verb is one of ordering, requiring, or expecting:

- **The regulations require that you *be* over five feet tall and in good general health.**
- **The chair has recommended that the committee *consider* this proposal immediately.**

The kind of condition represented by sentences [27] and [28] is called a **real condition,** since its fulfillment is a possibility. (Perhaps the vehicle actually does weigh over two tons.) Another kind of conditional is represented by:

[29] If the vehicle *had weighed* over two tons, a special permit would have been needed

This is an **unreal condition,** since the condition cannot under any circumstances be fulfilled. Unreal conditions have the auxiliary *had* in the *if*-clause and the modal *would* in the main clause. Sometimes the *would* is also found in the *if*-clause:

[30] ?If the vehicle would have weighed over two tons, a special permit would have been needed

Although frequently heard, the usage represented by [30] should be avoided in the formal written register.

Adverbial Clauses of Reason/Cause

Reason and cause are closely linked, and it is convenient to treat them together. The most important complementizers for reason/cause are *because, since,* and *as.* They can be pre- or postcore adverbials:

[31] *Because the winter snow was exceptionally heavy*, we can expect flooding of the river valleys in the spring

[32] We will have to cancel the class, *as the students have not shown up*

Reason/cause clauses have the peculiarity that they can refer not to the main clause itself, but to the *evidence* for the main clause:

[33] Jack is lying, *because his left ear is twitching*

The *because* clause in such cases always follows the main clause (that is, it is a postcore phrase). In writing, such "evidential" clauses are separated from the main clause by a comma.

Adverbial Clauses of Concession

Concession is typically signaled with *although:*

[34] Although Dr. Shooter is a little eccentric, she has nonetheless made some important discoveries

However, various other complementizers, including *if* and *while,* can also be used to mark concessive clauses:

[35] If Dr. Shooter is a little eccentric, she has nonetheless made some important discoveries

[36] While Dr. Shooter is a little eccentric, she has nonetheless made some important discoveries

Concessive clauses are closely related in meaning to coordinated clauses with *but,* as is shown by the following:

[37] (a) Although inflation is low, they have recommended an increase in the prime rate

(b) Inflation is low, but they have recommended an increase in the prime rate

The complementizer *although* is abbreviated to *though* when there is ellipsis of the verb in the subordinate clause:

[38] (a) The summer climate is warm, though humid

(b) The summer climate is warm, although it tends to be humid

Adverbial Clauses of Purpose

The most basic clause of purpose is not a full clause but an infinitive:

[39] Schultz took a job in a restaurant *to improve his Italian*

In order to can substitute for *to*. The deleted subject of the adverbial clause is understood to be the same as the subject of the main clause. When the subject is different, it must be introduced by *for:*

[40] His father worked at three jobs *in order for him to go to college.*

Nonfinite clauses are discussed in more detail in 16.4. The use of a full clause with a *that* complementizer is very formal, and is also found mainly when the adverbial clause has a different subject from the main clause:

[41] *In order that the rural audiences might appreciate his humor,* Rolf told some of his jokes in the local dialect

If the subordinate clause is a full clause, the complementizer (or complementizer phrase) is *in order that* or *so that*. As in [41], the operator in the verb phrase in a full clause of purpose is often a modal such as *might* or *should*. The reason for the modal is that a purpose clause does not express something that actually happened, but something that is intended. The usual modals are *can* and *may* in the present, and *could* and *might* in the past.

Adverbial Clauses of Result

Result clauses look somewhat like purpose clauses and can even use the same complementizer *so that*:

[42] The summit party had spent the past few weeks at a high altitude, *so that they were already acclimatized for the final ascent*

Alternative complementizers are *so* and the more elaborate *with the result that*. *So* alone has much in common with a coordinator and is usually classified as one:

[43] The summit party had spent the past few weeks at a high altitude, so they were already acclimatized for the final ascent

Loosely related clauses such as those in [43] should therefore be diagrammed in the same way as *and* clauses (see Chapter 12), with *so* identified as a coordinator. However, it should also be noted that in the written standard *so* without *that* is slightly suspect, and is somewhat less formal than *so that*.

Two important differences between result clauses and purpose clauses are

- The purpose clause can either precede or follow the main clause, whereas the result clause can only follow:

  [44] *So that they were already acclimatized for the final ascent, the summit party had spent the past few weeks at a high altitude

  This sentence is not possible with a result meaning. Note that the natural interpretation of [44] would be as a purpose clause!

- A purpose clause normally has a modal such as *should* or *could*, whereas a result clause can have a verb phrase without auxiliaries. This difference clearly has to do with the fact that purpose clauses involve future intentions and reasons, rather than accomplished facts.

16.4 Nonfinite Adverbial Clauses

Nonfinite adverbial clauses can be used as pre- and postcore adverbials. (We will not attempt to diagram nonfinite clauses in detail.)

We have already seen the infinitive used for the expression of purpose, as in

[45] *In order to keep squirrels away from the bird feeder*, you should place the post as far as possible from trees and fences

[46] *To make a creamy bechamel sauce*, see the recipe on page 200

As with infinitive noun clauses, the subject of an infinitive purpose clause is preceded by *for:*

[47] In order for the employees to benefit equally from the new pension plan, the retirement age must now be raised to 67

The *-ing* form of the verb can also form adverbial adjuncts, as in

[48] *In lifting the canoe across the shallows*, Muffy had severely strained her right shoulder

[49] *Before checking out of the hotel*, Lefty made several long-distance phone calls

Adverbial clauses of this kind have a predicate whose verb phrase has a verb or operator in the *-ing* form.

In this type of adverbial clause, there is never a subject. (The *-ing* type of nonfinite adverbial clause differs in this respect both from noun clauses and from infinitive adverbial clauses.) Apparently the only exception to this rule is the case of *with* clauses:

[50] *With Ms. Marbles leading the way*, the strange procession wound its way down the cliff path to the beach

However, when the complementizer is absent, a nonfinite adverbial clause can take a subject:

[51] *Professor Weltreise having left for a sabbatical in Slovenia*, the survey of western culture course will be taught by Mr. Urvogel

The subject in the type of adverbial *-ing* clause that lacks a complementizer may also be omitted, *provided* it is elliptical for a subject that is the same as the subject of the main clause. Failure to observe this rule results in the infamous "dangling participle," with its many attendant grammar-class jokes. Thus [52] is correct because the elliptical subject of "having eaten" is the same as the subject of "hiked" ("we"); but in [53], "having" is a dangling participle that does not connect with the main clause subject:

[52] *Having eaten our sandwiches*, we hiked a few more miles along the stony trail

[53] *?Having eaten our sandwiches*, a friendly truck-driver stopped to offer us a ride

This *ought* to mean that the truck-driver ate our sandwiches. In practice even good writers sometimes ignore the rule without disastrous effects. A few *-ing* forms have become complementizers in their own right, and are never viewed as dangling participles:

[54] *Considering he is so short,* his skill at basketball is quite unexpected

[55] *Providing you leave your house before breakfast,* you should easily arrive in Columbus by noon

(*Providing* is not as good as *provided* here, but both are used.)

EXERCISES

Exercise 16.1

Identify the function of *where* or *when* in each of the following sentences as (i) complementizer for adverbial clause or noun clause, (ii) relative pronoun, or (iii) *wh*-subordinator for noun clause.

1. I asked them where they had hidden the gloves.
2. Unscrupulous dealers sold the icons in the West, where museums did not always ask questions.
3. Assistance can sometimes be obtained from the federal government when financial support for small businesses is not available locally.
4. Mr. Edgeworth was late for the meeting where the firm's bankruptcy was announced.
5. The stretch of rail where the accident had occurred had not been checked by the engineers.
6. An e-mail message informed us when the lecture would take place.
7. We especially enjoyed the place in his autobiography where he discussed his first marriage.
8. When the fourth earthquake hit, the family decided to move back to Rhode Island.
9. Gilbert knew of a restaurant where they served vegetarian food.
10. We remembered the last occasion when Ms. Redfern invited us to lunch.

Exercise 16.2

Identify the function of *if* as (i) conditional, (ii) concessive, or (iii) complementizer for noun clause.

1. If our boat is small, it is nonetheless seaworthy.
2. I asked them if he could come with us.
3. If the blizzard dies down, we can continue our journey.

4. We would be obliged if you would write a letter to your member of Congress supporting our position.

5. If you think your government is an overblown bureaucracy, you should live for a year in Ruritania.

6. None of us could discover if they really believed in the existence of Bigfoot.

7. The union organizers would be pleased if the rank-and-file members found a cause to fight for.

8. The attorney asked if anyone had already seen the will.

9. If the verb is transitive, its subject must have the ergative case suffix.

10. If conditions in the federal penitentiary are grim, they are better than those in the county jail.

Exercise 16.3

Diagram the following sentences.

1. Since your grant has been approved by the foundation, you should now apply for a leave of absence.

2. The firefighters could not escape because the flames had come up the valley behind them.

Exercise 16.4

Identify the type of adverbial clause.

1. Wherever the funny man with the flute went, he was followed by crowds of children.

2. The defense attorney objected whenever the footprints were mentioned.

3. It had rained heavily the night before, so that the field was now a quagmire.

4. Granted that we do not have the cultural opportunities of a larger city, the prosperity and neighborliness of Oldville keep our population stable.

5. The instant he said the words "property values," a hush fell over the auditorium.

6. The French horn players were placed offstage so that the music would have the distant quality the composer was striving for.

7. The negotiators cannot change this condition for the simple reason that their mandate explicitly forbids it.

8. Provided you arrive in Sacramento on the 14th, you are free to take any route you like.

9. She has argued her case well, considering she has had no legal training.

10. So as to cover themselves against a flood, they had purchased multiple policies.

Exercise 16.5

(For class discussion) The following sentences, which include both compound and complex sentences, are anomalous in some way. Explain the anomalies in grammatical terms. How would you improve them?

1. Although her propeller shaft had snapped and her rudder had splintered, the fishing boat was drifting helplessly in the high seas.

2. That the end was lost to view over the horizon, the line of people in front of the palace was so long.

3. The voters considered it imperative that the deficit was reduced.

4. Geraldine tore the page out of her diary until a faint light on the horizon heralded the dawn.

5. If Lincoln lost the election, the Southern states would not have seceded.

6. If they would not have noticed the leak in time, the boat would have sunk.

7. If Elsie Goodenough was chair of the board, we would see a more favorable reaction from the stockholders.

8. But the tickets were definitely missing, in desperation we searched through every inch of our suitcases.

9. The legislators were relying on that the inflation rate would remain low.

10. The tourists had expected visiting Angkor Wat before they left.

17

GRAMMAR AND DISCOURSE

17.0 Grammar and Discourse

We began this course with the premise that grammar was the study of sentence structure, and that a sentence was completely analyzed once we had identified the phrases of which it was composed and seen the rules for putting these phrases together into a correct sentence.

From time to time, however, we have seen hints that there is something more to the various constructions we have diagrammed. We saw, for example, that sentences are often correct for one register (level of formality) but incorrect for another. This means that we may not be able to reject a sentence as absolutely wrong, but only as wrong for the style of writing at which we are aiming; there may be other styles for which the sentence is completely appropriate. We have seen, too, that some rules of grammar are disputed. That is to say, good writers may disagree about whether a given sentence is grammatical, and usage may be in flux. And we have seen sometimes how context can influence which grammatical construction is chosen for the best stylistic effect.

In this final chapter, we will look at some more ways in which discourse can be seen to affect the choice of a grammatical construction. By "discourse" we mean two or more sentences put together to make a meaningful text. Each of the sentences in a text has a **context**, the other sentences that make up the text. A sentence can be perfectly grammatical and yet inappropriate for its context. The mistake that has been made in writing a correct but inappropriate sentence is not a grammatical one but a *stylistic* one. This chapter can be seen as a transition into the wider questions of style that follow the study of grammar.

A simple example of the way discourse influences our grammatical decisions is the choice of a lexical noun or a pronoun. On the face of it there is nothing wrong with the sentence

[1] Steve's doctor had prescribed a sedative

But if there is an immediately preceding sentence or coordinate clause in which "Steve's doctor" is also the subject, we need to replace "Steve's doctor" in [1] with a pronoun. Instead of

[2] ?Steve's doctor had examined him that morning. Steve's doctor had prescribed a sedative

we should therefore write:

[3] Steve's doctor had examined him that morning. She had prescribed a sedative

Pronominalization, the replacement of a lexical noun with a pronoun, is one of the grammatical effects that derives from discourse context. We will consider a small number of examples from a field that is currently the subject of much important research in linguistics.

17.1 Balancing Information

Like all languages, Written English is acutely sensitive to the way information is delivered in a sentence. New and important information is kept distinct from old and less important information. Suppose, for example, I am asked the following question:

[4] When do the street lights come on?

I might answer, using a full sentence:

[5] The street lights come on *at four o'clock*

Clearly the phrase that supplies the answer to the question is the most important one, and it is the one that contains new information: "at four o'clock." In sentence [5], "the street lights come on" is uninformative (old) because it merely repeats part of the question sentence [4].

But to answer the question [4] with:

[6] ?At four o'clock the street lights come on

would be quite odd. The reason for its oddness is that speakers of English expect that if the answer to a question is contained in an adverbial, the adverbial will precede rather than follow the core.

This expectation by English speakers is part of a much more general stylistic principle. This general principle is

Older information goes closer to the start of the sentence; newer information goes closer to the end.

Or:

Start———>OLDER———>NEWER———>End

Against this ideal picture stands the fact that the order of words in English is to a large extent fixed by grammatical rules. (This is much less true, for example, of Latin and Russian.) In English the subject *must* come before the verb, and the verb must come before the indirect and direct objects and any adverbial complements. Prepositional complements *must* follow the preposition. And so on. The relatively fixed word order of English works against the ideal word order suggested by the general principle given above. We can't just arrange the words so that the older information comes first and the newer last.

There are several ways of getting around this difficulty in English.

Intonation

Words that convey new information can be pronounced louder and at a higher pitch than words that convey older, more redundant information. It is true that written words do not normally show the differences in loudness and pitch in different parts of a sentence, but the use of special typefaces such as italics and capital letters can help. In sentences like

[7] *Mary* carried the suitcases

the subject is written in italics, to indicate to us that it is unexpected that Mary should have carried the suitcases. In sentences of this kind, the newer, more emphatic information comes first, and, when spoken out loud, is said louder and with a special intonation (identified to the reader in this example by the use of italics). Special fonts are not always used, however; if they were, we would have unsightly printed pages in which every sentence contained two or more distinct typefaces. Experienced readers of English learn to identify the positions of emphasis in a written sentence by their understanding of the context. And good writers of English learn to craft their sentences in such a way as to convey to the reader unambiguously how new and old information are distributed.

Word Order

Although word order is generally inflexible in English, a few options do exist. For example, as we saw in the previous discussion, we can usually choose whether to place a prepositional phrase before or after the core sentence. We can also place a direct object before or after the preposition of a phrasal verb (that is, we can say either "I pumped up the tires" or "I pumped the tires up"). Word order change, however, is a rather minor option in English.

Special Grammatical Constructions

By far the most important means of expressing the old-new distinction in an

English sentence is by means of special grammatical constructions. We will deal with several of these in the present chapter. It should be borne in mind, however, that we are venturing into the realm of style, and no exhaustive treatment can be offered in this book. Our presentation of style is limited to a few of the areas of English where grammar reflects distinct stylistic options.

17.2 New and Old Information in the English Sentence

Let us look at a few of the ways that English deals with the distinction between new and old information in its sentence structure.

Definite and Indefinite Articles

Because of the overwhelming frequency of the articles *the* and *a/an* in texts, the discourse functions of these words are difficult to pin down. One important use of the articles, however, is to indicate that a noun is old to the discourse (*the*) or new to the discourse (*a/an*). In

[8] *The* fire in the museum destroyed *a* painting by Van Dyck

the reader is told that the fire has already been mentioned before, and that the painting has not been mentioned before. By reversing the positions of *the* and *a* the opposite effect is gained:

[9] *A* fire in the museum destroyed *the* painting by Van Dyck

The reader now gets the impression that the fire has not been mentioned before, but that the painting by Van Dyck is already familiar. The definite article *the*, then, signals that the noun it precedes is known to both the reader and the writer—that is, it is old. The indefinite article *a/an*, on the other hand, suggests that the writer is introducing the noun for the first time, and that the writer has reason to believe the reader isn't familiar with this item. The indefinite article introduces items that are new.

Although it is the most frequent, the definite article is not the only means for signaling definiteness. The possessive pronouns *my, your, his, her,* and so on may replace the definite article, as may a noun in the possessive case (*Dr. Hammer's, John's*). The same is true of the demonstratives *this* and *that*. The use of any of these forms suggests that the writer assumes familiarity with the noun on the part of the reader.

Nouns and Pronouns

As we have seen, pronouns are generally old: when writers use a pronoun where they might have used a noun, there is an assumption that what the pronoun refers to is known to the reader.

Since, obviously, when we repeat a noun, the repeated form is automatically old, one common way of using pronouns is to avoid repetition of a noun. But some care is needed here. While a pronoun can serve to avoid repeating the same noun, a problem may arise for the reader when several nouns compete as the antecedent (the form to which the pronoun refers):

[10] The manufacturers of these products have failed to consult consumer groups, and as a result *they* are rarely satisfied

"They" must refer back to a plural noun, but the preceding clause contains three different plural nouns, two of which could plausibly be the antecedent of "they." The sentence can be remedied by repeating the appropriate noun (either "the manufacturers are rarely satisfied" or "the consumers are rarely satisfied").

Phrasal Verbs

A phrasal verb, if it is transitive, has three components: the verb itself, a preposition, and a noun phrase functioning as a direct object:

[11] Earlier in the year the two brothers *had held up a convenience store*

In our earlier discussion of phrasal verbs like *hold up,* we noted that the direct object may appear on either side of the preposition with very little difference in meaning:

[12] Earlier in the year the two brothers had held a convenience store up

Yet [11] sounds more natural than [12], and it can be seen that the principle of old and new information is more closely followed in [11]. *The more the direct object of a phrasal verb is new, the more likely it is to follow rather than precede the preposition.* If we had been talking about a certain convenience store rather than about the two brothers, we might have had the following:

[13] Earlier in the year two brothers had held the convenience store up

In [13], "the" has been dropped from in front of "two brothers," and "the" has replaced "a" in front of "convenience store." Notice that [13] sounds more natural than [12]. But even [12] is better than the ungrammatical

[14] *Earlier in the year the two brothers had held up it

(compared to the grammatical "had held it up"). We saw in Chapter 7 that if the direct object of a phrasal verb is a pronoun, the direct object *must* precede the preposition. We can now see that this rule is merely an extension into the grammar of a general stylistic rule: in a phrasal verb construction, place the direct object before the preposition if it is old, and after the preposition if it is new. Pronouns are always old, and will therefore always precede the preposition. What looked like an arbitrary rule from the point of view of the simple sentence becomes clearly motivated when seen from a discourse perspective.

Active and Passive

We saw in Chapter 11 that, far from being a taboo construction, the passive, when used correctly, can contribute to a smoothly flowing paragraph. In that chapter, we discussed the use of the passive as a device to enable the *theme* of a paragraph to appear in the subject position. If, in an active sentence, the object of the verb is the theme, the passive permits it to appear where themes ought to be—that is, as subject. The principle of old and new information is simply a restatement of the idea of the theme. The theme of a paragraph is, whenever it appears in a sentence, *old*. In

[15] This house was designed by Frank Lloyd Wright

"this house" is old information, and "Frank Lloyd Wright" is new. The corresponding active sentence,

[16] Frank Lloyd Wright designed this house

is of course perfectly grammatical, but in a paragraph where the house is the theme, it is stylistically less preferable because the new information (the identity of the architect) comes first and the old information ("this house") last.

There and the Anticipated Subject

Sentences like [16], in which the subject is new, are possible in English because the subject has a special intonation when spoken aloud. As we have noted, however, intonation is not systematically represented in Written English. Readers must infer from the context when this kind of emphasis has to be supplied. Good stylists strive to make clear in the absence of a speaker where the new and old information is located. At the same time, they vary their sentence types to make for more interesting prose. For both these reasons good writers need to be aware of the range of constructions available in Written English that allow the balance of new and old information to be altered in ways that will keep the reader's attention.

One of these constructions is represented in sentences like the following:

[17] There are wolves in Minnesota

In such sentences there is a new subject ("wolves") that is placed after the verb. The word "there" is a dummy element that serves only to hold down the subject position in anticipation of the true subject. Notice that the verb agrees with the actual subject (rather than the dummy subject) even though the subject follows the verb; thus, in

[18] There is a raccoon on our compost heap

"raccoon" is singular, and so the verb ("is") is also singular. The anticipated subject normally has the indefinite article (*a/an* for singular count nouns, zero for plurals and mass nouns). This fact follows, of course, from the fact that the subject is new.

The *there is/are* construction is sometimes known as the **existential** construction. The existential construction can be used together with a relative clause or *-ing* form to create more complex sentences with new subjects:

[19] (a) There was a bystander who was telling the police about the accident

     (b) There was a bystander telling the police about the accident

Both of these have approximately the same meaning as

[20] A bystander was telling the police about the accident

Cleft and Pseudocleft Sentences

Sentence [20] can be compared to the sentences in [19] in the following way: the subject and predicate in [20] have, in [19], been placed in different clauses. The subject (of [20]) is in the *there* clause of [19], and the predicate (of [20]) is in the relative clause of [19a]. **Cleft** and **pseudocleft** sentences work similarly to provide different clauses for subject and predicate. They are exemplified as follows:

Cleft sentences. Look at the following pair of sentences:

[21] (a) Catherine rescued the cat

     (b) It was Catherine who rescued the cat

In both of them we are told that Catherine rescued the cat; but in [21a] the reader must choose whether or not to emphasize "Catherine," whereas in [21b] the reader has no choice: "Catherine" is unambiguously to be emphasized. The type of sentence in [21b] is known as a cleft sentence, because the subject ("Catherine") and the predicate ("rescued the cat") are split and placed in two different clauses. The cleft sentence can be useful stylistically when the writer wishes to throw the subject of the sentence into relief. The emphasized subject (in [21], "Catherine") is **contrasted** with another possible subject (in [21b], some other potential cat-rescuer); it is a contrastive NP.

The cleft sentence consists of the following formula:

    it+*Be*+Contrastive NP+Relative Pronoun+Predicate Phrase

The dummy subject is always *it*, and (unlike in the *there* type of sentence) the verb agrees with *it*, and is therefore always third-person singular. The contrastive subject NP follows and is modified by a relative clause. The predicate of this relative clause is what is being predicated of the contrastive NP. It is, by the way, possible to have NPs in other functions than subject, such as

[22] It was a harmonica that Heather wanted for her birthday

(compare "Heather wanted a harmonica for her birthday"). But such sentences are ungainly, precisely because the cleft sentence exists in order to give

special emphasis to the subject, not the direct object. A more natural way to focus attention on the direct object is the next construction, the *pseudocleft sentence.*

Pseudocleft sentences. The pseudocleft sentence is shown in the following example:

[23] What Heather wanted for her birthday was a harmonica

As with the cleft sentence, it is useful to think of the pseudocleft as being related to a simpler sentence, in this case "Heather wanted a harmonica for her birthday," in which some special emphasis is given to one of the NPs in the predicate, usually (as here) the direct object. The formula for a pseudocleft sentence of this kind is

what+Subject/Predicate Phrase+*be*+Emphasized NP

In the pseudocleft, one of the NPs is taken out of the basic sentence and put at the end of the sentence, the position of maximum newness. The emphasized NP in the pseudocleft may be in contrast with another potential NP ("a harmonica, not an accordion"), but this is not necessarily so; it may simply be placed there for its surprise value.

In [24] below, the cleft sentence comes at the end of a narrative in which the direct object "cat" and the verb "to rescue" are already part of the discourse, and the reader needs only to be told who brought the cat down:

[24] The ladder got caught in the branches and the firemen began quarreling among themselves over who was to blame. Eventually it was Catherine who rescued the cat.

Catherine is here being contrasted with the firemen, who might have rescued the cat but didn't. In the next example

[25] He isn't worried about the assistant manager's resignation, nor the loss of several important customers. What keeps him awake at night is the budget deficit.

the pseudocleft sentence in [25] focuses on the budget deficit by delaying this item to the very end of the sentence and thus placing it in the position of maximum prominence.

Indirect Objects and Adverbial Complements

In earlier chapters we have presented the indirect object as a noun phrase that precedes the direct object and does not have a preposition:

[26] He sold *the parking valet* the lottery ticket

The indirect object "the parking valet" could have been made into an adverbial complement, as in [27]:

[27] He sold the lottery ticket *to the parking valet*

Again it is the balance of new and old information that determines which of these two constructions is to be used. Although the difference between [26] and [27] is slight, using a noun phrase as an indirect object does impart some extra familiarity to it. This can be seen from the fact that substituting indefinite for definite articles results in clear differences in acceptability:

[28] He sold the parking valet a lottery ticket

[29] ?He sold a parking valet the lottery ticket

Many people would prefer [28], in which old information ("the parking valet") precedes new ("a lottery ticket"), over [29], where the reverse is the case. This difference in acceptability is in accordance with the principle of new and old information: old comes before new. A better way to write [29] would be:

[30] He sold the lottery ticket to a parking valet

Prepositional verbs sometimes allow different constructions according to how new and old information are to be distributed in the sentence.

> **REMINDER!**
>
> **Prepositional verbs are verbs that are followed by an adverbial complement whose preposition is selected just for that verb. Prepositional verbs may be transitive (that is, may have a direct object), such as *to deprive someone of something*, or intransitive (lacking a direct object), such as *to insist on something*.**

The verb *to introduce,* for example, can have two NPs, one of which is old and the other new:

[31] (a) I introduced my cousin to Professor Watson

      (b) I introduced Professor Watson to my cousin

In [31a], "my cousin" is old and "Professor Watson" is new. But in [31b] it is the reverse: "Professor Watson" is old and "my cousin" is new. (Notice, however, that social conventions crisscross grammar here—we are supposed to introduce the less important person to the more important person.) The verb *to load* is less sensitive to custom:

[32] (a) They loaded the station wagon with furniture

      (b) They loaded the furniture onto a station wagon

In all such cases, the adverbial complement comes last and contains the new NP, while the direct object precedes the adverbial complement and is old. In a small number of intransitive prepositional verbs, old information is in the subject and new information is in the adverbial complement:

[33] (a) The killer bees were swarming on our back porch

(b) Our back porch was swarming with killer bees

Some other verbs that behave this way are *to teem, to abound, to overflow, to mill, to flow,* and *to stream.*

17.3 Pre- and Postcore Adverbial Phrases

Grammatical constructions may respond not only to the distribution of new and old information within the sentence, but to wider contexts. One well-known example of this is the expression *Once upon a time,* which opens long narratives, especially fairy tales. We will consider here the discourse functions of pre- and postcore adverbial phrases (that is, adverbial phrases that precede the subject or follow the predicate).

Various kinds of prepositional phrases, infinitive phrases, and adverbial clauses can be placed before or after the core subject-predicate sentence. Thus, we can write, apparently with no change of meaning, either

[34] We receive our salary checks on the last day of the month

or

[35] On the last day of the month we receive our salary checks

Yet we have seen that discourse contexts exist in which the one or the other would be more appropriate. In answer to the question "When do you receive your salary checks?" only [34], not [35], is appropriate.

There is a more general stylistic difference between pre- and postcore phrases. It is this: a precore phrase has an effect over several subsequent clauses and sentences, whereas a postcore phrase closes off the current topic and allows a new topic to be introduced. Consider, for example, the following set of instructions in [36] for assembling a bird feeder:

[36] *To make sure that squirrels do not get at the bird feeder,* you should place the post as far as possible from trees and fences. Bolt the protective anti-squirrel hood firmly to the roof of the tray. The wire netting around the climb-proof pole should be loose. See "Choosing the Right Birdseed" on page 5 for advice on selecting food that is less attractive to squirrels.

Here the purpose phrase "to make sure that squirrels do not get at the bird feeder" is a precore adverbial. Notice that what comes after the purpose phrase tells you not just one but several things you can do to keep squirrels away. In the next passage [37], however, the same infinitive phrase follows the predicate:

[37] You should place the post as far as possible from trees and fences *to make sure that squirrels do not get at the bird feeder.* Attach the water bath to the feeding tray before bolting the tray to the platform at the top of the post.

Now, by presenting the infinitive phrase after the core sentence, the writer has closed off the problem of squirrels and permitted a new topic, attaching the feeding tray, to be started.

17.4 Conclusion: Grammar as Control and Opportunity

In this book we have seen that the study of grammar makes us aware of the conventions for writing sentences and can help us avoid what would be, from the point of view of formal written English, wrong and inappropriate ways of writing things. We have also seen that correctness is to be seen in a context. What is right for the variety of English referred to here as Standard Written English may not hold for other styles such as speaking or informal writing, or for specific genres such as fiction. Grammar as it has been presented in this book can be seen as a form of *control* over the conventions and norms that govern writing in formal settings, such as commercial, medical, and academic institutions, and in the written media, such as journalism and book publishing.

But in this final chapter we have glimpsed another face of grammar, a less authoritarian one. It is the face of grammar as *opportunity:* the expanding of our awareness of the full resources of a marvelously supple and expressive language, and of the ways in which we can deploy these resources to bring about freedom of voice.

EXERCISES

Exercise 17.1

Which of the following sentences contain new subjects?

1. A police detective stood in the doorway.
2. The president has decided to veto the bill.
3. We have arranged a surprise party for the graduating seniors.
4. Your guests have arrived.
5. Just before dawn a light rain began to fall.
6. The sun was shining brightly on the red roofs of the farms.
7. My parents had recently bought a summer cottage in Michigan.

8. There were several people knocking on doors in our neighborhood this morning.

9. It was the cost of renovating the damaged rooms that changed our minds.

10. The committee on nominations has asked you to stand for vice president.

Exercise 17.2

Convert the following sentences into (a) cleft sentences, (b) pseudocleft sentences, or (c) existential (*there is/are*) sentences, as indicated.

1. I need a few days' vacation in the Caribbean. (pseudocleft)

2. The Republicans were more embarrassed by the incident. (cleft)

3. A student is waiting to see you. (existential)

4. Several potholes are in the main street. (existential)

5. We found that the earlier results were wrong. (pseudocleft)

6. Toxic chemicals, not a virus, were responsible for the strange symptoms. (cleft)

7. The songbird population was most seriously affected by the new fertilizers. (cleft)

8. By the end of the decade, no one except a few of the older villagers was still illiterate. (existential)

9. Instead the government economists proposed a further tax increase. (pseudocleft)

10. Administrative inefficiency, not the poor harvest, brought about the food shortages. (cleft)

Exercise 17.3

Rephrase each of the following sentences so that, as far as possible, the principle of older and newer information is observed.

1. At his retirement party they presented a gold watch to him.

2. The farmers are blaming unusually heavy rainfall in the spring for the bad harvest.

3. Manfred looked "rheostat" up.

4. The sailors threw a rope tied in a bowline to me.

5. A tidal wave swamped the village in the early spring.

6. He sold a naive realtor from the city his farm.

7. They will provide board and accommodation for three nights to you.

8. Mike has been teaching inner-city schoolchildren from poor families French.

9. Gloria was so disgusted that she turned her resignation in.

10. A recount of the votes was demanded by the losing candidate.

Exercise 17.4

The following opening paragraph of a story contains sentences that are formulated in ways that are inappropriate to the function they serve. Rewrite the passage so that it makes sense and reads smoothly. For example, you will need to change cleft and pseudocleft sentences, passives and actives, pronouns and nouns, and the positions of prepositional phrases. (Do not, however, change the order of the sentences.)

A king of Ruritania once was, and three sons were had by him. The oldest son, Prince Gerald, was the crown prince. In the army through his own merit the oldest son, Prince Gerald, became a senior officer. It was the daughter of a high-ranking courtier that the oldest son married and what they had was several children. Prince Gerald traveled widely in his youth, and many modern ideas were brought to Ruritania by Prince Gerald. There was the second son, Prince Gundolf, who was a quiet man with intellectual interests, and it was he who painted. What was played by him was the flute, and books on literature and philosophy were read by the second son, Prince Gundolf. The second son, Prince Gundolf, had a pleasant and humane disposition. Although the crown prince, Prince Gerald, the oldest son, was much admired by the people, he was the best loved by the people. But if the two older sons were successful, the youngest son was a wastrel and a drunkard. Prince Garth, the youngest son, was a constant embarrassment to the king and to his brothers, and the courtiers despised Prince Garth. When on maneuvers Gerald was away, and what Gundolf was engrossed in establishing was museums, art galleries, and universities, after for days at a time in the taverns of the cities the youngest son, Prince Garth, had disappeared, a sodden wreck, the youngest son would return.

Exercise 17.5

(For class discussion) In Chapter 1 some of the characteristic differences between spoken and written English were discussed. A table of these differences, taken from the work of Chafe and Danieliwicz, was displayed. Turn back to this table and work through the list of features of written language, contrasting them with the features of spoken language. You should find that many of the grammatical terms in these lists are now familiar to you. Find examples of the features of written English in texts from various genres. When do the features of the spoken language appear in the written language? When writers use the spoken constructions unintentionally, does the writing seem immature and stylistically poor?

TERMS AND ABBREVIATIONS USED IN FORM-FUNCTION DIAGRAMS

Functions		Forms	
Adjectival Complement	AdjComp	Adjectival Phrase	AdjPhr
Adverbial	Advbl	Adjective	Adj
Adverbial Complement	AdvComp	Adverb	Adv
Adverbial Phrase		Adverbial Phrase	AdvPhr
Agentive	Agtv	Article	Art
Central Determiner		Auxiliary	Aux
Complement of Preposition	PrepComp	Complementizer	Czr
Coordinator	Coord	Demonstrative	Dem
Declaration		Determiner Phrase	DetPhr
Determiner	Det	Noun	N
Direct Object	DO	Noun Phrase	NP
Generic Past of X	GenPast	Predicate Phrase	PredPhr
Indirect Object	IO	Preposition	Prep
Modal of X	Modal	Prepositional Phrase	PrepPhr
Modifier	Modif	Pronoun	Pron
Negator		Quantifier	
Object Complement	OC	Verb	V
Operator		Verb Phrase	VP
Perfect of X	Perf		
Post-Adjunct			
Pre-Adjunct			
Pre-Determiner			
Predicate	Pred		
Progressive of X	Prog		
Sentence	S		
Subject	Subj		
Subject Complement	SC		

INDEX

Abstract nouns, 145–46
Accents, regional and ethnic, 6
Active sentence, 186, 191, 275
  making a passive sentence from an,
    186–87
Adjectival complements, 163–65, 246
  noun clauses as, 246–47
Adjectival phrases, 49, 162–70
  attributive, 162–63
  defined, 162
  diagramming, 44–45
  as object complement, diagramming,
    81
  predicative, 162–63
Adjectives:
  attributive, 30
  comparison of, 165–69
    adjectives with special forms, 165
    case of pronoun following than,
      165–66
    diagramming, 167–68
    different from/than/to, 166–67
    morphological comparatives, 165,
      167
    periphrastic comparatives, 165,
      168–69
    standard of, 165
    superlative degree, 169
  conjoined, 169–70
  coordination of, 204–05
  examples of, 29
  predicative, 30
  purpose of, 29
  superlative degree of comparison, 169
Adjuncts, *see* Post-adjunct phrases; Pre-
    adjuncts
Adverbial adjuncts, 266
Adverbial clauses, 256–67
  of concession, 264
  of condition, 262–63
  finite, 260–65
  functioning as adverbial, 213, 258–59
  nonfinite, 260, 265–67
  of place, 262
  as pre- and post-core phrases,
    256–57, 258–60
  of purpose, 264–65
  of reason/cause, 263–64
  of result, 265
  subordinators in, 257–58, 259, 261,

262, 264–65
  of time, 260–61
Adverbial complements, 71–73, 119–21
  diagramming multiple, 125–26
  new and old information in the sen-
    tence and, 278–79
  the passive of, 191–92
Adverbial reference, 243
Adverbials, 49
  adverbial clauses functioning as, 213,
    258–59
  adverbial complements distinguished
    from, 71–73
  discourse function of pre- and post-
    core, 279–80
  inside the core sentence, 128–30
  as postcore phrases, 70–71, 191–92
    diagramming, 71
  as precore phrases, 67–68
    diagramming, 68–69
  within the verb phrase, 129–30
Adverbs, 30, 92, 114–15
  adding suffix *-ly* to adjectives to form,
    30–31
  "marooned" prepositions, distin-
    guished from, 32, 114–15, 121,
    123–25
  negators, 176, 179
    adverb-operator inversion, 182,
      207
  uses of, 30
Affirmative declarative statements, 176
  see also Negation
Agentives, 187
Agentless passive, 190–91
Agreement:
  quantifier-verb, 151–52
  subject-verb, 94–95, 136–37
    apparent conjunctions, 208
    conjoined subjects, 208–09
    disjoint subjects, 208–09
ain't, 178
Alphabets, 10–11
Ambiguity:
  agentless passive and, 190–91
  in compound noun phrase containing
    an adjective, 159–60
  indirect statements and, 243–44
  modifying prepositional phrases and,
    170–71

Ambiguity (*continued*)
possessive nouns and, 161–62
*American Usage and Style: The
Consensus* (Copperud), 16, 223
Antecedent of pronouns, 143
Apostrophe, 146–47
Appositions, 172–73
noun clauses as, 247–49
Articles, 33–34
definite, 33
indefinite, 33–34
Aspect, 96, 99–101, 107–10, 243
defined, 99
perfect, 94, 99–101, 185
in the passive, 189–90
progressive, 96, 99, 101, 185
distinguishing gerundal *-ing* form
from progressive *-ing* form,
172
in the passive, 189–90
tense combined with, 101, 107–110
Aspects of Language (Bolinger), 8
Audience and register, 7–8
Auxiliary verbs, 29, 92
aspect, *see* Aspect
modal, 29, 101–103, 107–10, 112–13
in adverbial clauses of purpose,
264–65
in indirect statements, 243
periphrastic form of, 250–51
the operator, *see* Operator
tense and, 28, 29, 96
-verb homophony, 106

Balancing sentences, 194, 271–73
new and old information, *see* New
and old information in the
English sentence
barely, as negator, 179
Basic English movement, 122
be, 93
as linking verbs, 83
negation and, 179
in the passive form, *see* Passive, the
be able followed by the infinitive, 108
be going followed by the infinitive, 109
be supposed with the infinitive, 109
Biography of the English Language, A
(Millward), 6
Branching nodes, 50
British spellings, 11, 97–98
British usage:
coordination of adjectives, use of
commas in, 204–05

different from/than/to, 166–67
have as main verb in negation, 179
idioms, 183

can not, cannot, can't, 178
Cardinal numbers, 152
Case:
of personal pronouns, 135–36,
138–41
of relative pronouns, 215–17
whoever/whomever in a clause that is
the complement of a preposition, 237–38
see also Nominative case; Objective
case; Possessive case
Categories of words, 24–36
adjectives, 29–30
adverbs, 30–31
the categories, 25–26
conjunctions, 34–35
determiners, 33–34
difficulty in classifying a word in isolation, 25
grammatical, 26
lexical, 26
meanings of, 24–25
nouns and pronouns, 26–27
prepositions, 31–33
pronouns and nouns, 26–27
summary, 35–36
variation in defining, 25
verbs and auxiliaries, 27–29
see also specific categories
Category names, 41
Clause(s):
adverbial, *see* Adverbial clauses
complement, 35
defined, 197, 213, 256
finite, 260
main, *see* Main (matrix) clause
nonfinite, 260
noun, *see* Noun clauses
relative, *see* Relative clauses
subordinate, *see* Subordinate clauses
subordination of, *see* Subordination
Cleft sentences, 276–77
Commands:
imperatives for, 56–57
indirect, 246
Comma(s):
in appositional noun phrase, 172–73
in coordination of adjectives, 204–05
in nonrestrictive relative clauses, 221
in precore phrases, 70

with series, 204–06
Comparison of adjectives, *see* Adjectives,
    comparison of
Complement, 49, 78, 231
Complement clause, 35
Complementizers, 35
    with adverbial clauses, 257–58, 259,
        261, 262, 264–65
    compound, 259
    with noun clauses, 229–30, 231–32,
        234
Complements:
    see also Adjectival complements;
        Adverbial complements; Object
        complements; Prepositional
        complements; Subject comple-
        ments
Complex sentences, 212–13
    defined, 198
    with noun clauses, *see* Noun clauses
    with relative clauses, *see* Relative
        clauses
Compound nouns, 158–61
    ambiguity problems, 159–61
    hyphens, use of, 159
    written as single word, 158, 159
Compound sentences, 198–99
    defined, 198
    diagramming, 198–99
Concession, adverbial clauses of, 264
Concrete nouns, 145–46
Conditional clauses, 232–33, 262–63
Conjoined adjectives, 169–70
Conjunctions, 34–35
    coordinating, *see* Coordinating con-
        junctions (coordinators)
    purpose of, 34
    subordinating, *see* Subordinators
        (subordinating conjunctions)
Context, 270, 279
    grammar and, 270
Coordinating conjunctions (coordina-
    tors), 35, 200
    apparent conjunctions and subject-
        verb agreement, 208
Coordination, 198–209
    of adjectives, 204–05
    ambiguities arising from, 204
    disjunction, *see* Disjunction
    of full sentences, 198–99
    on the one hand...on the other hand,
        use of, 204
    of phrases, 199–206
        noun phrases, 203–05

predicate phrases, 199–200
    series of phrases, 205–06
    verb phrases, 201–03
respectively, use of, 204
subordination distinguished from,
    212
Correctness, 12, 270
    of speech, 6, 8–9, 12–13
    Standard Written English and, 8–9
    usage and, 15–16
Count nouns, 144–45
Cyrillic alphabet, 10

Declarative statements, 39–40, 43,
    55–56
    affirmative, 176
    examples of, 56
    negative, *see* Negation
Definite articles, 273
Deixis, 243, 244
Demonstrative pronouns, 143
Demonstratives, 34, 273
    distal, 34
    proximal, 34
Deontic interpretation, 102
Dependents, 49, 50, 162
Determiner phrases, 50, 150, 152–53
    diagramming, 153
Determiners, 33–34, 144, 150–53
    central, 150–51
    post-determiners, 152
    pre-determiners, 151–52
    see also Articles; Demonstratives;
        Quantifiers
Diagramming, 40–42, 43
    form-function, 41, 42, 43–48
        basic example of, 43–48
        filling in functions, 43–44
        pruning, 77–78
        starting, 43
        terms and abbreviations used in,
            45, 50, 70, 77, 283
        tips on drawing, 53–54
    note about, 69
    terms and abbreviations used in, 45,
        50, 70, 77, 283
    tree diagram, 40, 41, 42
        relationships in, 50
    triangle convention for abbreviating a
        tree, 47–48
    underlining diagram, 40, 41, 42
    *see also specific categories of words,
        phrases, and sentences*
Different from/than/to, 166–67

Direct object, 73, 80
    noun clauses functioning as, 234–35
Discourse, 270–80
    balancing sentences, 194, 271–73
    new and old information, *see* New
        and old information in the
        English sentence
    defined, 99, 270
    function of the passive in, 192–94, 275
    grammar and, 270–71
    pre- and postcore adverbial phrases
        in, 279–80
Disjunction, 206–08
    negative, 207–08
    positive, 206–07
Distal demonstratives, 34
Distancing of the perspective, 243
do:
    as auxiliary, 105
    as "dummy" operator in forming the
        negative, 105, 177–78, 179,
        207, 208
Dominates, 50, 77
Double negatives, 179–80

either...or, 206–07
Ellipsis, 62
    in relative clauses, 224
Emphatic pronouns, 141–42
English:
    as analytical language, 5
    categories of words in, *see* Categories
        of words
    origins of, 3–6
    spoken, *see* Speech
    Standard Written English, *see*
        Standard Written English
    word order in, 271
    as world language, 3
    written, *see* Writing
Epistemic interpretation, 102
Ethnic accents, 6
Exclamative sentences, 60–61
Exhaustively dominates, 82, 83
Existential construction, 276
Extraposition of the subject noun clause,
    233

Family names, confusion between posses-
    sive and plural forms of, 146
fewer/less, 16
Finite clauses, 260–65
    defined, 260
Formality and register, *see* Register

Form-function diagrams, *see*
        Diagramming, form-function
Form versus function, grammatical, 41,
    42, 68
Fractions, 151
Fragments, sentence, 59–60
Function names, 41, 42
Function versus form, 41, 42, 68
Future tense, 96
    prospective tense as, 109

Gender:
    nouns and, 148
    pronouns and, 137–38
    styles of speech and, 7
Generic past tense, 109
Genre, 14
Geographical names, 144
Germanic family of languages, 4
Gerunds, 95
    as modifier, 171–72
    nonfinite noun clauses, 249, 250–51
    subject of, 251
Grammar:
    context and, 270
    conventions and changes in, 17–19
    discourse and, 270–71
    as form of control, 280
    kinds of, 15
    as opportunity, 280
    style and, 16–17, 194, 270
    word order in English, 272
    of writing, 15–16
        characteristics of, 13
        grammar of speech versus, 13–14
        usage and, 15–16
Grammatical categories of words, 26
Greek-based alphabets, 10
Greek words, plurals and, 148–49

hardly, as negator, 179
have:
    as main verb, 179
    followed by the infinitive, 108
    negation and, 179
Headless relative clauses, 225
Head of a phrase, 44, 49–51, 163
    function of, 44, 47, 75
High registers, 7–8
Homophony, verb-auxiliary, 106
Hortatives, 61
Hyphens, compound nouns and, 159

Idiomatic expressions, 122

negative, 182
phrasal verbs with idiomatic meaning, 122
if:
   as complementizer, 231–33
   in conditional clause, 232–33, 262–63
Immediately dominates, 50, 77
Imperative sentences, 56–57
Indefinite articles, 273
Independent possessive pronouns, 140–41
Indirect commands, 246
Indirect object, 78–79, 80, 277–78
Indirect questions, 244–46
   if/whether to introduce, 232
Indirect statements, 242–44
Infinitives:
   as adjectival complement, 163–64
   defined, 74, 165
   for indirect commands, 246
   as modifier, 171
   nonfinite noun clauses, 249, 251–52
   in purpose clauses, 264, 265–66
   special verb phrases, 107–10
   "split," 252
Integrated text, 13
International language, English as, 3
Interrogative sentences, 58–59
   closed, 58
   open, 59
   the operator in, 105
Intonation, 272, 275
Intransitive phrasal verbs, 123
Intransitive prepositional verbs, 278, 279
Intransitive sentences, 73
   diagramming, 75–78
Intransitive verbs, 73–78
Inversion, 58, 59
   adverb-operator, 182, 207
it, it's, 139–40
it-replacement test for noun clauses, 228–29, 258

keep and *keep on*, with the verb followed by *-ing*, 108

Latin words, plurals of, 148–49
lay/lie, 106–107
less/fewer, 16
Lexical categories of words, 26
Lexical verbs, 28–29, 49, 92
lie/lay, 106–107
like followed by the infinitive or gerund, 108

Linking verbs, 28, 83–84
Low registers, 7–8
   sentence fragments in, 60

Main (matrix) clause, 34, 197, 212, 213
"Marooned" prepositions, *see* Prepositions, "marooned"
Mass nouns, 144–45, 146
Matrix clause, *see* Main (matrix) clause
Modality, 101–104, 107–10
Modals, *see* Auxiliary verbs, modal
Modification function, 42
Morphological comparatives, 165, 169
Morphological possessive form, 146–47
Multiple negatives, 179–80
Multipliers, 151

Names (proper nouns), 144
need followed by the infinitive, 108
Negation, 105, 176–83, 261
   double negatives, 179–80
   idioms, 182–83
   in other parts of the sentence, 179–83
      adverb-operator inversion, 182, 207
      negative idioms, 182
      negative verbs, 180–81
      negative words, 179–80
      scope of negation, 181–82
   overview of, 176
   in the verb phrase, 176–79
      have and *be* as main verbs, 179
      not, 176–79
      other negators, 179
Negators, 176, 179
   see also Negation
neither...nor, 207
"Network English," 6
never, as negator, 179
New and old information in the English sentence , 271–72, 273–79
   active and passive, 275
   adverbial complements, 277–78
   cleft and pseudocleft sentences, 276–77
   definite and indefinite articles, 273
   indirect objects, 277–79
   intonation and, 272, 275
   nouns and pronouns, 273–74
   phrasal verbs, 274
   prepositional verbs, 278–79
   special grammatical constructions and, 272–73

New and old information in the English
sentence (*continued*)
there and the anticipated subject,
275–76
word order options, 272
Nodes, 50, 77
Nominalizations, 171–72
Nominative case, 217
of personal pronouns, 136, 138
pronoun following *than* in comparisons, 165–66
Noncore phrases, *see* Postcore phrases;
Precore phrases
Nonfinite clauses, 265–67
defined, 260
Nonrestrictive relative clauses, 221–22
Non-tensed (nonfinite) verbs, 29, 93, 189
not, forming the negative with, 176–78
Noun clauses, 213, 228–52
as adjectival complements, 246–47
as appositions, 247–49
basic functions of, 213, 228, 233–39
as complements of prepositions,
237–39
diagramming, 234–35
that complementizer as, 237
whoever or *whomever*, 237–39
defined, 233
as indirect commands, 246
as indirect questions, 244–45
as indirect statements, 242–44
it-replacement test for, 228–29, 258
nonfinite, 249–52
gerunds, 249, 250–51
infinitives, 249, 251–52
as subject complements, 247
subordinators and, 229–33
Noun phrases, 48–49, 135–73
coordination of, 203–05
defined, 135
modifiers of the head noun, 158–74
prepositional phrases modifying,
115–18
simple, 135–53
Nouns, 144–50
abstract, 145–46
characteristics of, 26–27
compound, *see* Compound nouns
concrete, 145–46
examples of, 26
gender divisions in, 148
kinds of, 147–46
mass/count distinction, 144–45, 146
modifiers of:

adjectival phrases, 162–70
compound nouns, 158–61
gerunds, 171–72
infinitives, 171
-ing form as, 95–96
possessive nouns, 161–63
prepositional phrases, 114–18,
170–71
relative clauses, 213–15
new and old information in the
English sentence, 273–74
plurals, 148–50
Latin and Greek, 148–50
possessive, 146–47, 161–63
morphological form of, 146–47
periphrastic form of, 146–47
proper, 144
as referring form, 26–27
Number:
conflict in disjoint subjects, 208–09
of personal pronouns, 93
Numbers as determiners, 152

Object complements, 78, 81, 158
Objective case:
of personal pronouns, 138–39
pronoun following *than* in comparisons, 165–66
of relative pronouns, 216–17
Objects, 73–81
direct, 73, 80
indirect, 78–79, 80, 277–78
Old and new information in a sentence,
placement of, *see* New and old
information in the English sentence
one as impersonal pronoun, 143
"On Language," 16
on the one hand...on the other hand, use
in coordination of, 204
Operator, 104–05, 130, 136
-adverb inversion, 182, 207
do as "dummy" operator in forming
the negative, 105, 177–78, 179,
207, 208
Ordinal numbers, 152

Participles, 163
Particles, 32–33, 115
Parts of speech, *see* Categories of words
Passive, the, 185–94
of adverbial complements, 191–92
agentless, 190–91
the agent of, 190–91

to be followed by verb in -en form, 186

the by-phrase in, 186–87

in discourse, functions of, 192–94, 275

with other tenses and aspects, 186–87

of the prepositional verb, 191–92

structure of sentences in, 186–87

Past, or second subjunctive, 104, 262–63

Past tense, 93, 96, 97–99

(-ed) to form, 97

Perfect aspect, 94, 99–101, 185

in the passive, 188

Periphrastic, defined, 251

Periphrastic comparatives, 165, 167–68

Periphrastic forms of modal auxiliaries, 250–51

Periphrastic possessive form, 146–47

Person, *see* Personal pronouns, person

Personal pronouns, 93, 135–41

cases of, 135–36, 138–39

gender-marked, 137–38

nominative case, 136, 138

objective case, 138–39

person, 93, 135, 136

possessive case, 139–41, 273

Phrasal verbs, 121–26

with idiomatic meaning, 122

new and old information in the English sentence, 273–74

prepositional-, 127–28

diagramming, 129–30

transitive and intransitive, 122–26

Phrases, 38–50

adjectival, *see* Adjectival phrases

adverbial, *see* Adverbials

clause distinguished from, 256

coordination of, *see* Coordination, of phrases

definitions, 38, 82–83, 162

dependents in, *see* Dependents

determiner, *see* Determiner phrases

diagramming, *see* Diagramming; specific types of phrases

form and function of, 41, 42, 43

in grammar, 38–39, 43

head of, *see* Head of a phrase

noncore, *see* Postcore phrases; Precore phrases

noun, *see* Noun phrases

postcore, *see* Postcore phrases

precore, *see* Precore phrases

predicate, *see* Predicate phrases

prepositional, *see* Prepositional phrases

series of, coordination of, 205–06

verb, *see* Verb phrases

Place, adverbial clauses of, 262

Pluperfect, 244

Plurals, 148–50

Latin and Greek, 148–50

Possessive case:

of nouns, *see* Possessive nouns

of personal pronouns, 139–41, 273

independent, 140–41

of relative pronouns, 215, 217

Possessive nouns, 146–47, 161–63, 273

morphological form of, 146–47

periphrastic form of, 146–47

Post-adjunct phrases, 70, 192

Postcore phrases, 66, 70–73, 119, 192

adverbial clauses as, 256–57, 258–60

adverbial phrases, function in discourse of, 279–80

prepositional phrases as, 119, 121

Pre-adjuncts, 67–68

diagramming, 69

Precative sentences, 60–61

Precore phrases, 66–71

adverbial clauses as, 256–57, 258–60

adverbial phrases, function in discourse of, 279–80

adverbials as, 67–69

diagramming, 68–69

diagramming, 69–71

pre-adjuncts, 66–67

diagramming, 68

prepositional phrases as, 119

punctuating, 70

Predicate, 27, 42, 66

defined, 38

Predicate phrases, 49

coordination of, 204–05

Prepositional complements, 31, 42

noun clauses as, *see* Nouns clauses, as complements of prepositions

relative clauses based on, 217–21

Prepositional phrases, 31, 50, 117

as adjectival complement, 163–64

as adverbial complements, 119–21

by-phrase in the passive, 186–87

function of, 115–21

modifying noun or noun phrase, 114–18, 170–71

as noncore phrases, 119, 121

structure of, 116

Prepositional verbs, 126–29

characteristics of, 126

Prepositional verbs (*continued*)
  intransitive, 278, 279
  new and old information in the sentence and, 278, 279
  the passive of, 191–92
  phrasal—, 127–28
    diagramming, 129–30
  transitive, 127, 278
Prepositions, 31–33, 114–15
  examples of, 31
  "marooned," 31–32, 50
    distinguished from adverbs, 32, 114–15, 123–25
    as particles, 32, 115
    phrasal verbs and, *see* Phrasal verbs
    in relative clauses, 218–19
  in phrasal verbs, 121–26
Present tense, 96–97
Progressive aspect, 96, 99, 101, 185
  distinguishing gerundal *-ing* form from progressive *-ing* form, 172
  in the passive, 189–90
Prohibitions, 57
Pronominalization, 271
Pronoun reference, 243
Pronouns, 135–43
  agreement of verb with, 136–37
  antecedent of, 143
  case of, 135–36
  characteristics of, 26–27
  demonstrative, 143
  emphatic, 141–42
  examples of, 26
  gender-marked, 137–38
  impersonal pronoun *one*, 143
  new and old information in the English sentence, 273–74
  nominative case of, 136, 138
  objective case, 138–39
  one as impersonal pronoun, 143
  personal, *see* Personal pronouns
  possessive case, 139–41
  reciprocal, 141, 142
  as referring form, 26–27
  reflexive, 142, 143
  special, 141–43
Proper nouns, 144
Prospective tense, 109
Proto-Germanic language, 4–5
Proximal demonstratives, 34
Pruning form-function diagrams, 77–78
Pseudocleft sentences, 276, 277
Punctual verb, 261

Purpose, adverbial clauses of, 264–65

Quantifiers, 34, 151
  verb agreement, 151–52
Questions:
  indirect, *see* Indirect questions
  interrogatives for asking, 58–59

rarely, as negator, 179
Real condition, 263
Reason/cause, adverbial clauses of, 263–64
Reciprocal pronouns, 141, 142
Reciprocal sentences, 75
Reflexive pronouns, 142, 143
Reflexive sentences, 75
Regional accents, 6
Register, 7–8, 13, 60, 61, 178, 180, 270
Relative clauses, 212–25
  appositional noun clauses distinguished from, 247–49
  based on prepositional complements, 217–21
  elliptical, 224
  embedded, 213, 215
  function of, 213–15
  "headless," 225
  nonrestrictive, 221–22
  omitting a relative pronoun in, 222, 223–24
  pointers on diagramming, 221
  restrictive, 221–23
    omitting a relative pronoun in, 222, 223–324
    who/that rule, 223
  that refer to a whole clause, 222
Relative pronouns:
  case of, 215–17
  functions of, 213–14
  in nonrestrictive relative clauses, 221
  omission of, 221, 223–24
  position in the relative clause, 214
  in restrictive relative clauses, 223
  wh-words, 215, 224–25
respectively, use in coordination of, 204
Restrictive relative clauses, 221–23
  omitting a relative pronoun in, 222, 223–24
  who/that rule, 223
Result, adverbial clauses of, 265

scarcely, as negator, 179
Second, or past subjunctive, 104, 262–63
seldom, as negator, 179

Sentences:
  balancing, 197, 271–73
  classification of types of, 55–61
  complex, *see* Complex sentences
  coordination, *see* Coordination
  core of, 66
  declarative statements, *see* Declarative
       statements
  definitions of, 55
  diagramming, 62–63
       see also Diagramming
  exclamative, 60–61
  fragments, 59–60
  hortatives, 61
  imperatives, *see* Imperative sentences
  interrogatives, *see* Interrogative sen-
       tences
  intransitive, *see* Intransitive sentences
  negative, *see* Negation
  new and old information, *see* New
       and old information in the
       English sentence
  in the passive, *see* Passive, the
  patterns, basic, 85–86, 125, 131
  precative, 60–61
  reciprocal, 75
  reflexive, 75
  subordination, *see* Subordination
  transitive, *see* Transitive sentences
  verbless interrogatories with *wh-*
       word, 61
Series of phrases, coordination of a,
     205–06
set/sit, 107
Short History of Linguistics, A (Robins),
     24
sit/set, 107
Speech:
  audience and, 7–8
  correctness of, 6, 8–9, 12–13
  grammar of, 13–14
  regional and ethnic influences on, 6
  register and, 7–8, 180
  relationship to writing, 12–14, 179
  social influences on, 6
  whom used in, 220
Speech involvement, 13
Spelling:
  apostrophe in forming possessive
       form, 146–47
  differences in British and American,
       11, 97–98
  uniformity of, 11
"Split" infinitives, 252

Standard of the comparison, 165
Standard Written English, 9–10, 280
  grammar of, *see* Grammar, of writing
  see also Register
Style and grammar, 16–17, 194, 270
Subject, 39, 41
  agreement of verb with, 94–95, 136–37
       apparent conjunctions, 208
       conjoined subjects, 208–09
       disjoint subjects, 208–09
  conjoined subjects, agreement of verb
       and, 208–09
  noun clauses functioning as, 228,
       233–34
Subject complements, 83–85, 158
  diagramming sentences with, 84
  noun clauses as, 247
Subjunctive, 101, 103–04
  for indirect commands, 246
  past, or second, 104, 262–63
  present, 103–04
Subordinate clauses, 34, 212–13
  adverbial clauses, 213, 256–67
  functions and names of, 212–13
  noun clauses, 228–67
  relative clause, *see* Relative clauses
Subordinating conjunctions, *see*
       Subordinators (subordinating
       conjunctions)
Subordination, 197–98
  adverbial clauses, 256–67
  coordination distinguished from,
       212
  noun clauses, 213, 228–67
  relative clauses, *see* Relative clauses
Subordinators (subordinating conjunc-
       tions), 34–35, 229–33
  in adverbial clauses, 257–58, 259,
       261, 262, 264–65
  complementizers, 35
       with adverbial clauses, 257–58,
            259, 261, 262, 264–65
       with noun clause, 229–30,
            231–32, 234
  with noun clauses, 229–35
  wh-subordinators, 229
       with noun clauses, 229, 230,
            233–34, 235–36
supposed to, pronunciation of, 109–10
Syntax, 15

Talking from Nine to Five (Tannen), 7
Tense, 28, 96–99, 243
  aspect combined with, 101, 107–10

Tense (*continued*)
    auxiliary verbs and, 28, 29, 96
    future, 96
        prospective tense as, 109
    generic past, 109
    in indirect questions, 244
    in indirect statements, 242–43
    past, 93, 96, 96–99
        (*-ed*) to form, 97
    present, 96–97
    prospective, 109
Tensed (finite) verbs, 93
Tense reference, 243
Teutonic languages, 5
that:
    in appositional noun clause, 247–49
    as complementizer, 229, 231, 234
        as complement of a prepositions,
            237
    the fact that in place of, 237
    in relative clause, 247–48
    in restrictive relative clauses, 222
that clauses as adjectival complements,
    246–47
the fact that in place of that, 237
Theme, 193–94, 275
there and the anticipated subject, 275–76
Time, adverbial clauses of, 260–61
Time-and-place reference (deixis), 243,
    244
to ..., *see* Infinitives; *specific verbs*, e.g.
    Be
Transitive prepositional verbs, 127–28
Transitive sentences, 73
    diagramming, 75–76, 79–82
Transitive verbs, 73–75
    prepositional verbs, 126–27, 278
Tree diagram, 40, 41, 42
    relationships in, 50
try following by the infinitive of *-ing*,
    107–108

Underlining diagram, 40, 41, 42
"Understood object" sentence, 75
Unreal condition, 263
Usage, grammar and written, 15–16
used with the infinitive, 109
    pronunciation of *used to*, 109–10

Verbless interrogatives with *wh-* word,
    61
Verb phrases, 49, 75, 92–110

aspect of, *see* Aspect
coordination of, 201–03
defined, 92
diagramming, 112–13
formula for, 185, 189
modality of, 101–04, 107–10
negation in, *see* Negation, in the verb
    phrase
the operator in, 104–05
tense of, *see* Tense
Verbs, 92–110
    agreement of quantifier and, 151–52
    agreement of subject with, 94–95,
        136–37
        apparent conjunctions, 208
        conjoined subjects, 208–09
        disjoint subjects, 208–09
    auxiliary, *see* Auxiliary verbs
    base form of, 92, 93, 94
    -en forms of, 92, 94, 185, 188
        in the passive, *see* Passive, the
    examples of, 27
    forms of, 28–29, 92–96
        dictionary lists of, 99
    general present, 92, 93, 94
    gerunds, 95
    homophony of auxiliaries and, 106
    infinitives, *see* Infinitives
    -ing form, 92, 108–10, 185
        as gerund, 95
        as modifier, 95–96
    intransitive, *see* Intransitive verbs
    lexical, 28–29, 49, 92
    linking, 28, 82–83
    meanings of, 27–28
    negative, 180–81
    non-tensed (nonfinite), 29, 93, 189
    phrasal, *see* Phrasal verbs
    prepositional, *see* Prepositional verbs
    problematic, 106–07
    punctual, 261
    purpose of, 27
    -s form of, 93, 94, 95
    strong, 94, 98
    tensed (finite), 93
    tense of, *see* Tense
    transitive, *see* Transitive verbs
    weak, 94, 98
Voice, *see* Active sentence; Passive, the

want followed by the infinitive, 107
whether as complementizer, 231, 232

which:
in nonrestrictive relative clauses, 221
in restrictive relative clauses, 223
/*which*/*whose*, 220
/*who*, 217, 220
"WHIZ-deletion," 224
who:
in nonrestrictive relative clauses, 221
in restrictive relative clauses, 223
/*which*, 217, 220
/*whom*/*whose*, 220
whoever/*whomever*, 237–38
whom:
after prepositions, 220
as prepositional complements, 237–39
wh- words:
in interrogative sentences, 59, 61
to introduce adverbial clauses, 259
relative pronouns, 215, 224–25
as subordinators with noun clauses,
229, 230, 234–35

Words:
categories of, *see* Categories of words
wh-words, *see wh-words*
word order, 272
World language, English as, 3
Writing:
grammar of speech distinguished from
that of, 13–14, 184
historical background, 10–11
register and, 7–8
relationship to speech, 12–14
Standard Written English, *see*
Standard Written English
uniformity of present-day written
English, 11
*Writing Systems: A Linguistic
Introduction* (Sampson), 11
Writing Systems of the World (Coulmas),
11

You Just Don't Understand! (Tannen), 7